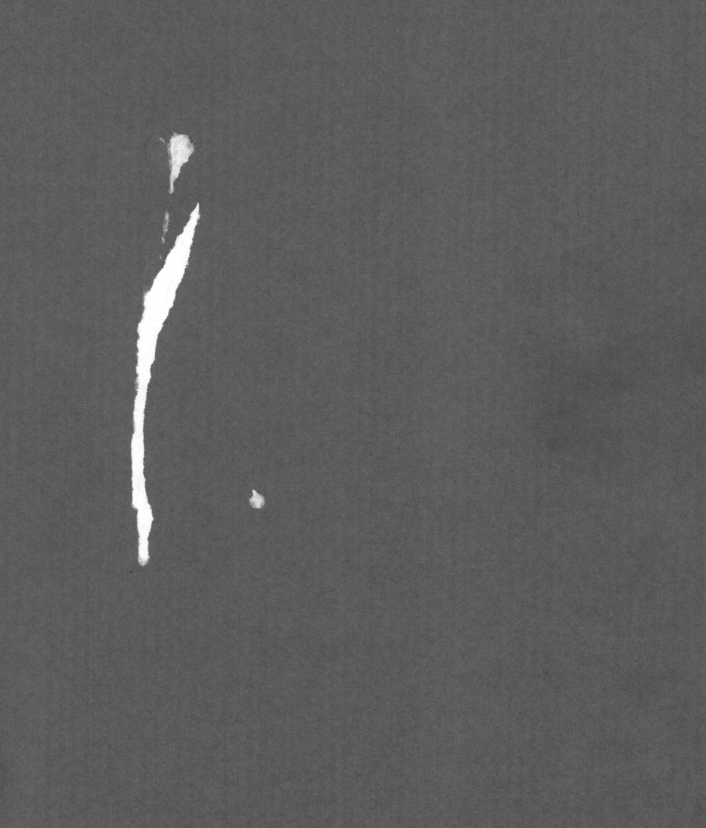

THE
100 GREATEST OLYMPIANS
AND PARALYMPIANS

First published by Carlton Books Limited 2011
Copyright © 2011 Carlton Books Limited

London 2012 emblems: © The London Organising Committee of the Olympic
Games and Paralympic Games Ltd (LOCOG) 2007. All rights reserved.

Carlton Books Limited
20 Mortimer Street
London, W1T 3JW

A CIP catalogue record for this book is available from the British Library.
10 9 8 7 6 5 4 3 2 1

ISBN: 978-1-84732-701-7

FSC
www.fsc.org
MIX
Paper from
responsible sources
FSC® C101537

Printed in China

Senior Editor: Conor Kilgallon
Design Direction: Darren Jordan
Design: Ben Ruocco, Brian Flynn
Picture Research: Paul Langan
Production: Karin Kolbe

Picture captions
Page 5: Usain Bolt of Jamaica races clear to win gold in the Men's
100m Final in Beijing 2008, setting a world-record time of 9.69
seconds in the process.

Pages 8/9: Michael Phelps (second left) in action for the USA in the
Men's 4 x 100m Freestyle Relay Final in Beijing 2008. The USA took
gold in a world-record time of 3:08.24. Phelps won a total of eight
gold medals in this single Olympic Games, also a record.

THE
100 GREATEST OLYMPIANS
AND PARALYMPIANS

FOREWORD BY SEBASTIAN COE KBE

NICK CALLOW

AN OFFICIAL LONDON 2012 OLYMPIC
AND PARALYMPIC GAMES PUBLICATION

CARLTON

CONTENTS

FOREWORD 6

INTRODUCTION 8

REBECCA **ADLINGTON** 10
BEN **AINSLIE** 12
VASILY **ALEKSEYEV** 14
NIKOLAI **ANDRIANOV** 16
EVELYN **ASHFORD** 18
BOB **BEAMON** 20
ABEBE **BIKILA** 22
MATT **BIONDI** 24
FANNY **BLANKERS-KOEN** 26
ARNOLD **BOLDT** 28
USAIN **BOLT** 30
VALERY **BORZOV** 32
VALERIE **BRISCO-HOOKS** 34
CASSIUS **CLAY** 36
SEBASTIAN **COE** 38
NADIA **COMANECI** 40
PHILIP **CRAVEN** 42
BETTY **CUTHBERT** 44
DAVID **DOUILLET** 46
NATALIE **DU TOIT** 48
TERESA **EDWARDS** 50
HICHAM **EL-GUERROUJ** 52
RAY **EWRY** 54
BIRGIT **FISCHER** 56
DICK **FOSBURY** 58
GERT **FREDRIKSSON** 60
FU MINGXIA 62
ROBERT 'BOB' **GARRETT** 64
HAILE **GEBRSELASSIE** 66
TORBEN **GRAEL** 68
TANNI **GREY-THOMPSON** 70
HARRY **HILLMAN** 72
KELLY **HOLMES** 74
CHRIS **HOY** 76
JIRI **JEZEK** 78

MICHAEL **JOHNSON** 80
JACKIE **JOYNER-KERSEE** 82
ALEKSANDR **KARELIN** 84
SAWAO **KATO** 86
KIPCHOGE 'KIP' **KEINO** 88
DARREN **KENNY** 90
KIM SOO-NYUNG 92
CAROLINA **KLUFT** 94
OLGA **KORBUT** 96
ALVIN 'AL' **KRAENZLEIN** 98
LARISSA **LATYNINA** 100
CARL **LEWIS** 102
JEANNIE **LONGO** 104
GREG **LOUGANIS** 106
EDOARDO **MANGIAROTTI** 108
ALAIN **MIMOUN** 110
EDWIN 'ED' **MOSES** 112
ALEXEI **NEMOV** 114
ISABEL **NEWSTEAD** 116
TADAHIRO **NOMURA** 118
PAAVO **NURMI** 120
AL **OERTER** 122
ELISABETA **OLENIUC-LIPA** 124
MERLENE **OTTEY** 126
JAMES 'JESSE' **OWENS** 128
LEE **PEARSON** 130
MARIE-JOSE **PEREC** 132
CHANTEL **PETITCLERC** 134
MICHAEL **PHELPS** 136
MATTHEW **PINSENT** 138
OSCAR **PISTORIUS** 140
STANISLAV **POZDNIAKOV** 142
STEVE **REDGRAVE** 144
VILLE **RITOLA** 146
DAVID **ROBERTS** 148

WILMA **RUDOLPH** 150
RICARDO **SANTOS** 152
LOUISE **SAUVAGE** 154
BORIS **SHAKHLIN** 156
UDHAM **SINGH** 158
PETER **SNELL** 160
MARK **SPITZ** 162
TEOFILO **STEVENSON** 164
SARAH **STOREY** 166
SHIRLEY **STRICKLAND** 168
NAIM **SULEYMANOGLU** 170
SUSI **SUSANTI** 172
IRENA **SZEWINSKA** 174
RYOKO **TANI** 176
DALEY **THOMPSON** 178
JENNY **THOMPSON** 180
IAN **THORPE** 182
JIM **THORPE** 184
GWEN **TORRENCE** 186
DARA **TORRES** 188
HUBERT **VAN INNIS** 190
ESTHER **VERGEER** 192
VALENTINA **VEZZALI** 194
LASSE **VIREN** 196
WANG NAN 198
ISABELL **WERTH** 200
HANS GUNTER **WINKLER** 202
EMIL **ZATOPEK** 204
JAN **ZELEZNY** 206
TRISCHA **ZORN** 208

OLYMPIC AND PARALYMPIC
GAMES RECORDS 210
INDEX 220
ACKNOWLEDGEMENTS 224

FOREWORD

The Olympic and Paralympic Games are the pinnacle of the sporting world. These global events of sporting and cultural significance bring together thousands of athletes and millions of spectators from every nation. The ideals of the ancient Greeks are still held dear as athletes strive to live up to the Olympic motto: faster, higher, stronger.

The modern Olympic Games were reborn in Athens in 1896 and were joined by the Stoke Mandeville Games (the precursor to today's Paralympic Games) in 1948. Together, they have produced competitors whose achievements have become the stuff of legend. Tales of spectacular new records, superhuman performances and medals won (and lost) against the odds fill the pages of this book. Some of these competitors were my peers – athletes I've known, watched, admired and competed against. The men and women competing in every Olympic and Paralympic sport continue to be a source of wonder.

The scale and complexity of this four-yearly event is extraordinary. Around 15,000 athletes, housed in a purpose-built Athletes' Village, now compete in 26 sports in the Olympic Games and 20 sports in the Paralympic Games. The intensity of the competition this generates in sports as diverse as Archery, Swimming, Athletics and Equestrian remains an inspiration. Drama, intrigue and sporting prowess stand alongside acts of magnanimity, goodwill and friendship, with each successive edition adding to the history of the Games.

Olympians and Paralympians train for years for the privilege of standing on top of the podium as a gold medal is hung around their necks. They also observe the spirit of the Olympic Creed: 'the most important thing in life is not the triumph, but the fight; the essential thing is not to have won, but to have fought well'.

The Olympians and Paralympians in this book have shared similar experiences and you will read about many of the names that are so familiar today. However, as well as Jesse Owens, Nadia Comaneci and Oscar Pistorius there are many others who may be less familiar but whose achievements have still propelled them into the ranks of the greats: Fanny Blankers-Koen, Kip Keino and Trischa Zorn, to mention but a few.

This account of the achievements of the greatest Olympic and Paralympic athletes reflects the stories and struggles of the modern Games. It is a fascinating tale of those who have made this most compelling of events the greatest show on earth.

Sebastian Coe KBE

INTRODUCTION

There is no greater test for an athlete than competing in the Olympic or Paralympic Games. The chance to shine comes only once every four years and, for some, just once in a lifetime. So it takes a huge amount of preparation and nerve, under the scrutiny of a global audience, for competitors to try to immortalise their sporting careers during such a brief spell of competition.

Some of the biggest names in sport have crumbled under the pressure or succumbed to injury just when it mattered most. But the truly great have risen to the occasion and left their legacy on the greatest sporting stage of them all. This book celebrates the men and women who have left their mark on the Summer Olympic and Paralympic Games.

The amazing feats of athletes such as Usain Bolt and Michael Phelps are recorded here, but it's not just those who went faster, higher and longer who appear on these pages. To list only these would be to suggest that only modern Olympians and Paralympians, with their hi-tech equipment and superb training techniques, are worthy of inclusion. Instead, there are many athletes from across all ages whose achievements, in the context of the era in which they competed, still stand up to scrutiny, making them worthy Olympic and Paralympic legends. Ray Ewry, Fanny Blankers-Koen and Arnold Boldt are just three. Also, there are several other athletes who may not feature in any medals table yet whose influence completely changed the face of their events. Olga Korbut, Dick Fosbury and Al Kraenzlein must be considered among the pantheon of greats.

And great Olympians and Paralympians do not just come from the Athletics track or the Swimming pool. *Judoka* such as Tadahiro Nomura, cyclists such as Sarah Storey and weightlifters such as Vasily Alekseyev all deserve their place alongside more familiar names such as Carl Lewis and Larissa Latynina, the most successful female Olympian of all time. So included here are fantastic stories to read from a wide variety of sports, from Archery and Beach Volleyball to Tennis and Wrestling.

Another inherent beauty of the Olympic and Paralympic Games is that they are not just for sports fans – spirit, endeavour and drama are as important as crossing the finishing line first. This book highlights the moments of great wonder that transcend the sporting world and cross over into everyday life, creating the stuff of legend.

Here then, are the 100 Greatest Olympians and Paralympians, in all their glory.

Nick Callow

REBECCA **ADLINGTON** GREAT BRITAIN
AQUATICS – SWIMMING

Rebecca Adlington OBE got her fair share of 'teenage kicks' at the Beijing 2008 Games when, at the tender age of 19, she won gold in the Women's 400m and 800m Freestyle swimming events, breaking the 800m Freestyle world record in the process.

Adlington took to the swimming pool at just four years old, making her competitive debut at 10. Nine years later she triumphantly returned home an Olympic gold medallist. Twenty thousand people lined the streets of Mansfield, where she was born and grew up, to watch an open-top bus tour before Adlington was later given the freedom of the town. Adlington is a member of Mansfield's Nova Centurion Swimming Club, which is also home to Paralympic gold medallist Sam Hynd. She is just one of a crop of young swimmers successfully nurtured by the club's head coach, Bill Furniss.

At the age of 12, in her first national age-group championships, she highlighted her potential when she won five medals, including gold in the 800m and 200m Individual Medley. Her first taste of international competition came in 2003 when she appeared at the European Youth Olympic Festival in Paris, picking up silver medals in the 400m and 800m Freestyle. She took on stiffer competition at 17 years of age at the 2006 European Championships in Budapest, where she won a silver medal in the 800m Freestyle.

Her senior world swimming debut did not prove to be quite as fruitful, as she failed to qualify for the final at the 2007 Swimming World Championships in Melbourne. A year later, Adlington bounced back to win gold at the World Short Course Championships in Manchester, less than 60 miles from her Mansfield home. The biggest moment in Adlington's career so far came in Beijing 2008 when she made a late burst to pip the USA's Katie Hoff by seven 100ths of a second to clinch gold in the 400m Freestyle. She followed up that first Olympic gold in emphatic style just days later, when she finished 2.12 seconds inside the previous world record to claim gold in the 800m Freestyle.

Adlington's exploits in Beijing 2008 meant she was the first British woman to win an Olympic Swimming gold medal since Anita Lonsbrough's triumph nearly half a century earlier, in 1960. In doing so she also became the first British swimmer to win two gold medals at a single Olympic Games in 100 years. In honour of her triumph, Adlington's local pool underwent a £5-million refurbishment and reopened as the Rebecca Adlington Swimming Centre in January

Statistics
Born: 17 February 1989, Mansfield, Nottinghamshire, England
Height: 5ft 10½in (1.79m)
Weight: 154lb (70kg)

Olympic Games Medals
Beijing 2008
Women's 400m Freestyle.................Gold
Women's 800m Freestyle.................Gold

Below: The Mansfield teenager is one of only five women swimmers in the history of the Olympic Games to have won two gold medals at a single Games.

Right: The British swimmer powers her way to victory in the 800m Freestyle, winning her second gold medal of the Beijing 2008 Games.

2010. Yates Bar in Mansfield was renamed The Adlington Arms for a short while. Adlington's achievements were not just recognised at local level, though. She received an OBE as Britain's Beijing 2008 heroes were acknowledged in the 2009 sporting New Year's Honours List.

However, there was almost bound to be a slight dip in her form following the highs of 2008, and Adlington was not quite as successful in the 2009 World Championships in Rome: she won a bronze medal in the 400m Freestyle and another bronze in the 4 x 200m Freestyle Relay. But she put in impressive performances at the 2010 British Swimming Championships in Nottingham, storming to victory in the 200m, 400m and 800m Freestyle, then won two gold and two bronze medals at the Commonwealth Games and a gold and a bronze at the European Championships. It all bodes well for domestic medal hopes when the Olympic Games relocate to London in 2012.

As Adlington spends a substantial chunk of her time barefooted in a swimming pool, some might find it odd that she is obsessed with shoes. Her Olympic victories were in part propelled by a promise of new shoes as a present from her mother if she did well enough.

'My first major event of the year was the Olympic trials. Without any doubt, the most emotionally draining domestic event I've ever experienced. Everywhere I looked I saw athletes crying, either because they had missed out on the GB Olympic Team, or through sheer elation and relief at making it.'

BEN **AINSLIE**
SAILING

Having won three consecutive Olympic gold medals and five world titles, there is no doubt that Ben Ainslie CBE is Britain's most successful sailor ever, reflected by the fact that, at the age of 33 in 2010, he had already been named ISAF World Sailor of the Year three times and British Yachtsman of the Year five times.

The son of Roderick 'Roddy' Ainslie, who skippered *Second Life* in the first Whitbread Round the World Race in 1973, Ben Ainslie has spent almost all his life on the water and been involved in Sailing since he was an eight-year-old boy growing up in Cornwall, England.

Even so, it has taken incredible dedication and a strong competitive spirit to take him to unprecedented heights in the sport. He was a Laser Radial World Champion by the age of 16 and won his first Olympic medal at just 19, taking silver in Atlanta 1996.

As his rivals will testify he is a determined and fearless opponent, winning gold in Sydney 2000 before switching from the Laser to the larger Finn class four years later. Since sailing a Finn-class boat requires a lot more strength, Ainslie needed to put on a lot of extra muscle bulk. In fact, he increased his body weight by 33lb (15kg) to pursue his new dream. His gruelling training programme paid dividends in 2002 when, a little over a year after changing classes, he won his first Finn World Championship. By the time he reached the Athens 2004 Games he had been crowned World Champion three years in a row and few commentators were surprised when he added Olympic gold to the tally.

After a spell with Emirates Team New Zealand, competing in the America's Cup, he returned to the Olympic circuit in 2007, winning an unprecedented fifth world title before going on to triumph at the Beijing 2008 Games a year later. This was possibly his toughest Games, not least because he was unfortunate enough to contract mumps just days before the opening race and had to battle illness as well as the elements to win his third consecutive gold medal.

If statistics were ever needed to prove the fact, the result confirmed him as Britain's most successful sailor of all time, surpassing Rodney Pattison's record of two golds and one silver Olympic medal. Since Beijing 2008, Ainslie has been made a CBE in the Queen's New Year Honours List, having already been awarded an MBE in 2001 and an OBE in 2005.

Statistics

Born: 5 February 1977, Macclesfield, England
Height: 6ft 1in (1.85m)
Weight: 203lb (92kg)

Olympic Games Medals

Atlanta 1996
Laser (one-person dinghy) .... Silver

Sydney 2000
Laser (one-person dinghy) .... Gold

Athens 2004
Finn (one-person dinghy [heavyweight]) .... Gold

Beijing 2008
Finn (one-person dinghy [heavyweight]) .... Gold

Below: Ainslie shows off his second Olympic gold medal, which he won at the Athens 2004 Games, competing in the Finn (one-person dinghy [heavyweight]) class.

Right: Flying the flag to celebrate his gold-medal victory for Team GB at the Beijing 2008 Games, Ainslie showed that he was once again the man to beat in the Finn class.

'My greatest strength is that I never give up.'

VASILY **ALEKSEYEV**
WEIGHTLIFTING

USSR

Giant Soviet weightlifter Vasily Alekseyev is generally regarded as the greatest exponent of super-heavyweight lifting in history. He won two Olympic gold medals, in Munich 1972 and Montreal 1976, during an eight-year unbeaten spell that began in 1970. He set an incredible 80 world records during his career.

It is probably a coincidence that Vasily Alekseyev married a woman called Olympiada, but at the same time, it could not be more apt for the most successful weightlifter of all time, and a double Olympic champion. Not only was Alekseyev a larger-than-life character but, weighing 353lb (160kg), he was also a colossal physical specimen. His undeniably large stomach became the subject of jokes throughout his career, but it no doubt contributed to Alekseyev's awesome strength, an unequalled power that allowed him to break world records seemingly at will.

Alekseyev's accomplishments in Weightlifting were groundbreaking – no lifter has even come close to replicating his achievements either before or since. Perhaps the most impressive of all his successes came in March 1970, when he became the first man to lift the combined weight of 600kg in three movements: the Snatch, Clean and Jerk, and the Clean and Press. That was the first indicator, the sign of something special, and the beginning of his eight years of utter domination

of the sport of Weightlifting, he is dubbed the world's strongest man.

The son of a lumberjack and vodka distiller, by the age of 12 he was felling trees and lifting logs for exercise, and had the body of a fully grown man by the time he turned 14. Alekseyev joined the forestry commission before becoming a mining engineer and army commander, and it was not until he was 18 that he began practising Weightlifting to any serious degree. A rigorous training regime saw him develop into a physical colossus and by 1970, when he turned 28, he was competing for the Soviet Union and setting his first world record. At one stage, Alekseyev declared he wanted to set 100 world records, and he craftily broke each of his marks by the smallest of margins to give himself the best chance of bettering it again in the future. It was a smart move, but Alekseyev's fellow competitors must have felt as though he was toying with them.

At the Munich 1972 Olympic Games, he lifted a total of 640kg in the three events, a massive 30kg more than the silver medallist, Rudolf

Statistics
Born: 7 January 1942,
       Pokrovo-Shishkino, Ryazan,
       Russia
Height: 6ft 1in (1.85m)
Weight: 353lb (160kg)

Olympic Games Medals
Munich 1972
Men's Over 105kg...............................Gold

Montreal 1976
Men's Over 105kg...............................Gold

Left: The colossal Soviet weightlifter won 18 World, European and Olympic titles in an undefeated run between 1970 and 1978.

Right: Alekseyev was only 12 when he exercised by chopping down trees and lifting logs. At 14 he was wrestling colleagues of his lumberjack father.

Mang of West Germany. He was in even more impressive form in Montreal four years later, where he retained his title by lifting world records in the Snatch (185kg) and the Jerk (255kg), finishing a total of 35kg ahead of second-placed East German, Gerd Bonk. After an incredible eight years of knowing nothing but victory, Alekseyev was finally beaten at the 1978 World

Championships, when he competed with an injury, and his almost super-human abilities finally started to wane.

He knew his time was up when he was unable to lift his opening weight in the Snatch at the Moscow 1980 Olympic Games. His 38-year-old body was telling him to call it a day and he retired after the competition. No damage could be

done to the reputation of the most remarkable weightlifter in history. In addition to his two Olympic triumphs, Alekseyev's roll of honour included eight golds in both the World and European Championships. He remains an icon in Russia and coached the Unified Team to nine medals – including five golds – at the Barcelona 1992 Games.

'The more complex the situation, the more
threatening my rivals, the more I spread my wings
in defiance of everything.'

NIKOLAI **ANDRIANOV**

GYMNASTICS – ARTISTIC

Until Michael Phelps' performance in Beijing 2008, Soviet gymnast Nikolai Andrianov had tasted Olympic success more times than any other male athlete in history. A total of 15 medals over three Olympic Games is an astonishing return, and one that looked unlikely to be beaten until the American's incredible success in the pool in 2008 saw him take his Olympic medal tally to 16.

One of the most interesting things about Nikolai Andrianov's sterling Olympic career is that he was not expected even to be a contender for the Munich 1972 Olympic Games. He was only the USSR's reserve for the 1970 World Championships, but his impressive performance at the following year's European Championships guaranteed him a place in the team for Munich 1972, which started him on the road to greatness.

Indeed, much of Andrianov's stunning success came against the odds. An unruly child who regularly skipped school, the seven-time Olympic champion was first spotted, aged 11, by coach Nikolai Tolkachyov, who became his mentor. The young Andrianov struggled in his early years, though, and charged off the podium in tears at his first ever event as a 14-year-old. Gradually, however, the burgeoning talent began to flourish, and by the time the Madrid European Championships of 1971 came around, it was clear that he was a star in the making. He returned from the Championships with six medals to his name, two of them gold, and was to continue that form a year later.

Despite being aged just 19, he returned from the 1972 Games with a full set of medals, having claimed gold in the Floor Competition, silver in the Team Competition and finally a bronze in the Vault. And he soon proved that those successes were no freak event. Over the next three World and European Championships he won a stunning 17 gold medals, and appeared to be the man to watch as the eyes of the world turned towards Montreal 1976.

The Soviet star's fans were not disappointed: Andrianov produced brilliant performances in front of an impressed Canadian audience, with his most remarkable display coming in the Individual All-Around, where he went up against Sawao Kato, who had won the gold medal in

1968 and 1972. In the end, the Japanese gymnast barely challenged Andrianov, who won the title by the largest margin for 42 years.

But he was not finished there. Further golds followed in the Floor Competition, Vault and the Rings, while he added two silvers in the Team Competition and Parallel Bars. To complete a remarkable medal haul, Andrianov went on to win a bronze on the Pommel Horse.

Statistics

Born: 14 October 1952, Vladimir, Russia
Height: 5ft 5in (1.65m)
Weight: 132lb (60kg)

Olympic Games Medals

Munich 1972

Men's Floor Competition	Gold
Men's Team Competition	Silver
Men's Vault Competition	Bronze

Montreal 1976

Men's Individual All-Around Competition	Gold
Men's Floor Competition	Gold
Men's Vault Competition	Gold
Men's Rings Competition	Gold
Men's Team Competition	Silver
Men's Parallel Bars Competition	Silver
Men's Pommel Horse Competition	Bronze

Moscow 1980

Men's Team Competition	Gold
Men's Vault Competition	Gold
Men's Individual All-Around Competition	Silver
Men's Floor Competition	Silver
Men's Horizontal Bars Competition	Bronze

Left: Andrianov acknowledges the cheers of the crowd as he awaits the presentation of a gold medal in the Individual All-Around Competition at the Montreal 1976 Games.

Right: Andrianov in action on the rings in Montreal 1976, on the way to winning one of four gold medals at the Games.

With Gymnastics generally being a sport for youngsters, some thought his best days were behind him by the time the Olympic Games arrived on home soil, in Moscow 1980. The sign of true greatness, though, is an athlete's ability to raise himself for one final performance, and that is exactly what Andrianov did. He finally won

gold in the Team Competition, and retained his Vault title. Two more silvers, in the Individual All-Around and the Floor Competitions, as well as a bronze in the Horizontal Bars, brought his final medal tally to 15, an Olympic record that stood for 28 years. He is also the only man to win three medals in the Vault and Floor Competitions.

A spell in the Far East as a coach followed retirement, where his golden touch continued as he guided Naoya Tsukahara to the top step of the podium as part of Japan's victorious 2004 Men's Team Competition squad. With 15 medals as a competitor and one as a coach, Andrianov is a true Olympic legend.

*'I never perform an element in competition if I'm not sure
I've completely mastered it.'*

EVELYN **ASHFORD**

ATHLETICS

USA

Evelyn Ashford is the only female athlete in American track history to have won four Olympic gold medals. She set an Olympic record at the Los Angeles 1984 Games when she won the 100 metres in under 11 seconds, and also won a gold medal at the age of 35 in the Women's 4 x 100m Relay.

Statistics

Born: 15 April 1957, Shreveport,
Louisiana, USA
Height: 5ft 5in (1.65m)
Weight: 115lb (52kg)

Olympic Games Medals

Los Angeles 1984

Women's 100m ....Gold
Women's 4 x 100m Relay...................Gold

Seoul 1988

Women's 4 x 100m Relay...................Gold
Women's 100m .... Silver

Barcelona 1992

Women's 4 x 100m Relay...................Gold

Regarded as one of the most accomplished sprinters of her generation, Evelyn Ashford can look back at her distinguished career with a great deal of pride. Ashford was not only dominant in her individual sport, but she was able to switch her attention to the team events and play her part in helping the USA to come away with gold medals.

Born in Louisiana, she was raised in Sacramento, California, as her father was in the air force and her family were often on the move. She attended Roseville High School and it was there that she showed the potential to blossom into one of the most talented athletes America would ever produce. She was first spotted running during her PE class by the school football coach, who challenged her to race his fastest player. She duly beat the school's star running back in a 50m dash.

Ashford later became one of the first women to be offered an athletics scholarship at the University of California. That was where she came into contact with Pat Connolly – a coach who was a three-time Olympian and who was taken aback by her ability on the track. Connolly was so impressed with her timings that she put her forward for the 1976 US Olympic trials. Ashford never let her down, managing to finish third and qualifying for her first Olympic Games in Montreal 1976. Although she had to settle for fifth place in the 100m final, she still managed to beat her more experienced US team-mate Chandra Cheeseborough and East Germany's Marlies Gohr.

Ashford left college in 1978 to train full-time in preparation for the Moscow 1980 Games, and managed to beat the world-record holders in the 100m and 200m in 1979, but she suffered heartache when the US boycotted the Games. She bounced back from her disappointment and set a new world record in 1983 at the National Sports Festival in Colorado Springs, when she ran the 100m in 10.79 seconds.

Ashford was determined to take that form into Los Angeles 1984 and, although she had to pull out of the 200m heats with a minor injury, she saved her best for the 100m and set an Olympic record of 10.97 seconds to clinch her first gold medal. Things were to get even better when she

Left: Ashford was devastated by her country's decision to boycott the Moscow 1980 Games, and soon responded by proving she was the world's best.

Right: Ashford's remarkable stamina, coupled with strength training, enabled her to run at her top speed for far longer than nearly all her rivals.

'I can feel the wind go by when I run. It feels good. It feels fast. Whatever muscles I have are the product of my own hard work and nothing else.'

picked up another gold in the 4 x 100m Relay, the US team winning by one of the biggest margins in the history of the Games. Ashford broke her own world record again later that season, beating her close rival Gohr to win the 100m in 10.76 seconds, which was her career best.

One of the highlights of her career was being the flag bearer for the United States during the opening ceremony of the Seoul 1988 Olympic Games. But she failed to retain her gold medal in the 100m when she lost out to Florence Griffith-Joyner, and had to settle for a silver medal. More success was to come in the 4 x 100m Relay, though, when she collected her second consecutive gold medal.

Many people in the sport thought that this might be the moment for Ashford to retire, but she defied all the odds when she came back for the Barcelona 1992 Olympic Games at the age of 35. She was knocked out of the 100m in the semi-finals but managed to win her third consecutive Olympic 4 x 100m Relay gold, becoming only one of four women to have won four gold medals for track and field athletics in the history of the Olympic Games. After announcing her retirement from the sport, Ashford was inducted into the National Track and Field Hall of Fame.

BOB **BEAMON**
ATHLETICS

USA

Less than a year before Neil Armstrong made a 'giant leap for mankind' with his first footstep on the moon, Bob Beamon took another historic leap of a completely different kind, shattering the world Long Jump record at the Mexico City 1968 Olympic Games.

Statistics

Born: 29 August 1946, New York City, USA
Height: 6ft 3in (1.9m)
Weight: 154lb (70kg)

Olympic Games Medals

Mexico City 1968
Men's Long Jump..................................Gold

It is one of sport's most enduring images: the look on Bob Beamon's face as he flies through the air, arms and legs flailing, on his way to immortality. That split-second in Mexico City, on 18 October 1968, was literally the zenith of Beamon's career, the halfway point between hitting the take-off board an ordinary man and landing in the sand a superstar.

His jump of 8.90m not only shattered the world record by 55cm – almost two feet – but created a new adjective: 'Beamonesque' now stands for an athletic feat that raises the bar by a huge margin. It is what Beamon did with his leap in the rarefied air of Mexico City that day, and one of his rivals, the defending champion Lynn Davies, told him so: 'You have destroyed this event,' he said. And indeed his record was to stand for 23 years until Mike Powell finally overtook it in 1991.

Beamon had a tough childhood, brought up in post-war New York by his grandmother after his mother died when he was just eight months old. He did not excel at school but his aptitude for athletics, and the Long Jump in particular, was noticed by coach Larry Ellis, a famous talent-spotter. Beamon broke school records in Long Jump and Triple Jump, and eventually won a scholarship to the University of El Paso in Texas by the time of the Mexico City 1968 Games.

There, where the air is thinner because of the high altitude, the conditions were ripe for breaking world records. Yet he nearly did not make it past the opening day's jumping. Although he was among the favourites to win gold, he had a reputation for inconsistency and, indeed, his first two qualifying jumps of the competition were fouls, as he overstepped the mark both times. A third would have put him out of the Olympic Games, so he desperately asked his team-mate and training partner Ralph Boston, who shared the world record with Russian Igor Ter-Ovanesyan, what to do. Boston advised Beamon to take off well before the mark, which he did, and he qualified comfortably to progress in the competition.

Conditions on the day of the final were perfect. It was cool, and Beamon ran up for his first jump with the strongest permissible following wind. Even so, no one could have imagined what would happen next, not least the officials using a new optical measuring device, which ran along a track at the far end of the pit. His leap was so massive that the measuring device ran out of track, and the officials had to use an old-fashioned tape to gauge the distance. Beamon sprang straight up and ambled away casually, conscious he'd had a good jump but not aware just how good, because it was announced in metric measurements. It was only when Boston told him what it meant that he collapsed on the ground and had to be helped to his feet by fellow athletes.

It was the first jump of the final, and no one else came close; Klaus Beer won the silver medal with 8.19m. When Mike Powell eventually broke Beamon's record in 1991, it had stood for 23 years, the second longest period after Jesse Owens' 25-year record, from 1936 to 1961. Beamon returned to college a hero, but even he could never get near his record again. He later retired from jumping to move into social work and motivational speaking.

Left: Beamon (centre) competed in only one Olympic Games, but his performance was enough for him to go down as one of sports all-time greats.

Right: Beamon's jump of 8.90m broke the old world record by 55cm, and stood for an impressive 23 years.

ABEBE **BIKILA**
ATHLETICS

Abebe Bikila is widely regarded as the greatest marathon runner in history and a key pioneer for Ethiopian athletics. He won back-to-back Olympic gold medals in Rome 1960 and Tokyo 1964 – the first Marathon athlete to do so – as well as two World Championship gold medals during his illustrious career.

Statistics
Born: 7 August 1932, Jato, Ethiopia
Died: 25 October 1973
Height: 5ft 10in (1.78m)
Weight: 126lb (57kg)

Olympic Games Medals
Rome 1960
Men's Marathon.....................................Gold

Tokyo 1964
Men's Marathon.....................................Gold

Born in the mountain town of Jato, central Ethiopia, in 1932 it was not until Abebe Bikila was well into his twenties that he first experienced a taste for athletics. After walking the more than 100 miles (160km) to the capital, Addis Ababa, in order to join the Imperial Guard in 1952, his desire was sparked by watching a parade of Ethiopian athletes on their return from the Melbourne 1956 Olympic Games.

Soon after joining the Imperial Guard athletics squad, he was spotted by Swedish coach Onni Niskanen, who noticed that Bikila had a natural flair for running and took on the task of nurturing his talent. His athletic ability, twinned with having grown up 6,000 metres above sea level, gave

would soon endear him to the crowds: he competed without wearing shoes.

Just a few hours before the gruelling 26.2-mile race, Bikila ditched his unfamiliar footwear as it was too uncomfortable. This was not new to him, as he had grown accustomed to running barefoot while training around his mountain home. As his competitors looked on in disbelief, he puffed out his chest in defiance, ready to embrace the pain.

He ran most of the race alongside rival Rhadi Ben Abdesselam, but with around 500 metres to go, a sudden burst of adrenaline pushed Bikila away from the Moroccan and into the record books. Footwear or no footwear, it did not matter – he was a champion, finishing with a world-record time of 2:15:16.2.

him an immense physiological aptitude for long-distance running.

Abede won his first three marathons in nearby Addis Ababa, which was when Niskanen realised that the Ethiopian had the potential to be a world-class athlete and he subsequently entered him in the Rome 1960 Olympic Games – a Marathon that would confirm him as an unrivalled talent. He may have been an unknown quantity going into the event but one striking part of his appearance

He returned to defend his title at the Tokyo 1964 Olympic Games. Worryingly for his rivals, his form was ominous: he had won all three previous marathons he had entered with the exception of the 1963 Boston Marathon.

At one point, after falling ill with appendicitis, Abede's bid for a second Olympic gold had appeared to be in the balance. But what was to follow would serve as an inspiration to anyone faced by adversity in any walk of life.

Above: Bikila celebrates after winning the first of his Olympic gold medals in the Men's Marathon at the Rome 1960 Olympic Games.

Right: Bikila makes the decisive move, barefooted, in the Men's Marathon at the Rome 1960 Games, pulling away from Rhadi Ben Abdesselam in sight of the finish.

The marathon man, against all the odds and in the stifling Tokyo humidity, claimed his second Olympic gold with a new world-record time of 2:12:11.2. Abede Bikila had the world at his bare feet, but in the lead-up to the Mexico 1968 Olympic Games a stress fracture of his foot denied him the chance of even completing a third successive Marathon, let alone of winning Olympic gold. He bravely started the race, even though he knew there was little or no chance of winning without enduring incredible pain, but pulled out mid-way through the race.

Barely a year later, he was involved in a car crash while driving in Addis Ababa, which left him a paraplegic. After 26 marathons, his career was over, but in true Bikila spirit he still competed in sports such as Archery.

The world lost a true Athletics hero four years later when Abede died aged just 41, and despite a tragically short career, he is an inspiration to those looking to follow in his footsteps.

'I wanted the world to know that my country, Ethiopia, has always won with determination and heroism.'

MATT **BIONDI**
AQUATICS – SWIMMING

Having won 11 Olympic medals, eight of them gold, Matt Biondi is considered one of the greatest ever swimmers in the history of the Olympic Games. His total equals the haul of his countryman Mark Spitz, the man whose record he tried to emulate when he went for seven golds at the Seoul 1988 Olympic Games.

Matt Biondi was always going to be a major star in the water; his father was a top Water Polo player and taught him how to float from an early age. Like his dad, Biondi got his competitive start in the pool by playing water polo before he became the top schoolboy sprinter in the United States with a National High School record of 20.40 seconds in the 50yd Freestyle. A league above his fellow competitors, Biondi then turned out to be one of the greatest ever swimmers at the University of California, Berkeley, where he was Swimmer of the Year three times in a row and was part of three champion Water Polo squads.

From there, he secured his place in the American 4 x 100m Freestyle Relay team for the Los Angeles 1984 Olympic Games. Despite being just 18 and a relative newcomer to major tournaments, he managed to secure his first Olympic gold medal in the relay, with his team also recording a world-record time. Returning to Berkeley, he notched up further successes, winning five NCAA Championships and then bursting on to the international scene with dramatic effect. He became the first ever swimmer to win seven medals at the World Championships when he blew the opposition out of the Madrid pool in 1986.

Pressure was now mounting on him to repeat that amazing achievement on an even bigger stage, and to match the seven gold medals Mark Spitz had won at the Olympic Games back in Munich 1972. He did not get off to the best of starts at the Seoul 1988 Games, when he finished third in the 200m Freestyle. With so much expectation surrounding his every move, Biondi improved his performance by winning a silver medal in the 100m Butterfly.

But no one could have predicted what was going to happen next as the American swimmer blitzed his way through the remaining events. He managed to secure a gold medal in the 4 x 200m Freestyle Relay and helped set a world-record time in the process. More gold medals followed as he won the 50m Freestyle, beating his rival and close friend Tom Jager and managing to clock 22.14 seconds, which was the third time he had equalled or broken the world record. He also won gold in the 100m Freestyle, setting another Olympic record in the final – 48.63 seconds, the second-fastest time in history. Next came gold in both the 4 x 100m Freestyle Relay and 4 x 100m Medley Relay, which took his tally to seven medals and guaranteed him an entry in the record books. He had broken four world records in the process.

Following his amazing success in Seoul 1988, he announced his retirement from competitive swimming, but still took part in exhibition races and worked the celebrity circuit. There was to be a swansong, however, as he came out of retirement to participate in the Barcelona 1992 Olympic Games. The USA named one of the oldest swimming teams in the history of the Olympics but Biondi still managed to come away with gold medals in the 4 x 100m Freestyle Relay and the 4 x 100m Medley Relay. He also secured a silver medal in the 50m Freestyle to take his tally to a staggering 11 Olympic medals, ensuring him a place among the greatest ever Olympians to have participated in the Games.

Statistics

Born: 8 October 1965, Moraga, California, USA
Height: 6ft 7in (2m)
Weight: 209lb (95kg)

Olympic Games Medals

Los Angeles 1984

Men's 4 x 100m Freestyle Relay .....Gold

Seoul 1988

Men's 50m Freestyle ....Gold
Men's 100m Freestyle..........................Gold
Men's 4 x 100m Freestyle Relay .....Gold
Men's 4 x 200m Freestyle Relay.....Gold
Men's 4 x 100m Medley Relay.........Gold
Men's 100m Butterfly.......................Silver
Men's 200m Freestyle.................... Bronze

Barcelona 1992

Men's 4 x 100m Freestyle Relay .....Gold
Men's 4 x 100m Medley Relay.........Gold
Men's 50m Freestyle ....Silver

Above: Biondi will go down in history as one of the best swimmers of all time. Over his career, he won 11 Olympic medals, eight of which were gold.

Right: At his last Olympic Games, Barcelona 1992, Biondi went out in style, winning two gold medals, in the 4 x 100m Freestyle Relay and 4 x 100m Medley Relay.

'He has the ability to feel the water, much like an
artist feels the canvas and a pianist feels the keys.
Those are things you just don't teach people.'

Matt Biondi's coach, Nort Thornton

FANNY
BLANKERS-KOEN

NETHERLANDS

ATHLETICS

'The First Queen of Women's Olympics' is a title that belongs to no one but Fanny Blankers-Koen. She remains the first and only woman ever to have won four Athletics gold medals at a single Olympic Games, a feat she achieved in London 1948. In 1999 she was voted Female Athlete of the Century by the International Association of Athletics Federations (IAAF).

Whether she is called 'The Flying Housewife', 'The Flying Dutchwoman', 'Amazing Fanny' or 'The First Queen of Women's Olympics', the sobriquets used to describe an unsurpassable athlete cannot do her justice. Fanny Blankers-Koen is one of the finest all-round athletes in history and the most successful female athlete ever at a single Olympic Games, her haul of four gold medals matched only by that of the great American men Jesse Owens and Carl Lewis. And Blankers-Koen did it as a 30-year-old mother of two.

She stormed around the Wembley track at the London 1948 Olympic Games to triumph in the 100m, 200m, 80m Hurdles and 4 x 100m Relay, proving her detractors wrong and inspiring women around the world, even to this day, with her outstanding achievements.

After eight gruelling days of competition in London she returned to the Netherlands firmly established as 'The Flying Housewife', and was awarded with the slightly curious gift of a bicycle.

A remarkable athletics career, which lasted 20 years from 1935 to 1955, actually started in fairly unassuming circumstances. Swimming had been Blankers-Koen's first sport before she switched to the track in 1935 at the age of 17, and set a national record for the 800m in only her third competitive race. A year later, she was encouraged to enter the Olympic Games trials by her coach, and soon-to-be husband, Jan Blankers. At the 1936 Berlin Games she tied for sixth in the High Jump and the 4 x 100m Relay, but also managed to collect the autograph of her hero Jesse Owens.

She went on to win European titles and set multiple world records – a total that reached 20 over her whole career – but her best years were lost to World War II. Before the London 1948 Olympic Games, most thought that her chance had passed, that she was just a housewife in Amsterdam and too old to be a genuine contender in London. Others claimed she should stay at home and look after her children. Perhaps with those words ringing in her ears, Blankers-Koen won her first event – the 100m – charging through mud and rain to the finish line in a time of 11.90 seconds. It was the first Olympic Athletics gold ever for a Dutch person, and a second soon followed when Blankers-Koen beat Briton Maureen Gardner in the 80m Hurdles in a photo finish.

Homesickness almost derailed her attempt at the 200m, which she won by seven-tenths of a

Statistics

Born: 26 April 1918, Baarn, Utrecht, Netherlands
Died: 25 January 2004
Height: 5ft 9in (1.75m)
Weight: 139lb (63kg)

Olympic Games Medals

London 1948

Women's 100m .... Gold
Women's 200m .... Gold
Women's 80m Hurdles .... Gold
Women's 4 × 100m Relay .... Gold

Below: Blankers-Koen stretches out her leading arm to assist her jump during the 80m Hurdles at the London 1948 Olympic Games.

Right: Blankers-Koen displays the style that led the IAAF to name her the female athlete of the 20th century.

second in 24.40 seconds – still the largest margin of victory in an Olympic 200m final. More drama followed – on the day of the final of the 4 x 100m Relay, Blankers-Koen went missing. With time running out before the start of the race, it seems

she went out to buy a raincoat, arriving back at the track only just in time to compete. She still won her fourth and final gold, at the end of 11 heats and finals in eight days, running the anchor leg and taking the team from third place to first.

Blankers-Koen had won four of the nine women's Athletics events. It could have been more if she had been able to schedule in the Long Jump and High Jump. She was crowned the IAAF's Female Athlete of the 20th century.

'All I've done is run fast. I don't see why people should make much fuss about that.'

ARNOLD **BOLDT**
PARALYMPIC ATHLETICS

Arnold Boldt rewrote the record books during an astonishing career that saw him win gold medals at five successive Paralympic Games. The Canadian was one of the pre-eminent athletes of his or any other generation, with his dominance in the High Jump unlikely to be surpassed. Yet he was also superb at the Long Jump, winning two Paralympic golds and a silver medal during his illustrious career.

Arnold Boldt's astounding success in the Paralympic Games was achieved against all the odds, but from a young age it was clear that the Canadian was determined to overcome any obstacle in his pursuit of glory. As he lost his right leg in a farming accident at the age of three, one might not necessarily have expected Boldt to be sport-obsessed.

With nowhere to train, he could have been forgiven for concentrating on matters other than Athletics. But the youngster was certainly determined and practised wherever he could. His parents' basement was converted into a miniature High Jump arena, using a sofa as a crash mat. Bales of hay were placed to cushion his fall when he was practising outdoors, and his dedication certainly paid off.

His prosthetist had told him about the Paralympic Games, and Boldt was determined to star in the Toronto 1976 Games, in his home country. He entered the High Jump and Long Jump, and trounced the opposition. His winning mark in the High Jump was 1.86m – 21cm higher than second-placed Konrad Reisner of Austria – as Boldt claimed the first gold medal of his career.

It was a similar story in the Long Jump. Again Reisner was his closest challenger, with his mark of 2.64m enough to give him a silver medal. But Boldt was untouchable as he jumped an astonishing 2.96m to seal the second gold medal of his inaugural Paralympic campaign.

Boldt, who also played Wheelchair Basketball and Sitting Volleyball, continued to dominate his sport, and was invited to able-bodied Athletics meetings as well. His superiority was demonstrated once more in the Arnhem 1980 Paralympic Games, where he won gold again in the High Jump. This time he hopped to the bar and flew over it head first in his normal style to set a new world record height of 1.96m. Anthony Willis of Great Britain came second with a jump of 1.80m, but again the winning margin made it

CANADA

Statistics
Born: 16 September 1957, Osler, Saskatchewan, Canada

Paralympic Games Medals
Toronto 1976
Men's High Jump D ....Gold
Men's Long Jump D ....Gold

Arnhem 1980
Men's High Jump D ....Gold
Men's Long Jump D ....Gold

New York/Stoke Mandeville 1984
Men's High Jump A2 ....Gold

Seoul 1988
Men's High Jump A2A9 ....Gold
Men's Long Jump A2A9 .... Silver

Barcelona 1992
Men's High Jump A1............................Gold

'I was fairly well accepted for who I was; it was quite easy to be yourself and do what you wanted to do without people prejudging you.'

Left: Boldt was a World Champion, a world-record holder and seven-time Paralympic Games gold-medal winner, a true Athletics legend.

Right: Clearing the bar at 1.95m, Boldt wins another High Jump gold medal, this time at the New York/Stoke Mandeville 1984 Games.

clear that no one could get near him. Just as he had done four years earlier, Boldt doubled up events, also competing in the Long Jump – and again he was completely dominant. The Canadian jumped 2.92m, giving him a winning margin of 16cm over Bert Bottemanne of the Netherlands.

A year later Boldt registered a new personal best with a High Jump of 2.04m, a mark he improved on by 4cm in an indoor event in Winnipeg. He could not quite hit those heights in the New York/Stoke Mandeville 1984 Paralympic Games, but he did not need to: he returned home again with a gold medal to his name after a leap of 1.95m sealed the High Jump title. It was a gold medal he was to retain four years later in Seoul 1988 as he recorded a jump of 1.94m, yet he was beaten to gold in the Long Jump by Albert Mead, although the silver medal was still a consolation.

That meant Boldt had won gold medals in four successive Paralympic Games – and he made it five to crown his career in Barcelona 1992. He did not quite replicate the glory of previous years, but a jump of 1.80m was enough to secure an astonishing fifth High Jump gold. And it appears that his records and achievements are standing the test of time, a fitting tribute to an astonishing athlete.

USAIN **BOLT**
ATHLETICS

The 2008 Olympic Games will always be remembered for Usain Bolt's astonishing feats in the Bird's Nest in Beijing. The Jamaican became the first man to win both the Men's 100m and 200m titles since Carl Lewis in Los Angeles 1984, but it was the fact that he shattered the world records in both events that really took the breath away.

Chicken nuggets are hardly recommended by nutritionists as a pre-race meal, but Usain Bolt is not your average athlete. The Jamaican has dominated the world of sprinting since his mind-blowing performance in the Beijing 2008 Olympic Games, where he won three gold medals and became the first man to simultaneously hold the world record for the 100m, 200m and 4 x 100m Relay.

Bolt has come a long way since his childhood in Trelawny, where he was more focused on football and cricket until Pablo McNeil, a former Olympic sprinter, recognised his potential and encouraged him to take up athletics. The results have been remarkable. Despite a carefree attitude in his younger days, Bolt was always astonishingly fast, and he made his first serious impact at international level in 2002, when he became the youngest person ever to claim a gold medal in the World Junior Championships, when he won the 200m aged just 15. He turned professional in 2004, although the Olympic Games of that year were a disappointment as he was eliminated in the first round of the 200m.

Bolt was dogged by injury over the next couple of years but won six medals at the 2007 World Championships – albeit without a single gold – but it was in 2008 that he left an indelible mark on his sport and the history of the Olympic Games. In May he set a new 100m world record of 9.72 seconds, but that was just a warm-up for August's Games.

Having decided to double up in the 100m and 200m, he cruised through the heats in the former and was the strong favourite for the final. Yet few could have expected to see Bolt fly past the field, even having time to celebrate before reaching the finishing line – and all with one of his laces undone. A new world record of 9.69 was set and a star was born.

Four days later, he was even more impressive in the 200m. This time he really went for it and even

dipped his head at the line: he claimed another gold, setting a new world best time of 19.30 seconds, and left watching record holder Michael Johnson almost lost for words. Bolt's famous celebration, the 'Lightning Bolt', was unleashed yet again as the Beijing crowd rapturously applauded his achievements, so much so that the start of the next race had to be delayed. On 22 August, the record books were rewritten once more as Bolt, Nest Carter, Michael Frater and Asafa Powell won the 4 x 100m Relay in a world record 37.10.

The fact that the indisputable star of Beijing 2008 eats chicken nuggets before every race seems to sit perfectly with his laid-back persona. Athletes' stars can wane after their triumphs in major events, but Bolt's has continued to rise. Indeed, he even bettered his Beijing 2008 achievements in the 2009 World Championships

in Berlin. The statistics barely begin to tell the story as he won the 100m in 9.58 and the 200m in 19.19, taking over a tenth of a second off each of his own world records. Perhaps the scariest thing for Usain Bolt's rivals is that he will be just 25 by the time of the London 2012 Olympic Games, and he believes there is still room for improvement.

Statistics
Born: 21 August 1986, Trelawny, Jamaica
Height: 6ft 5in (1.95m)
Weight: 207lb (94kg)

Olympic Games Medals
Beijing 2008
Men's 100m	Gold
Men's 200m	Gold
Men's 4 x 100m Relay	Gold

'He's a gift to this earth. He's a blessing to the track game. I'm just waiting for the lights to flash "game over", because I felt like I was in a video game.'

American sprinter Shawn Crawford, who finished second to Bolt in Beijing 2008

Above: Usain Bolt brandishes his well-won gold medal on the podium after winning the Men's 100m at the Beijing 2008 Olympic Games.

Right: Bolt's famous reaction after winning the Men's 200m final in Beijing 2008, earning his media nickname 'Lightning Bolt'.

VALERY **BORZOV**
ATHLETICS

USSR

Valery Borzov has lived an Olympic career filled with politics and controversy, yet on the track he was a sensational sprinter. 'The Fastest Man in the East' won two golds and a silver at the Munich 1972 Olympic Games, and more medals in Montreal 1976 four years later.

The Men's 100m quarter-final heat at the Munich 1972 Olympic Games very nearly began without Valery Borzov in the starting line-up. However, luckily for the sleepy Ukrainian, he awoke from his pre-race nap just in time to make it to the starting line. It was an event that Borzov, who was representing the Soviet Union at the time, would go on to win, and an event which would make him a household name. In another fortunate twist, the American athletes – and favourites for Olympic sprint glory – Eddie Hart and Rey Robinson were both eliminated for missing their respective heats, and Borzov eased to success in the final, claiming his first Olympic gold medal.

The two American sprinters vowed revenge on the victorious Ukrainian, claiming they would beat him in the 200m final. However, Borzov was spurred on by the Americans' taunts, and won an incredible second gold of the Games,

setting a new European record of 20 seconds. He completed his success in Munich with a third and final medal, taking silver in the 4 x 100m Relay.

Four years on, in Montreal in the summer of 1976, he returned to the Olympic Games, striving to add to his already impressive medal collection. However, in extraordinary circumstances, he only managed two bronze medals, in the 100m and the 4 x 100m Relay, despite the fact that he was considered a strong favourite to claim gold. Perhaps he can be excused for not succeeding in the manner expected of him, given that he had stolen the lion's share of the headlines ahead of the Games, but for all the wrong reasons. There were reports that Borzov was about to defect from the Soviet Union team and request political asylum. As a result, he was on the receiving end of countless threatening phone calls, a number of which claimed he was going to be assassinated in the final of the 100m event.

Seen in this context, his bronze medal, which might otherwise have been questioned, can be regarded as a significant success. For a man with such pressure and fear resting on his shoulders to still claim a place in the top three and guarantee himself yet another Olympic Games medal is something of a sensation.

Borzov was unable to compete at the 1980 Olympic Games, held in his native Moscow, because of a persistent injury problem, and he therefore turned his attentions from athletics to politics, becoming the first president of the Ukrainian Olympic Committee. Before moving away from sport entirely, he was also the president of the Ukrainian Track and Field Federation. He then became a member of the Ukrainian parliament, a position he held for eight years before stepping down in 2006.

He is now settled and happily married to fellow Olympian Ludmila Tourischeva, who happens to be one of the most successful Olympic gymnasts of all time. Their trophy cabinet at home is bursting at the seams.

Statistics
Born: 20 October 1949, Lviv, Ukraine
Height: 6ft (1.83m)
Weight: 176lb (80kg)

Olympic Games Medals
Munich 1972
Men's 100m ....Gold
Men's 200m..Gold
Men's 4 x 100m Relay.......................... Silver

Montreal 1976
Men's 100m .... Bronze
Men's 4 x 100m Relay.................... Bronze

Left: Part of Borzov's success was down to using techniques such as visualisation, routinely used by athletes today.

Right: Borzov was unbeaten for two years before the Munich 1972 Olympic Games and won the 100m without ever looking troubled.

'I never considered quitting.
I will fight for an Olympic medal.'

VALERIE
BRISCO-HOOKS
ATHLETICS

USA

Valerie Brisco-Hooks took up athletics as a tribute to her brother Robert, who had been shot on a Los Angeles running track. But it was only after the birth of her son that she dedicated herself to greatness, exploding on to the scene in Los Angeles 1984 by becoming the first athlete of either sex to win both the 200m and 400m sprints in the same Olympic Games.

O ut of shape and more or less resigned to retirement two years prior to her landmark Olympic Games feat, Valerie Brisco-Hooks achieved something that has only ever been matched by two others – Marie-Jose Perec and Michael Johnson, both in 1996. Her coaches revealed that she was still some 39½lb (18kg) overweight in the build-up to the Los Angeles 1984 Olympic Games, following the birth of her son two years before, and her career in athletics looked over without ever really coming to fruition.

Although she was born in America's South, Brisco-Hooks was perhaps viewed as the clichéd girl from the inner city, growing up in the poorer urban areas of Los Angeles. She would come to realise, too, the difficulties of living in such deprived neighbourhoods. Her older brother Robert, a rising athletics star at junior level, fell victim to gun crime. He was tragically shot dead by a stray bullet while training when Brisco-Hooks was just 14 years old. With the support of those closest to her, she was persuaded to make it her lifelong aim to achieve her own athletics goals, vowing to make her brother proud: 'Someone has to carry on the family name, so they chose me,' she famously said.

This was not before she had to overcome further obstacles on her way to the world stage: Brisco-Hooks struggled with chronic weight gain after the birth of her son and it needed the concerted efforts of her American-football-star husband Alvin Hooks and coaches alike to encourage her out of her inertia and back into training. She eventually left the sofa and defied the odds to become one of the most famous sprinters of all time.

At the height of her powers and determination, the then-24-year-old bagged the 200m and 400m gold medals at the 1984 Olympic Games in her native Los Angeles, knocking aside every favourite along the way. In one of the most iconic Olympic scenes of all time, her coach Bobby Kersee dodged security to embrace her, causing them both to tumble, and the pair rolled around the Olympic field in an outpouring of raw emotion. She made it a hat-trick of gold medals for herself and America with the 4 x 400m Relay team and, despite fading into obscurity, her exploits lit a candle that will forever burn bright in the sprinting world.

No one really knows the true reasons behind Brisco-Hooks' decline. Maybe, psychologically, she had achieved what she set out to do – to fulfil the potential and carry on the reputation her brother had established for himself and, in so doing, obtain some sort of justice and retribution

Statistics

Born: 6 July 1960, Greenwood, Mississippi, USA
Height: 5ft 7in (1.7m)
Weight: 137lb (62kg)

Olympic Games Medals

Los Angeles 1984

Women's 200m ....Gold
Women's 400m.......................................Gold
Women's 4 x 400m Relay ....Gold

Seoul 1988

Women's 4 x 400m Relay .... Silver

Below: Brisco-Hooks (right) holds the American flag aloft with pride after winning the 200m at the Los Angeles 1984 Olympic Games.

Right: The American took up running in honour of her brother, Robert, and is pictured on her way to winning three Olympic gold medals in 1984.

'I was really big. It took me a while to really believe in myself and want to run, but Bobby kept coming to my house and saying, "Valerie, I know you have it in you."'

Valerie Brisco-Hooks returns to running after the birth of her child

for him. However, she would return to the Olympic Games, at Seoul 1988, aiming to defend her 400m title at least. After striving to stay with the field in the championships leading up to the Games, she finished second in the semi-finals with her best time of the year. Unfortunately for Brisco-Hooks, she could not take this form into the final, and did well to finish a creditable fourth. She did achieve a medal, though, winning silver in the women's 4 x 400m Relay team.

She continued to compete after the Seoul 1988 Games but subsequently retired from track and field in 1991. Despite a life littered with unfortunate and undeserved personal setbacks, Brisco-Hooks will take comfort from the fact that she will be remembered forever as one of the most respected sprinters in Olympic history, and certainly one of the most cherished.

CASSIUS **CLAY**
BOXING

USA

Cassius Clay, better known as Muhammad Ali in the years following his Olympic Games career, is regarded by many as the greatest-ever boxer in the history of the sport. The three-times heavyweight champion of the world was crowned Sportsman of the Century and is among the five most recognised faces on the planet.

Few if any can match the achievements of Cassius Clay during a memorable career in boxing. After his gold-medal Olympic success the American boxer – more commonly known as Muhammad Ali, following his name change in 1964 – not only dominated his sport, but he became an inspiration to millions of people across the world.

Clay was born in Kentucky in 1942 and was the elder of two boys. He was named after his father and wasted no time taking a keen interest in sport. He was encouraged to take up boxing by a Louisville police officer and boxing coach,

also enabling him to gain knowledge from the more experienced Stoner, who played a major role in his early development. Stoner helped him win six Kentucky Golden Gloves titles, two national Golden Gloves titles and an Amateur Athletic Union national title.

By the age of 18 he had already amassed a record of over 100 victories with just five defeats. This had put him in the perfect frame of mind as he prepared for his first major tournament at the Rome 1960 Olympic Games. Clay showed his true potential in the single elimination tournament when he blitzed his way past his

Statistics

Born: 17 January 1942, Louisville, Kentucky, USA
Height: 6ft 3in (1.89m)
Weight: 176lb (80kg)

Olympic Games Medals

Rome 1960
Men's Light Heavyweight...................Gold

Joe E. Martin, who came into contact with him when the boy was left fuming over the theft of his bicycle at the Columbia Auditorium. Clay took up boxing at the age of 12 and quickly worked his way through the amateur ranks. Unbeknown to Martin, Clay was also being coached by trainer Fred Stoner, who worked at the local community centre. The young boxer needed to do this as Martin was hosting a local weekly TV show called *Tomorrow's Champions*, which helped Clay earn $4 a week and get his name on the circuit, while

opponents in the qualifying rounds, and beat Poland's Zbigniew Pietrzykowski in the final to win a gold medal.

Clay turned professional immediately after Rome 1960 and easily won his first fight against fellow American Tunney Hunsaker. It was not long before he was working his way up the heavyweight ranks, and he continued his unbeaten run over the next three years, overcoming the likes of Archie Moore, Sonny Banks and Henry Cooper and often correctly predicting which round he would do it in.

Above: The Olympic Games are the peak for most athletes, but they were just the start for one gold-medal winning boxer as he towered over his rivals in 1960.

Right: Clay shows his punching power on his way to a unanimous points victory over Russia's Gennadiy Shatov in the Men's Light Heavyweight final.

Clay was the fastest heavyweight boxer anyone had ever seen and had an unorthodox style for such a tall athlete. He never threw any body shots and some say he had the most nimble legs in the history of the sport, which enabled him to float across the ring. His first heavyweight title match was against Sonny Liston in 1964 and, though few gave him a chance of victory, he won by a technical knockout in the seventh round.

Clay then changed his name to Muhammad Ali after telling the world he had embraced the Black Muslim faith. Ali went on to dominate the boxing world and was unbeaten through the 1960s, but

he caused controversy when he refused to be called up for induction into the armed services and had his fighting licence revoked.

After three and a half years away from the sport, Ali made his comeback but lost his heavyweight crown to Joe Frazier in what was billed as the 'fight of the century' in 1971. Ali quickly won back his belt when he defeated George Foreman, who was another Olympic champion, in the 'Rumble in the Jungle', the showdown fight held in Kinshasa, Zaire. He suffered more disappointment when he was defeated by the 1976 light heavyweight Olympic champion Leon Spinks, but he then won back the

heavyweight crown from the same opponent.

He is the only man in heavyweight history to have won the crown three times, and ended his career with a record of 56 wins (37 by knockout) and just five defeats.

Ali was diagnosed with Parkinson's disease in 1984, but he was given the ultimate accolade when he was asked to light the Olympic Flame at the opening ceremony of the Atlanta 1996 Games. After all those years as a professional, it illustrated perfectly what Cassius Clay had meant to the Olympic Games, and what the Olympic Games had done for him.

'I am the greatest; I said that even before I knew I was. I'm in a world of my own. Not only do I knock 'em out, I pick the round.'

SEBASTIAN COE
ATHLETICS

The golden boy from Britain's golden age of middle-distance running, Sebastian Coe (now Lord Coe) transfixed a generation with his style of running as well as the much-publicised duel with compatriot Steve Ovett throughout the late 1970s and early 1980s. He won 1,500m gold medals in both Moscow 1980 and Los Angeles 1984.

The sight of Sebastian Coe crossing the line at the finish of the 1,500m in Moscow 1980, arms raised above his head and eyes rolled towards the sky, is one of the most famous and iconic images in Olympic history. It was the culmination of a fascinating duel between the free-flowing runner who had revolutionised middle-distance running and his great rival Steve Ovett, who had matched him record for record.

Coe had earlier finished second behind Ovett in the 800m, his specialist event for which he had been a strong favourite, claiming afterwards that he had run the 'worst tactical race of my life'. So to come back from that low and win the 1,500m, inflicting Ovett's first defeat over that distance in three years, represented a momentous effort – and no wonder the BBC is planning to dramatise the race in a forthcoming film.

But there is far more to admire about Coe's career than just an intense rivalry with an international team-mate. He will go down in history as one of the greatest milers Athletics has ever produced, setting records with remarkable regularity. In 1979, in fact, he produced three world records in the space of just 41 days over 800m, 1,500m and the mile. In that year, and again in 1981, Coe – whose training was famously overseen by his father, Peter, who acted as his coach and motivator – was ranked number one in the world at both 800m and 1,500m, and during his career he set nine world records outdoors and three indoors.

He was also a phenomenal racer in major championships, famed for his incredible sprint finish. In fact, to see Coe surging for the front and effortlessly leaving his rivals for dead over the final 200 metres was one of the great sights of athletics for many years. He added to his 1,500m gold in Moscow 1980 by winning the same race four years later, setting an Olympic record of 3:32.53 in the process as he beat Steve Cram to the line, and once again finished second in the 800m.

His CV also includes 800m victories in European and World Championships and, although he inexplicably missed out on his third Olympic Games in 1988 after a poor run in the trials, he remains one of the greatest middle-distance runners of all time. Ten years after he retired in 1990 his world records at 800m and 1,500m still stood, a testimony to the calibre of his performances. His influence on the sport has not waned, either. Following a spell in politics, including several years as a British MP, he went on to lead London's successful bid for the London 2012 Games and is now chair of the London Organising Committee of the Olympic Games.

He was made a life peer in 2000, taking the title of Baron Coe of Ranmore, and has also been awarded an MBE and OBE.

Statistics

Born: 29 September 1956, London, England
Height: 5ft 9in (1.75m)
Weight: 119lb (54kg)

Olympic Games Medals

Moscow 1980

Men's 1,500m	Gold
Men's 800m	Silver

Los Angeles 1984

Men's 1,500m	Gold
Men's 800m	Silver

Below: Coe was gracious in defeat, twice winning silver in the 800m, behind Steve Ovett at Moscow 1980 and Joaquim Cruz of Brazil at Los Angeles 1984.

Right: Coe matched his 1980 gold medal in the 1,500m final at the Los Angeles 1984 Games, becoming the first athlete to win successive golds in that event.

*'On the day there was only one man, and on the day
Seb Coe was that man.'*

Steve Cram reflects on being beaten into second place in the 1,500m final in Los Angeles 1984

NADIA **COMANECI**
GYMNASTICS – ARTISTIC

This Romanian gymnast could have changed her name to 'Nadia Comaneci Perfect 10' and few would have complained. Comaneci became the first gymnast to be awarded the maximum mark at the Olympic Games, a feat she ultimately achieved six times. A total of nine Olympic medals, five of them gold, has made her a true legend of her sport.

Very few sportsmen or women can genuinely claim to have made history in the Olympic Games, but for gymnasts, Nadia Comaneci is the standard by which all performances are now judged. Her display on the Uneven Bars Competition in the Montreal 1976 Games was too good even for the scoreboard. As the crowd erupted at her performance, the digital scoreboard simply showed '1.00' as it only had space for three numerals and could not display '10.00'. Yet, astonishingly, it was one of seven perfect scores for the 14-year-old as she claimed three gold medals, a silver and a bronze.

Those performances were repeated four years later in Moscow 1980 when she returned home with two more golds and another two silvers, giving her an impressive tally of nine Olympic medals. It was fair to say that Comaneci had come a long way from her humble upbringing. She took up gymnastics at the age of six, and was swiftly taken under the wing of Bela Karolyi, who was to become a hugely respected and successful coach.

Within two years Comaneci had been crowned national champion and her reputation was spreading fast. She made her first real impact on an international stage in the 1975 European Championships, blowing away the competition and coming agonisingly close to winning a clean sweep of all the events. She eventually took gold in every event except the Floor Competition, in which she took silver. After a performance like that, it was no surprise that Comaneci was the favourite going into the Montreal 1976 Games. Tickets to get into the Montreal Forum, where the Gymnastics events were being held, were going for hundreds of dollars. And the audience, lucky enough to witness history, were not left feeling short-changed after Comaneci's performance on the Uneven Bars.

The Romanian has since said she never used to look at the scoreboard in the seconds after she finished her routine, but made an exception this time because the crowd erupted in celebration.

And the 14-year-old was not finished there. Six more perfect scores led to three golds, two silvers and a bronze medal, as she became the youngest ever winner of the Individual All-Around gold.

By her own high standards, the next four years were not as productive for the young star, although she did claim gold on the beam in the 1978 World Championships in Strasbourg, and the all-round title in the 1979 European Championships in Copenhagen. With gymnasts enjoying relatively short careers, many had questioned whether Comaneci, by now aged 18, could follow up her Olympic achievements at the Moscow 1980 Games. As it turned out, she was able to summon enough strength to rule the world again. She disappointed slightly in the Individual All-Around Competition, coming second, but retained her gold in the Balance Beam and also stood on top of the podium in the Floor Competition.

She may not have reached the heights attained in Montreal 1976, but it is hard to improve on perfection. Comaneci retired from the sport a year later and returned to Romania, before defecting to the US in 1989. She married fellow gold-winning gymnast Bart Conners, with whom she runs a gymnastics school. Having achieved perfection herself, she now develops future Olympic heroes.

Statistics
Born: 12 November 1961, Onesti, Romania
Height: 4ft 11in (1.5m)
Weight: 99lb (45kg)

Olympic Games Medals
Montreal 1976
Women's Uneven Bars Competition..Gold
Women's Balance Beam Competition..Gold
Women's Individual All-Around Competition..Gold
Women's Team Competition.........Silver
Women's Floor Competition.......Bronze

Moscow 1980
Women's Balance Beam Competition..Gold
Women's Floor Competition............Gold
Women's Individual All-Around Competition.......................................Silver
Women's Team Competition.........Silver

Above: With her performance on the Uneven Bars during the Team Competition at the Montreal 1976 Games, Comaneci became the first gymnast to score a perfect 10.

Right: Although Comaneci couldn't quite match her phenomenal medal haul of 1976, she won four medals at Moscow 1980, including gold on the Balance Beam.

*'Hard work has made it easy. That is my secret.
That is why I win.'*

PHILIP **CRAVEN**
WHEELCHAIR BASKETBALL

GREAT BRITAIN

Sir Philip Craven MBE may not have a cabinet bulging with Paralympic medals but his influence is undeniable. An accomplished Wheelchair Basketball player across five Paralympic Games, he is now President of the International Paralympic Committee (IPC).

Through his various official posts, whether it is his presidency of the IPC, his membership of the International Olympic Committee (IOC) or the legacy he helped to shape as a founding member of the World Anti-Doping Agency (WADA), Philip Craven has left an indelible mark on both the Olympic and Paralympic Games. And while he continues his sterling work as an influential administrator, it should be remembered that his involvement dates back to Heidelberg 1972, when he competed in the first of five Paralympic Games in Wheelchair Basketball.

Craven and the Great Britain team finished second in their group behind Argentina and pushed eventual champions, the USA, all the way in their semi-final clash before they lost 52–36. Argentina once again had the measure of Great Britain in the bronze-medal game, where they won 54–39, but it was clear that the team would remain a threat. However, not content with spearheading Great Britain's charge in Wheelchair Basketball, Craven also competed in Athletics events, as well as the Men's 50m Breaststroke at Heidelberg 1972.

His gold medal at the Commonwealth Games in 1970 and another in the European Championships a year before his Paralympic debut hinted at what was to come and, in 1973, his Great Britain side reigned supreme in the World Championships, claiming gold. In the lead-up to his second Paralympic Games in Toronto 1976, Craven won another gold medal in the European Championships as well as a bronze in the World Championships, but at the Toronto Paralympic Games he was unable to inspire Great Britain to glory as eventual silver-medallists Israel won 60–26 in the quarter-finals.

By the late 1970s, Craven's standing in the sport had grown to such an extent that it was only a matter of time before he received official recognition and, while still competing, he was appointed the Great Britain Wheelchair Basketball Association (GBWBA) chairman. His work off the court did not prevent him from tasting Paralympic competition again, but in Arnhem 1980 he could only watch as

Israel underlined their status as the world's best Wheelchair Basketball nation.

After stepping down as chairman of the GBWBA in 1980, Craven went on to complete two more successful terms serving the association as a Committee member, as well as competing in two more Paralympic Games. Although Paralympic glory continued to elude him, Craven and the Great Britain Wheelchair Basketball team were still a force to be reckoned with in the European Championships, as they claimed a silver in 1993, while a gold medal in the European Champions Cup followed a year later.

Statistics
Born: 4 July 1950, Bolton, England

Paralympic Games
Heidelberg 1972
Wheelchair Basketball, Swimming (50m Breaststroke 3) and Athletics (100m 3 and Slalom 3)
Toronto 1976, Arnhem 1980, New York/Stoke Mandeville 1984 and Seoul 1988
Wheelchair Basketball

Below: As IPC President, Craven appears at the opening ceremony of the Beijing 2008 Paralympic Games.

Right: Craven (centre) played Wheelchair Basketball for Great Britain, participating in five different Paralympic Games. He was also a swimmer and an athlete.

42

At the end of five successive Olympiads, in 1988, Craven strove to influence the game off the court and was the President of the International Wheelchair Basketball Federation from 1998 to 2002, as well as playing a crucial role in bringing the Olympic and Paralympic Games to London in 2012. He has been a board member of the London Organising Committee of the Olympic Games since 2005, the year of his knighthood, and has combined his role with numerous high-profile jobs elsewhere. The IPC President is also a member of the IOC as well as being on the board of the British Olympic Association since 2003.

With medals to his name and a wealth of experience to draw upon, he has possibly the most influential voice across both Olympic and Paralympic competition.

'The biggest accomplishment that the Movement has made while I've been president is we've moved from being a disability, with a big "D", sports organisation to a sports organisation where that "D" word doesn't exist.'

BETTY **CUTHBERT**
ATHLETICS

There can only be one 'Golden Girl'. Betty Cuthbert earned that moniker following her stunning performances at the Melbourne 1956 Olympic Games in her native Australia, where she won three sprinting gold medals. Another gold at Tokyo 1964 lifted her into the pantheon of Olympic greats.

Born in 1938, Elizabeth 'Betty' Cuthbert grew up during the Great Depression and would often train in between the rows of plants at her father's horticultural nursery. She won a plethora of sprinting trophies while at primary school and this would hint at further victories to come.

After meeting renowned athletics coach June Ferguson while at high school, a fruitful partnership was born. Cuthbert stood out at a young age and her tendency to run with her mouth open would be a trademark characteristic people would identify her by in the years to come, as well as her strawberry-blonde hair.

Ahead of the Melbourne 1956 Games, Cuthbert was so convinced she would not make the Australian team she originally bought tickets to watch as a spectator. Her modesty was mis-placed, however, and after breaking into the Athletics squad, she would proceed to have the very crowd she intended to sit with in raptures at her performances on the track.

Having set a world record in the 200m in the build-up to the Olympic Games, she was one of the favourites for that event. But, by her own admission, she did not rate her chances in the 100m. The Australian sprint sensation made a mockery of her pessimistic outlook and duly won the 100m, before winning her favoured event, the 200m, in a world-record time of 23.4 seconds.

In the short space of just nine days, the 18-year-old won the 100m, 200m and anchored the team that won the 4 x 100m Relay in a world-record time, which meant she had become the first Australian, male or female, to win three gold medals at a single Olympic Games. Cuthbert, at just 18, was world famous and a national hero. Australia loved her, with her striking appearance and open mouth further endearing her to the crowds. At the Rome 1960 Olympic Games four years later, Cuthbert was expected to sweep the board once again, but a torn leg muscle ruined her chances of emulating her Melbourne masterclass

and forced her out of the heats in the 100m. Then came news of her shock retirement.

A deeply religious woman, she announced her decision to return to athletics two years after retirement, claiming God told her to continue. 'I said "OK, you win", and as soon as I said that this wonderful feeling came right through my body, and I was mentally keen to want to do something again,' she later recalled.

Now 26, she returned to Olympic competition for the Tokyo 1964 Games, although she was written off by those who considered her injury lay-off too detrimental to her career. With her mouth gaping wide as always, she not only claimed her fourth Olympic gold in the 400m, but she did it with a time of 52 seconds – an Olympic record. It meant she was one of only three 20th-century Australian Olympians, alongside swimmers Dawn Fraser and Murray Rose, to win four Olympic golds.

Between 1956 and 1964 Cuthbert set or equalled 18 world records over 60m, 100m, 200m, 400m, the 4 x 100m and 4 x 220m Relays. Despite since battling multiple sclerosis, her determination and spirit to overcome illness were there for all to see when she helped carry the Olympic Torch at the opening ceremony at the Sydney 2000 Olympic Games.

Statistics

Born: 20 April 1938, Merrylands, New South Wales, Australia
Height: 5ft 7in (1.7m)
Weight: 125lb (57kg)

Olympic Games Medals

Melbourne 1956

Women's 100m..............................Gold
Women's 200m ....Gold
Women's 4 x 100m Relay................Gold

Tokyo 1964

Women's 400m.............................Gold

Below: Modest Cuthbert bought tickets to attend the Melbourne 1956 Games as she did not rate her chances of being chosen to represent Australia.

Right: Cuthbert (right) won three gold medals at the Melbourne 1956 Olympic Games. She pipped Britain's Heather Armitage to first place in the Women's 4 x 100m Relay, in a world record time of 44.5 seconds.

'While I was out I did the right thing, by being in the public [eye] and being noticed, but I loved to get home and have my little security.'

DAVID **DOUILLET**
JUDO

David Douillet was primed to become a heavyweight *judoka* from an early age – at 11 years old he stood 5ft 9in (1.8m) and weighed 176lb (80kg); at his peak, he was 6ft 5in (1.96m) tall and weighed (275lb) 125kg. Douillet's extraordinary natural physique, combined with a fiercely competitive nature, translated into a glittering career – a bronze medal at the Barcelona 1992 Games was soon trumped by gold medals in Atlanta 1996 and Sydney 2000, along with four World Championship titles.

D avid Douillet's steady success at junior level set him up nicely for senior action, and in 1991, aged 21, he won his first senior national title. The newly crowned French heavyweight champion then achieved a very respectable third place in his first senior European Championships.

In 1992, Douillet successfully defended his national title, cementing his position as his country's best heavyweight *judoka*. National recognition soon became international – Douillet won bronze at the Barcelona 1992 Games later that year, still aged just 22, after coming up against some tough competition in the shape of the Seoul 1988 silver medallist Henry Stöhr of Germany and four-time World Champion Naoya Ogawa of Japan.

Douillet went into the 1993 World Judo Championships in Hamilton, Ontario, knowing that he would probably have to defeat number one favourite, Georgian, David Khakhaleishvili to emerge as World Heavyweight Champion. Sure enough, Olympic and European Champion Khakhaleishvili was powerless to stop Douillet, who became the first French World Champion in the +95kg weight class. Douillet supplemented this great victory with his first European title the following year in Gdansk, Poland, when he defeated Pole, Rafal Kubacki, again in the +95kg category.

At the 1995 World Championships in Chiba, Japan, the French team competed in both Douillet's +95kg weight class and the Open category, which has no weight limit. Douillet was up to the challenge, emerging victorious in both classes; he even finished off his +95kg final opponent, German, Frank Möller in less than two minutes. Douillet became only the third *judoka* to achieve this special double victory.

Douillet's outstanding performances at these World Championships made him favourite for Olympic gold at the Atlanta 1996 Games. In Atlanta, Douillet's semi-final opponent was Naoya Ogawa, the Japanese *judoka* who had defeated him at the same stage in the Olympic competition four years earlier. This time, the Frenchman narrowly won before going on to easily defeat Spaniard Ernesto Pérez in the final, thus claiming his first Olympic gold.

Soon after his Olympic victory however, Douillet was seriously injured in a motorbike accident. Following eight months of rehabilitation, the Frenchman demonstrated tremendous strength of character to return to the judo ring and win a fourth World Championships in Paris in 1997.

Douillet suffered further injury setbacks over the next couple of years, and was mostly unable to compete. In spite of this, he bounced back from adversity yet again to take another Olympic gold at Sydney 2000, defeating Japanese Shinichi Shinohara in the final, the same man he had beaten in the World Championships final in Paris three years previously. Douillet retired immediately after the Games, leaving behind a legacy as one of the most decorated *judoka* of all time.

Statistics
Born: 17 February 1969, Rouen, Seine-Maritime, France
Height: 6ft 5in (1.96m)
Weight: 276lb (125kg)

Olympic Games Medals
Barcelona 1992
Men's Heavyweight........................ Bronze

Atlanta 1996
Men's Heavyweight.............................Gold

Sydney 2000
Men's Heavyweight.............................Gold

Left: Douillet celebrates his win in the Heavyweight class at the Atlanta 1996 Games. He beat Ernesto Pérez of Spain in the final.

Right: By the time Sydney 2000 came around, Douillet (right) was competing in his third Olympic Games. He still dominated the Heavyweight class, winning gold again.

*'I am happy because I won the gold medal but I am also sad because
I must now start a new chapter. The last chapter has taken up
half my life and now it has come to an end.'*

David Douillet after winning gold in Sydney 2000

NATALIE **DU TOIT**
PARALYMPIC SWIMMING

South African swimmer Natalie Du Toit is the true embodiment of the Olympic spirit. A promising swimmer at 16, she lost a leg in a car accident but has since gone on to become one of the most successful athletes with a disability of all time, as well as being a serious challenge to able-bodied competitors.

South Africa had a new star. Natalie Du Toit set multiple national age group records and, at 16, she came close to qualifying for the Sydney 2000 Olympic Games in three events. The future of women's swimming looked bright but, in 2001, she suffered a terrible setback.

A careless driver smashed straight into her left leg as she was riding her scooter to school and, despite the best efforts of doctors, there was no alternative but to amputate. For some, that would have been the end of their career right there. Not Du Toit. The accident merely marked a footnote in her illustrious ascent to stardom.

Du Toit took to the pool again as soon as she was discharged from hospital, desperate not to let the accident ruin her promising swimming career. And less than two years after the crash, she qualified for the finals of the Women's 800m Freestyle at the 2002 Commonwealth Games – the first time an amputee had raced in the finals of an able-bodied international swimming

competition in the modern era. It was not the only time she would face able-bodied swimmers: she won gold when she competed in the 800m Freestyle at the All-Africa Games in 2003. While she was unsuccessful in the able-bodied section of the Commonwealth Games, she successfully claimed gold medals in both the 50m and 100m Freestyle multi-disability events, and there were yet more challenges ahead.

Having just fallen short of qualification for the Athens 2004 Olympic Games, Du Toit was almost unbeatable in the Athens 2004 Paralympic Games, winning five gold medals and one silver in the swimming events. Never one to rest on her laurels, Du Toit turned her attention to meet the challenge that had previously defeated her – qualification for the coming Beijing 2008 Olympic Games. In May 2008, she realised her dream, becoming the first ever athlete to qualify for the Olympic and Paralympic Games as she finished fourth at the Open Water World Championships, just five seconds behind the winner.

Statistics

Born: 29 January 1984, Cape Town,
South Africa
Height: 5ft 9in (1.75m)
Weight: 159lb (72kg)

Paralympic Games Medals

Athens 2004
Women's 100m Butterfly S9............Gold
Women's 100m Freestyle S9............Gold
Women's 200m Individual
Medley SM9............Gold
Women's 400m Freestyle S9..........Gold
Women's 50m Freestyle S9..............Gold
Women's 100m Backstroke S9.... Silver

Beijing 2008
Women's 100m Butterfly S9............Gold
Women's 100m Freestyle S9...........Gold
Women's 200m Individual
Medley SM9............Gold
Women's 400m Freestyle S9..........Gold
Women's 50m Freestyle S9..............Gold

Left: In May 2008 Du Toit became the first athlete in history to qualify for both the Olympic Games and Paralympic Games in the same year.

Right: The South African won her first Paralympic gold medal in Butterfly.

'It doesn't matter if you look different. You're still the same as everybody else because you have the same dream.'

For some, just to have qualified would have represented a victory, but Du Toit was intent on pushing the boundaries. She was desperate to push herself into medal contention at Beijing 2008. Unfortunately for her, she finished 16th in the able-bodied event, but back in Paralympic competition Du Toit reigned supreme once again, with a haul of five gold medals. Before the London 2012 Games, the South African sensation had 11 Paralympic medals to her name, 10 of them gold.

Her story is as heartening as it is awe-inspiring. Not content with utter domination of the Paralympic circuit, Du Toit is battling – and looks a decent bet – to claim a medal in able-bodied Olympic competition at the London 2012 Games. Paralympic competition has come a long way since the American gymnast George Eyser became the first amputee to compete at the Summer Olympic Games. He won six medals at St Louis 1904, but now Paralympian competitors have Du Toit to look to for inspiration. It is no surprise she is in demand as a motivational speaker, too, although in her eyes the story is only half written.

TERESA **EDWARDS**
BASKETBALL

USA

The unique achievements of Teresa Edwards are encapsulated by her holding the record as both the youngest and oldest Olympic Games gold medallist in Women's Basketball. During an Olympic career that spanned five Olympic Games, from Los Angeles 1984 to Sydney 2000, she won four gold medals and one bronze as part of the American team.

She was once described as the Michael Jordan of women's basketball, and although she may not be a household name worldwide, she is the most decorated Olympic Basketball player ever. At the Sydney 2000 Games, Teresa Edwards became the first female Basketball player to compete in five Games, something only two of her male counterparts have ever managed to do. At those Olympic Games, she won her fourth gold medal, an achievement managed by no other Basketball player, male or female.

which she used to practise as a schoolgirl before beginning her career at the University of Georgia, where she was a two-time All-American.

She made her international debut in 1981 and at the Los Angeles 1984 Games, after her fresher year at Georgia, Edwards won her first Olympic gold medal as part of the dominant USA team that won all their games on the way to smashing South Korea 85–55 in the final. After graduating, and while continuing her international career, she played abroad for nine seasons in Europe until women's basketball eventually became professional in her home country.

In Seoul 1988, Edwards was at the heart of the USA triumph, with her points the key in their opening-game victory over Czechoslovakia, and their first ever win against the Soviet Union in the semi-final. In the final against Yugoslavia, she scored more points than any other player in a tense 77–70 win. She was forced to settle for bronze at the Barcelona 1992 Olympic Games, but the status quo was restored back on home soil at the 1996 Atlanta Games. In front of crowds of more than 30,000, Edwards was given rave reviews for a string of fine performances as the Americans trounced all before them on their way to regaining the gold.

In the build-up to the Sydney 2000 Games, Edwards announced that she wanted to have one last crack, one more attempt to win another gold medal. At the age of 36, it would be her final international competition, and she bowed out in fitting fashion. She used all her experience and savvy and played a key role as the Americans won all eight of their matches, and completely outclassed Australia 76–54 in the final.

Edwards would continue to play in domestic competition for the Minnesota Lynx, but she decided that her international career was over. She had set American records for matches played at Olympic Games (32), assists (143), steals (59) and – most importantly – medals (five).

Edwards became the youngest gold medallist in the event at Los Angeles 1984 when she was just 20, and 16 years later, at the age of 36, she received her final gold as the oldest. A Women's Basketball Hall of Famer, she was named Sportswoman of the Year in 1996 by the Women's Sports Foundation. A street in her home town is named after her, probably one of those on

Statistics
Born: 19 July 1964, Cairo, Georgia, USA
Height: 5ft 9in (1.75m)
Weight: 150lb (68kg)

Olympic Games Medals
Los Angeles 1984
Women's 12-Team Tournament.......Gold

Seoul 1988
Women's 12-Team Tournament.......Gold

Barcelona 1992
Women's 12-Team Tournament...Bronze

Atlanta 1996
Women's 12-Team Tournament.......Gold

Sydney 2000
Women's 12-Team Tournament.......Gold

'I'm at peace with where I am. If somehow my abilities and talents have been used to further the game, then it feels good.'

Left: Edwards first represented the USA at the age of 17, and is the youngest and oldest Basketball player to win Olympic gold medals.

Right: The American leaps to score a lay-up during the gold-medal game against Australia, during the Sydney 2000 Olympic Games.

HICHAM
EL-GUERROUJ
ATHLETICS

MOROCCO

Hicham El-Guerrouj is one of the finest middle-distance runners in history and is the world record-holder for the 1,500m and 2,000m. He became a double Olympic gold medallist at Athens 2004 in the 5,000m and 1,500m, the distance at which he previously won silver at the Sydney 2000 Games.

Statistics

Born: 14 September 1974, Berkane, Oriental, Morocco
Height: 5ft 9in (1.75m)
Weight: 128lb (58kg)

Olympic Games Medals

Sydney 2000

Men's 1,500m...Silver

Athens 2004

Men's 1,500m...Gold
Men's 5,000m..Gold

At the Athens 2004 Games, in the birthplace of the Olympic Games, Hicham El-Guerrouj produced a display of middle-distance running that will forever define his career. Much like Usain Bolt in the 100m four years later, El-Guerrouj's 1,500m and 5,000m double seemed to stretch the boundaries of possibility, to set such a historic mark on athletics that there seemed no immediate prospect of his accomplishments ever being bettered.

It was the first time in 80 years that an athlete had won both of those events at the same Games, replicating the achievement of Paavo Nurmi, the 'Flying Finn', at the Paris 1924 Games. 'He's the best I've seen by a long way,' explains Lord Coe, himself a two-time Olympic Games gold medallist. That standing within middle-distance running was established at a track meeting in Rome in July 1999. El-Guerrouj flew around a mile of track in a time of 3:43.13, smashing the world record held by Algerian Noureddine Morceli. Roger Bannister, the first man to break the four-minute mile in 1954, would have finished an astonishing 110 metres behind him.

Not only an idol for budding runners, El-Guerrouj is now regarded almost as a deity in his homeland. A symbol of national pride, from that moment onwards El-Guerrouj would be mobbed at airports and chased down every street. He dominated the 1,500m with ease, his relaxed style consistently making a mockery of the clock, his body perfectly tuned. His supremacy was marked when he became the first middle-distance runner to win four consecutive world titles, in 1997, 1999, 2001 and 2003. El-Guerrouj also became the first man to be named Athlete of the Year by the International Association of Athletics Federations (IAAF) in two consecutive seasons, 2001 and 2002, after remaining unbeaten in more than 20 races.

That puts El-Guerrouj's failure to win gold at his first Games in 2000 and his subsequent tears into

striking context. Perhaps affected by the weight of expectation, the Moroccan master could only come second, ironically finishing behind Kenyan Noah Ngeny, who had run as El-Guerrouj's pacemaker in one of his world record-breaking 1,500m runs in 1998. Yet El-Guerrouj's career record highlights an incredible longevity, and in the build-up to the Athens 2004 Games he knew he had one final shot at Olympic glory. For all his grace, El-Guerrouj needed absolute commitment, dedication and desire to become one of the great Olympians.

Just 20 days before the Men's 1,500m final, El-Guerrouj was beaten by the Kenyan athlete Bernard Lagat. Summoning all his reserves of mental strength he responded in the final with typical determination and won his first Olympic gold, beating Lagat by just 0.12 of a second. Four days later he was pointing his arms to the skies

after adding his second gold, in the 5,000m in a time of 13:14.39 after accelerating past Kenenisa Bekele in the final straight. It was his last action in international competition, a fitting end to a glorious career, the perfect coup de grâce. After being decorated with the Cordon de Commandeur by King Mohammed VI of Morocco and receiving the Prince of Asturias Award, El-Guerrouj announced his retirement in May 2006.

Above: The Moroccan could not hold back the tears as he stood on the podium to receive his gold medal at the Athens 2004 Games.

Right: El-Guerrouj remained undefeated at Athens 2004, confidently leading all of his rivals home on his way to golden glory.

'*It is finally complete. Four years ago in Sydney, I cried with sadness. Today I cry tears of joy. I'm living a moment of glory.*'

Hicham El-Guerrouj on his 1,500m triumph at Athens 2004

RAY **EWRY**
ATHLETICS

USA

After overcoming polio as a young boy, American standing jumper Ray Ewry then beat the odds to become one of the most successful Olympians of all time, winning eight gold medals between 1900 and 1908. Competing in the Standing Triple Jump, Standing Long Jump and Standing High Jump, he also won two golds in the 1906 interim Games in Athens.

The names of celebrated American athletes roll off the tongue almost as quickly as they once flew around the running track or cut through the swimming pool. Yet one of them, possibly the greatest of all, is often overlooked: Ray Ewry.

Born in the small town of Lafayette, Indiana, Ewry is as awe-inspiring for his personal journey as he is for his many sporting achievements. Orphaned at the age of five, he was delivered the most devastating news when he was just seven. He had polio and would never walk again. He was paralysed by the disease, confined to a wheelchair with the outlook seemingly bleak. Yet such was his indomitable spirit that he started, gradually but diligently, an exercise regime to build up the muscles in his legs, step by step, day by day.

That training, known as plyometrics, slowly but surely helped young Ewry to stand, then to walk, and finally to jump – not for medals, but because he could. He had defied the doctors and developed into a strapping all-American athlete

with long, strong legs. He attended Purdue University, captaining the track team before graduating and moving to New York, where he worked as a hydraulics engineer. At the New York Athletics Club it soon became clear that he was potentially the finest exponent of the Standing Jump in modern sporting history.

The events he competed in – the Standing Long Jump, Standing High Jump and Standing Triple Jump – have now been replaced with versions that incorporate a run-up. In July 1900, at the age of 26, he was sent to Paris for his first Olympic Games. It did not take him any time to show the world his talent. In the Standing High Jump he launched himself 5ft 5in (1.65m) into the Parisian air, leaving the locals gawping in wide-eyed amazement: one gold. Next up was the Standing Long Jump, where he leapt a distance of just under 11 ft (3.35m): two golds. By the time he stepped up for the Standing Triple Jump, Ewry was already the talk of the Games. After covering 34ft 8in (10.57m), the French were calling the American 'the human frog': three golds.

Statistics
Born: 14 October 1873, Lafayette, Indiana, USA
Died: 29 September 1937
Height: 6ft 1in (1.85m)
Weight: 174lb (79kg)

Olympic Games Medals
Paris 1900
Men's Standing High Jump...............Gold
Men's Standing Long Jump..............Gold
Men's Standing Triple Jump.............Gold

St Louis 1904
Men's Standing High Jump...............Gold
Men's Standing Long Jump..............Gold
Men's Standing Triple Jump.............Gold

London 1908
Men's Standing High Jump...............Gold
Men's Standing Long Jump..............Gold

Left: The American won gold in all of the Standing Jump events in which he competed, over the course of three Olympic Games.

Right: Ewry in training at the London 1908 Games. He won eight gold medals between 1900 and 1908.

Four years later, Ewry repeated his achievement of winning all three events at the St Louis 1904 Games, doubling his gold medal haul to six and setting a world record in the Standing Long Jump in the process. In 1906, Ewry took part in the Intercalated Games in Athens to celebrate 10 years of the modern Olympic Games. By this time the Standing Triple Jump had been discontinued, but he won gold medals in the Standing Long and High Jumps. The Intercalated Games were not official Olympic Games so the gold medals he won in Athens could not count towards his total.

Two more golds followed in London 1908 as he extended his record in the two remaining jumps to four straight Games without defeat; a quartet of championships without losing a single competition. He retired as by far the greatest jumper on earth, with 10 gold medals to his name and a small collection of Athens dirt, which he had scooped up after his final victory there. He remains the greatest jumper in Olympic history – all the more amazing an achievement, considering that at the age of seven he was not even supposed to be able to walk.

'Standing Jumps are the most natural form of athletics one can indulge in. The two things that decide success are perfect flexibility of the body and as near a perfect nervous system as possible.'

BIRGIT **FISCHER**
CANOE SPRINT

Considered to be the greatest female canoeist of all time, Birgit Fischer has made a career out of breaking records, claiming an astonishing eight gold medals over six Olympic Games, in a career spanning three decades. Her first gold came in Moscow 1980, while her most recent was won in Athens 2004.

To enjoy a 24-year career in any sport is one thing, but to remain the best in the world over that entire period of time is something that not many can claim to have achieved.

In 1980, Birgit Fischer became the youngest gold medallist in the history of Olympic Canoeing, when she won the gold for the K-1 at the age of just 18. Despite this great success at such a young age, very few would have predicted the career that lay ahead for Fischer.

Unfortunately for her, Fischer missed the Los Angeles 1984 Olympic Games because of East Germany's boycott, yet she returned four years later in Seoul in memorable fashion, adding two more gold medals to her growing collection, winning two events in the Canoe Sprint – the K-4 and the K-2.

She continued to build on her success, winning gold and silver medals in Barcelona in 1992, and then repeating her achievement in the Atlanta 1996 Games.

In Sydney 2000, she won two gold medals at the same Games for just the second time in her career, before announcing her retirement. However, following a change of heart and much to her opponents' disappointment, Fischer came back for one last Games, in which she won her eighth and final Olympic gold medal in Athens 2004 for the K-4, at the commendable age of 42, before hanging up her paddle for good.

Fischer's incredible career in canoeing has seen her acknowledged as the only female Olympian to win medals 24 years apart, and she also boasts the honour of being the only canoeist ever to have won 12 Olympic medals, eight of which were gold. One can only imagine what would have happened had there been no boycott of the Games in 1984. Her continuous sporting success also brought her recognition and accolades beyond canoeing, including being named German Female Sports Personality of the Year for 2004, although the award was just as much a celebration of her fantastic career.

Her achievements in the field of canoeing are remarkable to say the least, yet her records stand proud across all sports, as she is currently the second most successful Olympian of all time, behind Larissa Latynina, the gymnast who won 18 medals for the Soviet Union.

Fischer, who now claims to have given up for good, casts such a golden shadow over the sport that her rivals can never really afford to relax. After all, she also claimed to have retired in 2000, before returning to win gold again. Now, at 48 years of age, it is difficult to see her returning for the London 2012 Olympic Games, although if there is one thing she has taught opponents during her career it is to expect the unexpected.

It is impossible to rule out a comeback for the German veteran, although if she does decide to sit out London her niece, Fanny Fischer, is one to watch: she is tipped to add to the gold medal she won in Beijing 2008, also for Canoeing.

Statistics

Born: 25 February 1962, Brandenburg, Germany
Height: 5ft 8in (1.73m)
Weight: 152lb (69kg)

Olympic Games Medals

Moscow 1980
Women's K-1 500m ....Gold

Seoul 1988
Women's K-2 500m..............................Gold
Women's K-4 500m..............................Gold
Women's K-1 500m ....Silver

Barcelona 1992
Women's K-1 500m ....Gold
Women's K-4 500m...........................Silver

Atlanta 1996
Women's K-4 500m..............................Gold
Women's K-2 500m........................... Silver

Sydney 2000
Women's K-4 500m..............................Gold
Women's K-2 500m..............................Gold

Athens 2004
Women's K-4 500m...........................Gold
Women's K-2 500m........................... Silver

Left: Fischer picked up her second gold of the Sydney 2000 Games in the women's K-2 500m, becoming the first woman to win two medals at four summer Olympic Games.

Right: Fischer called time on her Olympic Games career after Athens 2004, where she became the oldest-ever Olympic canoeing champion at 42 years old.

Birgit Fischer

'If I were to get two medals here [Beijing 2008], two in 2012, two in 2016, then it might be possible. To be honest, I'm not sure I want to still be racing at 42, like my aunt.'

Birgit Fischer's niece, Fanny Fischer, contemplates how she might win as many medals as her aunt.

57

DICK **FOSBURY**
ATHLETICS

USA

Dick Fosbury not only won the gold medal at the Mexico City 1968 Olympic Games, he transformed the High Jump with his revolutionary technique. His method of jumping was truly ground breaking – he eschewed the traditional straddle or scissors action to twist in mid-air and go over the bar head first, before landing on his back. 'The Fosbury Flop' was born.

Statistics

Born: 6 March 1947, Portland, Oregon, USA
Height: 6ft 4in (1.93m)
Weight: 180lb (83kg)

Olympic Games Medals

Mexico City 1968
Men's High Jump ....Gold

Below: Fosbury's pioneering 'Fosbury Flop' jumping technique earned him worldwide fame from a young age. It has been universally adopted as the technique of choice.

Right: The American clears the bar at the Mexico City 1968 Olympic Games. He won with a jump of 2.24m.

Dick Fosbury came away from the Mexico City 1968 Olympic Games much like his fellow countryman Bob Beamon – with a gold medal, worldwide fame and his name in the athletics lexicon. Whereas Beamon's huge leap advanced the Long Jump world record so far that 'Beamonesque' came to stand for an athletic feat that went way past conventional boundaries, Fosbury's famous 'Flop' took the High Jump to new records in a different way.

It is perhaps hard for today's fans to imagine a time when no one went over the bar in the way Fosbury pioneered. But until the enterprising American decided that the only way to get greater height was to go over the bar backwards, the world of high jumping was used to the straddle technique. This was a complicated manoeuvre that required the athlete to go over the bar facing down, flicking the legs over individually. Fosbury struggled to become competitive using the straddle method, regularly failing to reach the required heights to qualify for high school events. So, aged just 16, he began to develop his own technique, a variation on 'the barrel roll', in which athletes would go over the bar sideways, rotating their body as they did so.

Fosbury has since admitted that he did not have a clear idea in mind when he started out with his innovation, but it gradually evolved and steadily became more successful. He was the only high jumper attempting this new style, but it was clearly working for him. At the start of high school, his finest jump was 1.61m. By the time he left he was jumping over half a metre higher. Yet major success had still eluded him as a youngster, and he was far from a household name going into the Mexico City 1968 Games.

Aged just 21, he had never jumped over 2m, but all that was to change in the year that transformed his life. He finally cleared the 2m mark during the 1968 indoor season, which was a major milestone for him. He proceeded to win the National Collegiate Athletic Association title while competing for Oregon State University, in the run-up to the Mexico City 1968 Olympic Games where he would make his name.

Yet Fosbury went into the Games with one hope – of reaching the final. Once he got there he realised he could go all the way, and so it proved. Clearing every height on his first attempt, the competition was whittled down to the final three as Fosbury, Ed Caruthers and Valentin Gavrilov all cleared 2.2m. But only one cleared 2.24m – the unheralded American, who beat compatriot Caruthers into second and Gavrilov into bronze.

The 'Fosbury Flop', as it became known, was swiftly adopted by the majority of high jumpers, and is the standard technique used today. Yet that victory in 1968 was almost the last that its inventor enjoyed. Fosbury returned from Mexico to a hero's reception, but he never overlooked his studies and graduated from Oregon. He attempted unsuccessfully to qualify for the Munich 1972 Olympics Games but, as he later confessed, his competitive thirst had been quenched. Indeed, he only took part in one Olympic Games and later found fulfilment in civil engineering and swing dancing; he even married his dancing instructor.

Just one Games, but how many athletes can say that they changed the face of their sport in one summer? Fosbury certainly can, which makes him a true Olympic legend.

'I adapted an antiquated style and modernised it to something that was efficient. I didn't know anyone else in the world would be able to use it and I never imagined it would revolutionise the event.'

GERT **FREDRIKSSON** SWEDEN
CANOE SPRINT

Gert Fredriksson is the most successful male canoeist in history and the only one ever to be recognised as the best sportsman in the world, when he was awarded the Mohammad Taher trophy by the International Olympic Committee in 1956. The 'Kayak King' won six gold medals, one silver and one bronze in four Olympic Games between 1948 and 1960.

The manner in which he won his first Olympic gold medal heralded a once-in-a-generation talent. Gert Fredriksson, a 29-year-old fireman from Sweden, won the K-1 1,000m at the London 1948 Games by the biggest winning margin in any Olympic Kayak final, other than the 10,000m. For Fredriksson, it was his first step on the way to becoming Sweden's most successful Olympian and the first of three consecutive Olympic Games triumphs in the K-1 1,000m. He made rocketing through the waters look ridiculously easy in one of the most physically demanding Olympic sports. He showed his superiority from the second he jumped into a kayak for his first Olympic heat, casually sitting in fourth place for the first 950 metres before sprinting the last 50 to finish first.

That he did not even own a kayak until he was 18 makes Fredriksson's achievements all the more remarkable. He started out by touring the Swedish lakes with his friends from the Nykoping canoe club, and over time it became clear that he was a special talent. World War II delayed the start of his international career – possibly costing him an even greater medal haul – but he burst on to the scene by taking total command at the London 1948 Games. Following his stunning triumph in the 1,000m, Fredriksson destroyed the field at Henley-on-Thames to storm to victory in the 10,000m. His 30.5-second margin of victory remains the largest in the sport's history.

Those two victories established a dominance on the water that lasted until his retirement in 1960 at the age of 41, following his sixth Olympic gold medal in Rome. During that time he also cleaned up at the World Championships with seven golds, but it was Olympic glory that mattered most to Fredriksson and he achieved it by training harder and longer than anyone else. He developed incredible strength and adjusted his technique to use his legs and body more than his competitors did. His day-job fighting fires certainly helped to keep him in peak physical condition, but the lack of sponsorship in canoeing meant he often had to pay considerable expenses out of his own pocket just to compete.

One of only 13 Olympians to have won gold medals at four or more consecutive Games, he

Statistics

Born: 21 November 1919, Nykoping, Sweden
Died: 5 July 2006
Height: 5ft 9in (1.75m)
Weight: 159lb (72kg)

Olympic Games Medals

London 1948
Men's K-1 1,000m .... Gold
Men's K-1 10,000m .... Gold

Helsinki 1952
Men's K-1 1,000m .... Gold
Men's K-1 10,000m .... Silver

Melbourne 1956
Men's K-1 1,000m .... Gold
Men's K-1 10,000m .... Gold

Rome 1960
Men's K-2 1,000m .... Gold
Men's K-1 1,000m .... Bronze

Left: The 'Super Swede' pictured at his last Games, in Rome 1960, when he won a bronze medal in the K-1 1,000m and a gold medal in the K-2 1,000m.

Right: Power, timing, determination and the sheer will to win were what propelled Fredriksson to record-breaking Olympic success in the water.

secured gold in the K-1 1,000m at Helsinki 1952 but misjudged his sprint finish in the K-1 10,000m, so had to settle for silver. He responded at the Melbourne 1956 Olympic Games by winning gold in both events, just as he had done at the London 1948 Games eight years earlier. It was in 1956 that he was awarded the Mohammad Taher trophy as the number one sportsman in the world for his success in canoeing.

At the Rome 1960 Games he could only manage bronze in the K-1 1,000m, but was victorious in the doubles event over the same distance, bringing the curtain down on an extraordinary career. Amazingly, he could have competed at the Mexico City 1968 Games but, aged 48, he chose to coach the team instead. Active in the sport until well into his seventies, including competing in the Marathon World's Masters, Fredriksson died in July 2006 after a battle with cancer. The ultimate sportsman, he remains an inspiration to all young canoeists.

'I missed the first one here back in 1938 and wouldn't be able to win the next so I really have to win this.'

Gert Fredriksson before the K-2 Marathon World's Masters in Vaxholm 1996

FU MINGXIA
AQUATICS – DIVING

CHINA

It is bewildering enough that Fu Mingxia competed in the Olympic Games aged 13. But, astonishingly, she won gold – becoming the youngest ever Olympian to do so when she triumphed at the Barcelona 1992 Games. In an incredible Olympic Games career, the indomitable Chinese diver won five medals, and the hearts of Olympics fans worldwide.

I t could have been a completely different story for Fu Mingxia. Growing up in Wuhan, in China's Hubei Province, she began learning gymnastics at the age of five, but her parents discouraged her from taking her interest further as she was not considered flexible enough. That opened up the route into swimming and diving, and it is fair to say Fu never looked back.

Fu took to diving before she was even able to swim; her coach would tie a rope around her to pull her back to safety after she had dived. At the tender age of nine years old, she moved to Beijing to step up her training, displaying a startling independence for a girl her age as she left her parents back at home in Wuhan. It was a tough education for Fu: she trained for 10 hours a day, seven days a week, while also keeping up with her studies. In 1990 she began competing in international events, and that year she won the Alamo Invitational at the age of 11.

A year later, Fu became the youngest competitor to win gold at the World Championships and the youngest World Champion ever in aquatic sports. She was so good that the rule-makers felt compelled to change the regulation that stipulated divers had to be 14 to compete in the World Championships, World Cup and Olympic Games. Fu was therefore prohibited from entering the 1991 World Cup, but a loophole allowed her to dive in the Barcelona 1992 Olympic Games. At just 13, she became the youngest ever Olympian to win a medal – a gold in fact – as she executed a stunning display of acrobatics in the Women's 10m Platform.

A star had undoubtedly been born, but it had not been without its sacrifices. Having bewildered the world by winning in Barcelona, three years of hard training in preparation for Atlanta took their toll, as Fu regularly broke down in tears under the strain and pressure of having to live up to the

Statistics
Born: 16 August 1978, Wuhan, Hubei
Province, China
Height: 5ft 3in (1.6m)
Weight: 106lb (48kg)

Olympic Games Medals
Barcelona 1992
Women's 10m Platform ....Gold

Atlanta 1996
Women's 10m Platform ....Gold
Women's 3m Springboard................Gold

Sydney 2000
Women's 3m Springboard................Gold
Women's Synchronised 3m
  Springboard... Silver

Left: Standing on the podium, the hard work and sacrifices were proved worth it – Fu had left home at the age of nine to train in Beijing for Olympic greatness.

Right: Pictured diving to Olympic glory at the Atlanta 1996 Games, Fu became the youngest World Champion ever in 1991 at the age of 12.

*'When I won in Barcelona and Atlanta, I was a child
and it was too easy. Winning at Sydney was a medal
I earned all by myself.'*

standard she set in Barcelona. She sought solace and escape in listening to and playing pop music and, by 1996, Fu was calling the tune. Having won the World Championships for the second time in 1994, a 17-year-old Fu went to the Atlanta 1996 Games with high hopes.

Once again she delivered, winning gold in the Women's 10m Platform and 3m Springboard events. Now a more rounded, stronger athlete than the fragile-looking girl who had dominated in Barcelona, Fu became the first woman to win those two events in the same Olympics since the feat of Ingrid Kramer at the Rome 1960 Games.

The pressure eventually became too much, and Fu retired after the Atlanta Games to study economics in Beijing. But she returned in time for Sydney 2000 and successfully defended her 3m Springboard crown as well as winning silver in the new event of Synchronised 3m Springboard with partner Guo Jingjing. Now on a par with Greg Louganis and Pat McCormick as the only divers to win four gold medals, Fu called time on her diving career after Sydney, retiring as one of the most awe-inspiring Olympians ever. And she found happiness away from the sport too, marrying the former financial secretary of the Hong Kong government and starting a family.

ROBERT 'BOB' GARRETT USA

ATHLETICS

One of the most celebrated athletes of all time, Robert Garrett was renowned for his versatility at the Olympic Games. He won two gold medals in Athens 1896, both in throwing events, while also boasting medals during his career for the Long Jump, High Jump and Triple Jump.

In the latter part of the 19th century, the discus throw was an unknown event in America, yet Robert Garrett, affectionately known as 'Bob', was determined to try his hand at as many events as possible. Coming from a prosperous background, Garrett was a student at Princeton University, and it was his history professor, William Milligan Sloane, who first suggested that he might attempt the 'new' event, simply by producing a drawing of an ancient Greek discus. Garrett then consulted a blacksmith, who had a model made for him, but his version weighed 10kg, five times more than the competitive implement, which weighed just two. Due to the ridiculously heavy weight, he soon gave up interest in the Discus Throw, as he could hardly throw it any distance. Yet in Athens in the Olympic Games of 1896, the young American picked up a competition disc and was so encouraged by its much lighter weight that he decided to have a go at entering the event, despite having had no preparation for it at all.

Regarded as a mere fanciful outsider, Garrett, much to everybody's surprise, took the gold medal, by launching his discus an impressive 29.15m. In the process he beat the local favourite, Panagiotis Paraskevopoulos, and his victory was certainly a huge disappointment to the home crowd: the Greeks prided themselves on their prowess in the Discus, as they believed the event to be as much an art form as it was a sport.

The following day, Garrett was back in action and won his second gold of the Games, claiming the Shot Put title with his very first effort. That came as less of a surprise to the spectators as it was considered to be his favoured event. But it was far from a foregone conclusion as the Shot Put competition took place just half an hour after the Long Jump, in which Garrett had won a silver medal. Not many athletes can claim to have won gold and silver medals in the space of an hour. He then rounded off what was a great Olympic Games, the first of the modern era, with his fourth and final medal, taking silver in the High Jump.

Having established himself as one of the greatest athletes in the world and certainly one of the most versatile, Garrett returned four years on, at the Paris 1900 Olympic Games, and this time also attempted the Triple Jump, in which he won a bronze medal. He added a second bronze for the Shot Put, although it could easily have been a gold had he not refused to compete in the final series of throws held on a Sunday because of his religious beliefs. His success in both Athens 1896 and Paris 1900 took his Olympic Games medals tally to six, a fantastic achievement, especially considering they were won over five different disciplines.

On retiring from track and field athletics, he pursued a career in investment banking. A wealthy man, he eventually began collecting ancient manuscripts from Africa and Asia, and in 1941 he became the chairman of the National Recreation Association. The unforgettable American, who was born and raised in Baltimore, Maryland, passed away in his home town at the age of 85, in 1961.

Statistics

Born: 24 May 1875, Baltimore County, Maryland, USA

Died: 25 April 1961

Height: 6ft 2in (1.88m)

Weight: 178lb (81kg)

Olympic Games Medals

Athens 1896

Men's Discus Throw	Gold
Men's Shot Put	Gold
Men's Long Jump	Silver
Men's High Jump	Silver

Paris 1900

Men's Triple Jump	Bronze
Men's Shot Put	Bronze

Below: Garrett (far right) was fêted on his return from Athens to the United States – this commemorative photograph was taken at Princeton University in 1897.

Right: Garrett won his first gold medal in the Discus at Athens 1896, upsetting the host nation by beating local favourite Panagiotis Paraskevopoulos.

*'The Greeks were overwhelmed by the superior skill and
daring of the Americans.'*

1896 Olympic Games spectator Burton Homes witnessing the reaction to Garrett's amazing feats

HAILE GEBRSELASSIE

ETHIOPIA

ATHLETICS

Haile Gebrselassie is considered one of the greatest distance runners of all time. The Ethiopian has broken no fewer than 27 world records during his career, with his two Olympic Games gold medals coming in the 10,000m in Atlanta 1996 and Sydney 2000. He has recorded victories at other major competitions at distances ranging from 1,500m to the Marathon.

So many magical moments has Haile Gebrselassie produced, so many minor miracles, that some regard him as the greatest living sportsman. As the years have advanced his dominance on the track has not waned. Young challengers have come and gone but Gebrselassie remains the godfather, peerless with his spikes on, an idol to the very people who try to dethrone him. He still runs with a crooked left arm, an enduring idiosyncrasy from the days when he used to run 10 kilometres to school every morning holding his books.

Gebrselassie rose to international prominence when he won the 5,000m and 10,000m World Junior Championships in 1992, and a year later he was mirroring that success in the senior tournament, winning gold in the 10,000m in Stuttgart. It was the first of four consecutive world titles in the 10,000m between 1993 and 1999, during which time he had a highly competitive rivalry with Kenyan athlete Daniel Komen.

In 1995, Gebrselassie set world records in the two-mile and 10,000m races within a week of each other, dramatically achieving the latter at a meeting in Hengelo in the Netherlands, in an astonishing time of 26:43.53. More world bests across the middle distances, both indoor and outdoor, quickly

followed as Gebrselassie's reputation grew race by race. He entered the Atlanta 1996 Olympic Games determined to emulate his childhood idol, Miruts Yifter, who won the 5,000m and 10,000m double at the Moscow 1980 Olympic Games. In the 10,000m, Gebrselassie timed to perfection his acceleration away from Paul Tergat in the final lap, to edge out the Kenyan in a time of 27:7.34.

For Gebrselassie, it was one dream accomplished but also the end of another. The hard track at Atlanta had caused his feet to blister badly and he was forced to withdraw from the 5,000m. It was a great disappointment for the ambitious athlete, who, nevertheless, returned to Ethiopia a hero. His reputation was further enhanced the following year when he even managed to set a world record in the 1,500m, an event in which he hardly ever competed. He was almost mocking the athletes who specialised over the distance.

He continued to produce consistently outstanding performances in the 5,000m and 10,000m for the next four years, including his triumph in the so-called 'Million Dollar Race' against Noureddine Morceli of Algeria in May 1997. At the Sydney 2000 Olympic Games, Gebrselassie once more produced a quite astonishing display of long-distance running as he retained his 10,000m crown, the third man in history to do so, again beating Tergat into second place. He was unable to win a third in a row in Athens 2004 four years later, only managing fifth in the 10,000m final as a consequence of an Achilles injury that prevented him from training in the weeks leading up to the Games.

Gebrselassie has indicated that London 2012 will be his last Olympic Games. The prize he is targeting is that of the Marathon, in which he set world-record times in 2007 and 2008, although he did not enter the event at the Beijing 2008 Games because of concerns over his health. There seems sure to be more to come from the Ethiopian marvel before he gives someone else a chance.

Statistics

Born: 18 April 1973, Asella, Oromia, Ethiopia
Height: 5ft 5in (1.65m)
Weight: 123lb (56kg)

Olympic Games Medals

Atlanta 1996
Men's 10,000m..Gold

Sydney 2000
Men's 10,000m..Gold

'Since I achieved something, running has exploded in my country. For me, sometimes it is difficult even to know who the athletes are who are competing at the highest level. There are thousands.'

Left: Gebrselassie proudly waves the flag for his country as he circles the Atlanta track after winning the 10,000m, celebrating more Olympic Games success.

Right: The smile says it all as the Ethiopian breaks clear to win his second successive 10,000m gold medal at the Sydney 2000 Games.

TORBEN **GRAEL**
SAILING

Nicknamed 'The Turbine', the Brazilian has swept up more Olympic medals than any other sailor in the world, and any other Brazilian Olympian in any sport. Torben Grael and his younger brother Lars came from a long line of sailors and made a formidable duo, raising the bar the world over. Grael's achievements remain the benchmark in his sport, even though his last appearance at the Olympic Games was at Athens 2004.

Statistics
Born: 22 July 1960, São Paulo, Brazil
Height: 6ft 1in (1.85m)
Weight: 194lb (88kg)

Olympic Games Medals
Los Angeles 1984
Open Soling (Keelboat) .... Silver

Seoul 1988
Open Star (Keelboat)..................... Bronze

Atlanta 1996
Open Star (Keelboat)..........................Gold

Sydney 2000
Open Star (Keelboat)..................... Bronze

Athens 2004
Men Star (Keelboat)...........................Gold

I t is generally considered that Brazil is the home of soccer. Yet, quietly, this nation has cause to claim a second sport in sailing, with a history of Olympic medal winners since the 1960s. Torben Grael is one of them and, with inspirational winners before him, no wonder this two-time Olympic champion has become one of the most famed sailors of all time.

Although born in São Paulo, Brazil, he is of Danish descent, and the sport has a long and prestigious tradition in Grael's family. He says that he first realised the esteem and significance of the Olympic Games at just five years old when his grandfather, Preben Schmidt – who pioneered the sport in Brazil after moving there from Denmark – took him sailing in his 6m-long boat *Aileen*. This was a famous vessel, having featured in an

in a boat away from their home in Niteroi, near Rio de Janeiro. The two of them would become Brazilian and international champions together before Grael's first Olympic Games, following in the footsteps of their Danish ancestors and their Brazilian-born uncles, Erik and Axel Preben-Schmidt, who competed in the Mexico City 1968 and Munich 1972 Olympic Games. Grael and Lars went their separate ways as a team before his first Games, Los Angeles 1984, so Grael teamed up with Daniel Adler and Ronaldo Senfft, trying to renew Brazil's success in the water.

They did so, and finished in the medal places in three of the seven arduous races that took place in the Soling class. That was enough to clinch an overall second place behind the USA and bring home the silver. Grael was 24 years old, relatively

Olympic gold-winning race in the Stockholm 1912 Games. Almost inevitably, his passion for sailing quickly took root.

His brother Lars would be just as fanatical about sailing and the two trained together in the Bay of Guanabara, nothing more than a hop

young for a sailor, and this would be just the start of his reign as one of the toughest competitors in the sport for many years. On the way to his second Olympic Games, he secured victories in a number of competitions, including his third World Championships in 1987, which provided the

Above: Elation on Grael's face (left) after another successful race, partnered by Marcelo Ferreira.

Right: Grael (right) and Ferreira won the gold medal in the Men's Star (Keelboat) class at the Athens 2004 Olympic Games.

'Winning a gold medal is always a peak in your career. The one in Athens was very special, being the second one and making me the best Olympic athlete in Brazil. It was really very special.'

perfect stream of confidence and belief ahead of the Seoul 1988 Games.

Grael opted to change class from his three-man Soling to the two-man Star (Keelboat) event, and took a new crew with him in the form of Nelson Falcao. They finished just 4.3 points behind the Great Britain team that won gold, but it would only be enough to take a bronze medal. That represented failure to the highly competitive Grael, and he was further frustrated by an 11th-place finish at the Barcelona 1992 Games.

'The Turbine' was as driven as ever and returned with partner Marcelo Ferreira to the Atlanta 1996 Olympic Games to finally clinch his first Olympic gold. The competition now comprised 10 races, and of these the Brazilians finished in the medal places five times, accumulating 41 points, which was enough to be crowned champions.

With a taste for gold and an ever-increasing résumé of competition victories, the pair won bronze at the Sydney 2000 Games before returning for their last Olympic Games outing in Athens 2004. As skipper, Grael led from the fourth round onwards and finished eight of the 10 races in the top place, securing him another gold medal and a permanent place as a true Olympic great.

He continues to sail and has amassed more than 30 national wins in many classes, not to mention a recent outstanding victory in the 2009 Volvo Ocean Race. For that, he is regarded as the world's most complete sailor.

TANNI
GREY-THOMPSON
PARALYMPIC ATHLETICS

Born with spina bifida, Baroness Tanni Grey-Thompson defied her disability to achieve enormous success both during and after her athletics career, on and off the track. She won 16 Paralympic medals, 11 of which are gold, in a Paralympic Games career spanning 16 years. She also holds the title of being Britain's most successful wheelchair athlete.

For Tanni Grey-Thompson, finishing in first place was something she grew accustomed to during a remarkably long and successful 23-year career. The inspirational British competitor was born and raised in Cardiff, Wales. She was christened Carys Davina but her two-year-old sister Sian called her 'Tiny', pronouncing it 'Tanni', and the name stuck. She wore callipers until the age of seven, when she used a wheelchair for the first time. Fiercely independent, she tried all sports and excelled at school in many of them, including horse riding, swimming and archery.

Having started out as a 100m sprinter for Wales in the 1984 Junior National Games, she began her Paralympic career four years later in Seoul 1988, where she won a bronze medal in her 400m category. Grey-Thompson then suffered a setback as she required spinal surgery, which put her out of action for a while. She came back fighting, though, and four years later won an incredible four

gold medals in her category, completing the set for the Women's 100m, 200m, 400m and 800m, not to mention a silver in the 4 x 100m Relay. This was a sensational achievement for the young Welsh star, who had instantly established herself as the greatest Paralympian athlete in the world. The fact that she had combined her athletic training with academic study, graduating from the University of Loughborough with a degree in politics just a year before the Games, only magnified her success.

In Atlanta 1996, Grey-Thompson bagged another haul of medals: a further gold and three silvers. Four years later, in Sydney 2000, she did the unthinkable and matched her magnificent achievement of Barcelona 1992, winning four more medals, but this time they were all gold. Now the undisputed world best in her Paralympic category, Grey-Thompson still had one more Games left in her, and she signed out in style, celebrating two more gold medals in Athens 2004 by winning the 100m and 400m events.

Statistics
Born: 26 July 1969, Cardiff, Wales

Paralympic Games Medals
Seoul 1988
Women's 400m 3 .... Bronze

Barcelona 1992
Women's 100m TW3 .... Gold
Women's 200m TW3 .... Gold
Women's 400m TW3 .... Gold
Women's 800m TW3 .... Gold
Women's 4 x 100m Relay TW3-4 .... Silver

Atlanta 1996
Women's 800m T52 .... Gold
Women's 100m T52 .... Silver
Women's 200m T52 .... Silver
Women's 400m T52 .... Silver

Sydney 2000
Women's 100m T53 .... Gold
Women's 200m T53 .... Gold
Women's 400m T53 .... Gold
Women's 800m T53 .... Gold

Athens 2004
Women's 100m T53 .... Gold
Women's 400m T53 .... Gold

Left: Grey-Thompson waves her last goodbye to the crowd at her fifth and final Games in Athens 2004, after finishing fourth in the 200m T54.

Right: Grey-Thompson shows the strength and determination that characterised her athletics career, crossing the line to win the Women's 100m T53 at the Athens 2004 Paralympic Games.

Despite her unremitting run of success as an athlete, Grey-Thompson had also been achieving off the track. In 2000, following her Sydney triumph, she received a host of awards, including an OBE and the prestigious Helen Rollason award for BBC Sports Personality of the Year, and was named Best Welsh Sportswoman of the previous 50 years. In 2002 she won her final London Marathon, making it six in total. A wonderful moment for her, coming as it did in front of her home fans. The accolades didn't stop there, however: she won the BBC Wales Sports Personality of the Year for the third time in 2004, having previously picked up the same award in 1992 and 2000. In 2005 she received her crowning honour, when she was made a Dame of the British Empire by Her Majesty The Queen.

Grey-Thompson's charity work and on-track achievements have made her a role model to all aspiring athletes, giving both hope and optimism to those with similar disabilities.

'If you put the hard work in, you have a chance of fulfilling your dream.'

HARRY **HILLMAN**
ATHLETICS

USA

Harry Hillman's greatest Olympic success came in St Louis, where the young American won an astonishing three gold medals, instantly making him one of the most renowned and well-remembered hurdlers of all time. Hillman also made it to the London 1908 Games, where he won his fourth and final medal, taking silver for the 400m Hurdles.

Statistics

Born: 8 September 1881, New York, USA
Died: 9 August 1945
Height: 5ft 11in (1.8m)
Weight: 145lb (66kg)

Olympic Games Medals

St Louis 1904

Men's 200m Hurdles...........................Gold
Men's 400m Hurdles...........................Gold
Men's 400m..Gold

London 1908

Men's 400m Hurdles.......................... Silver

Harry Hillman was not educated in a sportsman's diet, but he still knew that he needed to avoid sweets, cakes and tobacco if he wanted to be a successful athlete. However, he also advocated swallowing whole raw eggs, saying that it was 'excellent for the wind and stomach'.

Born and raised in Brooklyn, New York, in the late 19th century, Hillman chose to enter full-time employment as a young man as opposed to going to college, earning his trade by graft as a bank teller. However, following much success in amateur athletics, he focused sufficiently in time to reach the necessary standard to compete in the St Louis 1904 Games. He won two gold medals for his favoured event, the Hurdles, claiming both the 200m and the 400m titles. Despite being renowned for his achievements as a hurdler, he won a third and final gold medal in St Louis for the 400m.

In the 400m Hurdles, Hillman had shattered the existing world record with an outstanding 53-second run, but the new mark was not allowed to stand because not only did he knock over the eighth hurdle, but the hurdles themselves were not of the required height.

Hillman returned to the Olympic stage four years later, in London 1908, with high expectations, yet he left with just a single medal, the silver for the 400m Hurdles. This time, though, it was not a matter of Hillman being below par; in fact, his silver-medal performance was the fastest legitimate run of his career, at 55.3 seconds, beating his previous best of 56.4, a world record that he had set in the heats for the final. It was simply unfortunate for Hillman that he came up against fellow American Charles Bacon, who edged him out to win the gold in a time of 55 seconds.

Despite narrowly missing out on claiming any further world records in the Hurdles, Hillman was listed in the *Guinness World Records* for many years, for the rather unusual record of winning, with Olympic high jumper Lawson Robertson, the 100 yard three-legged race in just 11 seconds – a record that is yet to be beaten.

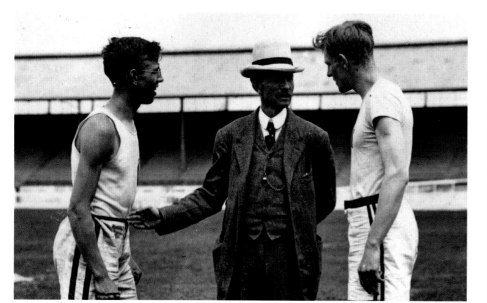

Left: Hillman, pictured on the left, takes advice from coach Mike Murphy (centre) at the London 1908 Games. His rival Charles Bacon (right) beat him in the 400m Hurdles.

Right: Hillman leaps a hurdle on the way to victory in the Men's 200m Hurdles at St Louis 1904, watched by inhabitants of St Louis from their windows.

Still to this day, over 100 years since Hillman's achievements, he is considered to be one of the greatest track and field athletes of all time, despite the fact that he had such a short-lived Olympic career. However, following his retirement as a competitor he remained in the sport for many years, joining his country's Olympic coaching staff for Paris 1924, Amsterdam 1928 and Los Angeles 1932. He remained in track and field as a coach at Dartmouth College right up until his death in 1945, aged 63. He spent 35 years at the college, where his role was to assist and inspire young, aspiring athletes, offering his unique help and insight to those who wanted to become Olympians. Raw eggs were always on the menu.

'Athletics gives one that needed virility demanded by modern business life.'

Harry Hillman advised on the merits of an athletics career

KELLY **HOLMES**
ATHLETICS

When Dame Kelly Holmes won the 800m and 1,500m middle-distance 'double' at the age of 34 in Athens 2004, the home of the Olympic Games, there cannot have been a better example to young athletes never to give up on their dream, no matter how many obstacles are placed in their way. Having overcome injury, depression and even self-harming, Holmes was now responsible for one of sport's most life-affirming moments.

Statistics

Born: 19 April 1970, Pembury, Kent, England
Height: 5ft 4in (1.63m)
Weight: 121lb (55kg)

Olympic Games Medals

Sydney 2000
Women's 800m .... Bronze

Athens 2004
Women's 800m ....Gold
Women's 1,500m ....Gold

Kelly Holmes was inspired to take up athletics as a teenager after watching Sebastian Coe win gold in Los Angeles 1984 and, although it took her nearly 16 years to emulate him, it was surely worth the wait.

The young runner's talent was obvious from a very early age but so many things stood in her way as she carved out a career on the track. For a start she did not compete seriously until she was 22, having opted to join the British Army first and becoming a blue belt in judo and a highly competent volleyball player. But when she did start to take athletics more seriously, she broke the English record for 800m at the World Championships in Stuttgart in 1993 at the first time of asking.

From that point on the middle-distance expert improved rapidly, but found fate often conspired against her when it came to major

record, was a particular low, one which left her badly depressed, and it was by no means her final setback.

Holmes later admitted that injury problems in the build-up to Athens 2004 had led her to self-harm, cutting herself on her wrists and chest. 'I thought I was cursed. It's the lowest I've ever, ever been,' she said. But the way she fought back through sheer determination won the hearts of the British public and of athletics fans across the world. Having failed to win a medal in Atlanta 1996 and taken bronze in the 800m in Sydney 2000, Holmes arrived in Greece with a chance to finish her career on a high – and it was an opportunity she grabbed in remarkable style.

At the age of 34 she was well aware that this would be her last Olympic Games, and she announced that she would only compete in one event, the 1,500m, in a bid to concentrate fully on

championships; in fact, injuries at key moments often left her feeling she was destined never to fulfil her true potential.

Rupturing her calf and tearing her Achilles tendon at the World Championships in 1997, when she was five seconds faster than anyone else in the sport and had just beaten the British

achieving her one final goal: winning an Olympic gold. But a victory over Slovenian athlete Jolanda Ceplak in the run-up to Athens 2004 proved she was still a real contender over the shorter distance and just five days before the 800m finals she dramatically changed her mind and opted to go for the 'double'.

Above: Holmes flies the flag for Great Britain after winning the gold medal in the Women's 800m final at the Athens 2004 Games.

Right: Five days later, Holmes celebrates as she crosses the line just ahead of Russia's Tatyana Tomashova in the 1,500m, winning her second gold medal at Athens 2004.

It was to prove a career-defining decision, because in a fascinating final she moved ahead of World Champion Maria de Lurdes-Mutola on the final bend and took gold ahead of Hasna Benhassi and Ceplak on the line. Holmes was only the second British woman to win an 800m gold medal at the Olympic Games, following in the footsteps of Ann Packer, who won in Tokyo 1964. But by

going on to win the 1,500m days later she carved out her own place in athletics history. Coming from the back of the field, she took the lead on the final straight and held off a strong challenge from World Champion Tatyana Tomashova of Russia to finish in a new British record time of 3:57.90.

Perseverance had, at last, paid off and the dream that began almost 16 years earlier had

finally been achieved, despite encountering so many obstacles along the way. Her success did not go unnoticed back home in Britain, where thousands of well-wishers lined the streets for an emotional 'welcome home' parade in her home town in Kent. Then, having retired in 2005, she became Dame Kelly Holmes in the New Year's Honours List.

'I dreamt of being Olympic champion ... after watching
Seb Coe win gold at the 1984 Olympics. Winning two gold
medals in Athens was more than a dream come true. It
made all the fighting worthwhile.'

CHRIS HOY
CYCLING – TRACK

Since the turn of the millennium, Sir Chris Hoy has gone from strength to strength as an Olympic cyclist, breaking several records along the way. His crowning achievement came when he finished the Beijing 2008 Games with three gold medals, becoming the first British athlete to achieve such a feat for 100 years and making the Scot the most successful male Olympic cyclist of all time.

For most children, *ET* was simply an uplifting film, full of fantasy and hope. For Chris Hoy, however, it was the inspiration which has since led to an illustrious career. Hoy, who was just six years old at the time, has since admitted that what first made him want to become a cyclist was the famous scene from *ET* in which a child magically cycles high into the air. A year later, at the age of seven, he turned his dreams into a reality, and took up BMX racing. Over the following seven years, he became the Scottish champion and the British number two, and also made the top 10 in the world rankings. Being a champion everyone wanted to beat was a position he would have to grow used to for the rest of his career.

When still a teenager, the determined Scot turned his attentions to Track Cycling, where he would become one of the greatest competitors ever to have graced the sport. Despite picking up 'only' a silver medal in the Sydney 2000 Olympic Games in the Team Sprint, Hoy came back four years later, in Athens 2004, and won the gold which he had been craving, for the 1km Time Trial, an event which has since been removed from the Olympic programme.

In the Beijing 2008 Games, Hoy did the unthinkable, picking up three gold medals, including the 'holy grail' of the Team sprint, an achievement of personal significance for Hoy, as he had narrowly missed out on the gold in the same event in Sydney 2000. He had now become the first British Olympian to win three gold medals at a single Olympic Games since Henry Taylor swam to victory in London 1908. Hoy's exceptional achievement also resulted in him being crowned as the most successful Scottish Olympian of all time, not to mention becoming the most successful male cyclist the Olympic Games have ever produced.

The final medal that Hoy collected, to round off his sensational Olympic summer, was in the Sprint, when he won the gold ahead of fellow Brit and team-mate Jason Kenny – a cause for double delight for British supporters and perhaps making the defeat easier for Kenny to swallow.

Since Beijing 2008, Hoy has received various personal awards, as the Scot was taken to the hearts of the British public. Within a month he was named Sportsman of the Year for 2008 by the Sports Journalists' Association of Great Britain, before picking up the prestigious BBC Sports Personality of the Year, becoming only the second cyclist to win the award, following Tom Simpson's success in 1965. Less than a year later he became Sir Chris Hoy, following his knighthood – a rare honour for a sportsman still considered to be at the peak of his career.

In London 2012, on home territory, he will be hoping to break even more records in an Olympic Games for which he is a key ambassador.

JIRI **JEZEK**
PARALYMPIC CYCLING – ROAD/TRACK

Jiří Ježek was born able-bodied but lost his right leg below the knee as a child. The Czech is now regarded as the best cyclist in the world after winning medals at each of the three Paralympic Games he has competed in, starting in Sydney 2000, securing five gold medals during that time.

Many of the great Paralympians are born with their disabilities. Some, like Jiří Ježek, have to recover from life-changing events, and through a combination of positivity and desire go on to become Paralympic champions. Ježek had no obvious sporting aspirations as a boy growing up in Prague. Then his life changed in an instant. He was 11 when he was involved in a car accident, the consequence of which was that his right leg was amputated below the knee. As a typically active youngster, cycling in the park had been a daily activity for Ježek when he was a child, but following the accident he did not get back on a bike until he was 18, after watching the Cycling events at the Barcelona 1992 Paralympics Games.

It started off as a hobby while he continued his job as a prosthetics technician, but by the age of 20 Ježek was cycling competitively. He competed in the LC2 category for locomotor disabilities and was entering international competitions by 1999, training relentlessly with the possibility of a Paralympic medal the following year in his sights.

He was still an amateur when he went to his first Paralympic Games, Sydney 2000, where he won the Mixed Individual Pursuit, going below five minutes, and set a world record time of 4:59.672. Ježek, a self-confessed 'Mr Nobody' at this time, won his second gold medal with a personal best in the Mixed 1km Time Trial and was only narrowly edged into second place in the Mixed Road Race by Australian Daniel Polson.

After his success in Sydney 2000, Ježek stepped up his training regime and became a professional cyclist, largely thanks to the financial input of sponsors as his popularity soared in the Czech Republic. He was determined to succeed and to create a legacy as the most successful cyclist with a physical disability of all time.

In 2004, shortly after turning professional, Ježek went some way to attaining that status by winning gold in the Men's Road Race at the Athens 2004 Paralympic Games. He also won silver in the Men's individual Pursuit and, post-Athens 2004, dominated cycling for athletes with a physical disability, winning numerous races and titles.

He was given the honour of captaining the Czech National Paralympic Team for Beijing 2008, where he added four more medals to his tally. Ježek was unable to retain his Men's Road Race title but won gold in the Men's Individual Time Trial and the Men's Individual Pursuit on the track. He also won silver in the 1km Time Trial on the track, and was the shining light of a Czech team that came third in the Men's Team Sprint.

After the Beijing 2008 Paralympic Games, Ježek began competing against able-bodied cyclists, insisting it would make him more competitive in the high-level Paralympic Games, which are almost as fast as their Olympic equivalent. He still cycles around 30,000km a year, including training, and competes in up to 75 races, 90 per cent of which are in able-bodied competition. He remains committed to charitable causes and is a motivational speaker, inspiring children to cycle and helping people with prosthetic limbs. With nine Paralympic medals and a heart-warming life story, few are better placed to do that.

Statistics

Born: 16 October 1974, Prague, Czech Republic
Height: 5ft 11in (1.81m)
Weight: 150lb (68kg)

Paralympic Games Medals

Sydney 2000
Track: Mixed 1 km Time Trial LC2 ...Gold
Track: Mixed Individual
   Pursuit LC2 ....Gold
Road: Mixed Road Race LC2 .... Silver

Athens 2004
Road: Men's Road Race/
   Time Trial LC2......................................Gold
Track: Men's Individual
   Pursuit LC2 .... Silver

Beijing 2008
Road: Men's Individual
   Time Trial LC2......................................Gold
Track: Men's Individual
   Pursuit LC2 ....Gold
Track: Men's 1km Time Trial LC2 ... Silver
Track: Men's Team Sprint
   LC1-4 CP3/4....................................... Bronze

Left: Beijing was a happy hunting ground for Ježek in at the Beijing 2008 Paralympic Games, as he won medals of every colour to add to his cycling collection.

Right: Ježek pedals for gold around the Laoshan Velodrome in the Men's individual pursuit (LC2) final at the Beijing 2008 Paralympic Games.

'I am not just cycling for the Czech Republic, but
also for all of those who suffer from a disability of
one sort or another.'

MICHAEL **JOHNSON**
ATHLETICS

USA

Michael Johnson was one of the greatest athletes the sport has ever known and arguably the greatest 400m runner in history. Dubbed 'The Man with the Golden Shoes', he was the first sprinter to win 200m and 400m golds at the same Olympic Games and also the first to successfully defend his 400m Olympic title, and he set a host of other records.

For an athlete who was labelled 'The World's Fastest Man' in 1997, Michael Johnson took a while to get into his stride in terms of Olympic gold medals. Having earned a reputation as a record-breaking runner at both 200m and 400m while still at Baylor College in his native Texas, Johnson missed the Seoul 1988 Games because of a stress fracture, and suffered food poisoning at Barcelona 1992 four years later. Already a world-record champion at 200m and ranked number one at both 200m and 400m, the loss of weight and power in 1992 meant he managed only one gold medal, in the Men's 4 x 400m Relay, and he even returned that when it later emerged that three of his team-mates had been caught up in a doping scandal.

At the 1995 World Championships he won the 200m and 400m and set a new world record in the 4 x 400m Relay, where his leg of 42.91 seconds remains the fastest split time in history. But it was not until the Atlanta 1996 Games that the man known by his rivals as 'Superman' and 'The Duck' – because of his unusual upright running style – truly struck Olympic gold. He went into Atlanta 1996 as World Champion at both 200m and 400m, a double no man had achieved before, and repeated this unique feat on home soil in the Olympic Games in thrilling style.

First came the 400m, where he walked out for the race in his trademark gold spikes. He took control by the halfway stage and kept pulling clear until he beat silver medallist Roger Black by almost a second and a 10-metre margin, the biggest for a century. He also set a new Olympic record time of 43.49 seconds. Now for the 200m, where he was world record-holder, having beaten Pietro Mennea's 17-year best at the US trials with a time of 19.66 seconds. He shattered that and the Olympic record at Atlanta 1996, shaving more than a third of a second off his own record with a winning time in the final of 19.32 seconds, which included running the first 100 metres in 10.35 seconds.

More medals and records followed, and by the time he reached the Sydney 2000 Games, Johnson had broken the 400m world record, achieved with a time of 43.18 seconds in the 1999 World Championships – a mark that still stands as a record today. He'd also won 57 of his previous 60 400m finals, including the preceding four world titles. No one had ever defended the Olympic 400m title, however, but Johnson was unbowed. Although he was last out of the blocks, he cruised through the gears and won by a four-metre margin. At 33, he became the oldest athlete ever to win Olympic gold at a distance under 5,000m.

He retired soon afterwards, and has since pursued a successful media career, as well as continuing his association with athletics as an agent for stars such as Jeremy Wariner, who inherited Johnson's 400m Olympic crown in Athens 2004, and also with his performance centre for young athletes in Texas.

Statistics
Born: 13 September 1967, Dallas, Texas, USA
Height: 6ft (1.83m)
Weight: 170lb (77kg)

Olympic Games Medals
Barcelona 1992
Men's 4 x 400m Relay ....Gold

Atlanta 1996
Men's 200m...Gold
Men's 400m...Gold

Sydney 2000
Men's 400m...Gold

Above: Johnson, aged 33, becomes the oldest gold medal winner in an Olympic sprint event, In Sydney 2000.

Right: The American sprinter appears calm as he displays his unique upright running style on his way to defending his 400m Olympic title at the Sydney 2000 Games.

'Life is often compared to a marathon, but I think it is more like being a sprinter; long stretches of hard work punctuated by brief moments in which we are given the opportunity to perform at our best.'

JACKIE
JOYNER-KERSEE
ATHLETICS

USA

One of the finest female athletes in sporting history, the American golden girl became the first heptathlete ever to achieve consecutive Olympic triumphs, having secured gold medals in the Seoul 1988 and Atlanta 1992 Games. With her knack of setting records, Jackie Joyner-Kersee also became the first American woman to win a gold medal in the Long Jump.

Named Jacqueline after the glamorous wife of President Kennedy because, in the eyes of her grandmother, 'someday this girl will be the First Lady of something', Jackie Joyner-Kersee made a career out of doing things first. Not even Sweden's Carolina Kluft, widely regarded as the greatest woman athlete today, seems to be able to get close to the world record of 7,291 points scored by Joyner-Kersee on the way to her first Heptathlon gold-medal success in Seoul 1988. She was the first woman in history to earn more than 7,000 points in the gruelling seven-discipline event, and her abilities were so outstanding that much of Joyner-Kersee's career was played out challenging the clock rather than the competition.

earned a basketball scholarship to the University of California at Los Angeles in 1980, where she was a starting forward for the UCLA Bruins as well as working on the track as a long jumper. Assistant track coach Bob Kersee put his job on the line to ensure he could take her under his wing, claiming he would quit if he was not given the chance to coach the prodigious talent. Luckily for the pair, the athletics department agreed to his plan.

Having qualified for the US Olympic team for the Los Angeles 1984 Games, Joyner-Kersee missed out on Heptathlon gold by a mere 0.06 seconds in her final event, the 800m. She settled for silver but the tears she shed were not in anguish at her defeat, but for joy at brother Al's victory in the Triple Jump. Somehow, she knew her time would come.

Statistics
Born: 3 March 1962, East St Louis, Illinois, USA
Height: 5ft 8in (1.73m)
Weight: 154lb (70kg)

Olympic Games Medals
Los Angeles 1984
Women's Heptathlon .... Silver

Seoul 1988
Women's Heptathlon .... Gold
Women's Long Jump .... Gold

Barcelona 1992
Women's Heptathlon .... Gold
Women's Long Jump .... Bronze

Atlanta 1996
Women's Long Jump .... Bronze

She caught the athletics bug watching the Montreal 1976 Games and, after embarrassing older brother Al on the track, it wasn't long before she was putting other competitors to shame; at the age of 14, she won the first of four straight national junior Pentathlon championships. She did not just dominate in track and field, however. Joyner-Kersee

While it came as no surprise when she won gold at Seoul 1988, the manner of the success was startling. Not only did she cruise to victory in the Heptathlon, she also flew over 24ft (7.32m) to claim the gold medal in the Long Jump. The Heptathlon score of 7,291 points was her fourth world record, with her achievements made all the

Above: Joyner-Kersee throws the javelin in the Heptathlon at Seoul 1988. As well as winning gold, she set a world record of 7,291 points in the event, which still stands.

Right: Joyner-Kersee stamped her authority on women's athletics with a second gold at the Seoul 1988 Games in the Women's Long Jump, setting an Olympic record of 7.40m.

more phenomenal by the fact that the multi-event competitions and the Long Jump had previously been dominated by the former Soviet bloc, whose athletes were not averse to using steroids. Ever the one for doing things first, Joyner-Kersee was the first American woman to win Long Jump gold, as well as the first athlete in 64 years to win gold in both a multi-discipline and single event.

Marrying long-term coach Bob in 1986 brought stability to her career and the couple's desire to go one step further was enough to seal another Heptathlon gold in the Barcelona 1992 Games.

Her Olympic farewell came at the Atlanta 1996 Games and this time she had to settle for another Long Jump bronze, while injury problems forced her to miss the Heptathlon and give the other athletes a chance to shine – and how grateful they must have been.

'Ask any athlete, we all hurt at times. I'm asking my body to go through seven different tasks. To ask it not to ache would be too much.'

ALEKSANDR **KARELIN** RUSSIA
WRESTLING – GRECO-ROMAN

This huge wrestler has had some of the most prestigious titles attached to his name. He is honoured by his country's highest decoration as a Hero of the Russian Federation, and is nicknamed 'Aleksandr the Great'. He is one of only four male wrestlers to have won three Olympic Games gold medals.

It is difficult to decide which nickname is more fitting for an athlete who is honoured by his country so highly that only a handful of Russian sportsmen can be considered his equal. He is 'Great' and his name is Aleksandr, he is a 'Russian Bear', sharing a similar physique to the woodland animal, and strikes fear into his opponents. When called 'The Experiment', one can only wonder whether his size-defying speed and agility, as well as his strength, are super-human.

Karelin was already huge at birth, weighing in at 6.8 kg (15 lb) in Novosibirsk, in the desolate region of Siberia. But he would not use his natural size and strength for sport until taking up wrestling at the age of 13, when he grew taller than his father, and trained by hunting on skis and hauling huge logs through the snow.

Under the tutelage of Viktor Kusnetzov, the only coach he ever had, his training was increased, running in huge depths of snow for hours on end. He is said to have carried a fridge up eight flights of stairs all by himself in one legendary exercise.

No wonder he quickly achieved success in Soviet junior tournaments. He became World Junior Champion in 1987, a feat that earned him a place on the Soviet national wrestling team.

As if this unique and ruthless training was not enough, Karelin and his coach refined a wrestling manoeuvre previously unthinkable for heavyweights to carry out – the reverse body-lift. With this in his arsenal, fellow opponents admitted to being scared of the great 'Russian Bear', describing an experience of intense fear at being lifted and dumped over his head.

Shortly before his first gold medal at just 21 years old at the Seoul 1988 Games, he was crowned European Champion and became a clear favourite to be ranked as Russia's prime Wrestling candidate for the upcoming Games. Few would have predicted, however, that this would become the start of an amazing 13-year winning streak. From 1990 he commenced on a 10-year consecutive run without ever losing a single point.

He won his first Olympic title in devastating fashion. Trailing Bulgarian Rangel Gerovski 3–0 with just seconds remaining, 'The Experiment' used his trademark finish to slam his opponent, scoring a five-point takedown to claim the gold medal. He won all three World Championships on the way to his second Olympic Games in Barcelona 1992, where again not a single opponent survived to the time limit until the final, which Karelin still won with apparent ease.

Four years later, with more emphatic victories the world over and six more major championships within his huge grasp, he became the first Olympic Games wrestler to win the same weight division three times. He took his third consecutive gold, extending his unprecedented tyranny over the sport by outscoring all five of his opponents 25–0.

His first defeat in well over a decade of competition would also prove to be his last. Karelin finally lost at the Sydney 2000 Olympic Games when a relatively unknown American wrestler by the name of Rulon Gardner achieved a 1–0 victory in added time. One of the most feared but revered Greco-Roman wrestlers of all time subsequently retired from the sport with a silver medal around his neck.

Statistics

Born: 19 September 1967,
Novosibirsk, Russia
Height: 6ft 4in (1.93m)
Weight: 218lb (99kg)

Olympic Games Medals

Seoul 1988
Men's 96–120kg Greco-Roman
Wrestling...Gold

Barcelona 1992
Men's 96–120kg Greco-Roman
Wrestling...Gold

Atlanta 1996
Men's 96–120kg Greco-Roman
Wrestling...Gold

Sydney 2000
Men's 96–120kg Greco-Roman
Wrestling... Silver

Below: Karelin's 13-year winning streak in Greco-Roman Wrestling was finally ended by America's Rulon Gardner, at the Sydney 2000 Games.

Right: The Russian grapples with America's Siamak Ghaffari in the 96–120kg Greco-Roman Wrestling final at the Atlanta 1996 Olympic Games.

'You consider this ancient sport and this monumental man who's had a perfect career, and the only thing you come up with is that he is to us what Hercules was to the ancient Greeks.'

American gold-medal-winning wrestler Jeff Blatnick on Karelin

SAWAO **KATO**
GYMNASTICS – ARTISTIC

Sawao Kato is one of the most successful Olympic gymnasts of all time, having won 12 medals, eight of which were gold. He is without question one of the best ever Japanese Olympians, and is one of only nine athletes to have won eight or more gold medals.

When it comes to discussing the most successful gymnasts in the history of the Olympic Games, Sawao Kato's name will always be mentioned. Few can match his achievements at the Olympic Games, where he won a memorable eight gold medals and was one of the greatest athletes to have taken part in the sport.

Kato was born shortly after World War II and was attracted to sport at an early age, enrolling as a student at Kuiku University. He was fortunate

Voronin, he managed to win gold medals in the Floor and Individual All-Around Competitions.

It was clear to see that Kato was going to be a major Olympic star, and his success story was to get even better when the Games moved to Munich in 1972. He won the Individual All-Around gold medal once again, becoming only the third gymnast in the history of the sport to win the title in two consecutive Olympic Games.

He was joined on the podium by two fellow countrymen who won silver and bronze,

that his teacher and coach, Akitomo Kaneko, had been a member of the Japanese team that finished a creditable fifth in the Helsinki 1952 Olympic Games.

There was a lot of pressure on Kato to succeed at his first Olympic Games, at Mexico City in 1968, since the Japanese team were dominant in international gymnastics. But he refused to let the hype surrounding his debut affect him and calmly helped Japan win the Team Competition with ease. Kato was also dominant in the individual events and, even though his main rival at the time was the frighteningly good Mikhail

demonstrating the strength of gymnastics in Japan at that time. He also managed to win gold in the Parallel Bars and played his part in Japan winning the Team Competition once again. But the medals did not stop there and he also picked up two silver medals for his display in the Horizontal Bars and Pommel Horse Competitions.

His quality was there for all to see but despite his dominance at the Olympic Games he failed to win a World Championships – even though that tournament provided him with one of the most memorable days of his career, in Varna in 1974. Kato left the crowd stunned when he fell off the

Statistics

Born: 11 October 1946, Niigata, Japan
Height: 5ft 4in (1.63m)
Weight: 130lb (59kg)

Olympic Games Medals

Mexico City 1968

Men's Individual All-Around Competition	Gold
Men's Team Competition	Gold
Men's Floor Competition	Gold
Men's Rings Competition	Bronze

Munich 1972

Men's Individual All-Around Competition	Gold
Men's Team Competition	Gold
Men's Parallel Bars Competition	Gold
Men's Horizontal Bars Competition	Silver
Men's Pommel Horse Competition	Silver

Montreal 1976

Men's Team Competition	Gold
Men's Parallel Bars Competition	Gold
Men's Individual All-Around Competition	Silver

Above: A combination of both physical and mental strength was required for Kato to be able to set 12 Olympic Games records.

Right: The Mexico City 1968 and Munich 1972 Olympic Games individual all-around champion enjoyed competing on the horizontal bar more than any other apparatus.

parallel bars and broke an arm. Most athletes would have called it a day, but after a lengthy spell just lying on the floor and holding his shoulder he somehow managed to pick himself up and signalled to his coach that he was okay to carry on. Grimacing through what must have been excruciating pain, he defied the odds to finish his exercise, displaying for all to see the commitment he had to his sport.

His last participation at the Olympic Games came in Montreal 1976. He was desperate to secure his third consecutive Individual All-Around gold medal, but standing in his way was the Soviet Union's Nikolai Andrianov. Regarded as one of the best young talents in the world, Andrianov took gold by just a single point. Kato eased his disappointment by helping Japan win the Team Competition once more, and closed out

his Olympic career by also claiming a gold medal in the Parallel Bars.

He was inducted into the International Gymnastics Hall of Fame in 2001. Most recently heard of working as a professor at the University of Tsukuba, Kato also appeared as an Olympic Games judge following competitive retirement, making headlines again with some controversial opinions at the Athens 2004 Games.

'Defeating Kato was the most difficult competition in my life.'

Nikolai Andrianov, the Olympic Games' most decorated athlete,
reveals that Kato was his toughest opponent

KIPCHOGE 'KIP' **KEINO** KENYA
ATHLETICS

Kip Keino inspired a dynasty of his fellow countrymen to follow him into long-distance running glory and Olympic greatness. He was one of the first of an era of Kenyan athletes who would continue to set new benchmarks for middle- and long-distance running, winning titles in every distance from 1,500m to 10,000m, including two Olympic gold medals.

T his Nandi tribesman from the Rift Valley area of western Kenya was, quite simply, born to run. But, not only this, he was born to be an Olympic gold medallist, and he cares so deeply about the prestige of this most ancient of traditions that he gave his first daughter the middle name of Olympia.

Keino's father was also a long-distance runner, who encouraged him to train in the high hills and plains of his native region while herding goats for his local tribe. The natural habitat of giraffes and zebras would prove to be an unrivalled training base, as the steep inclines, wide flat plains and searing heat provided the ideal conditions for stamina running. The added threat of lions and hyenas emerging from the undergrowth would surely have been an even greater incentive to keep on running at pace.

Orphaned as a child and raised by an aunt, Keino joined the local police force as a physical training instructor after leaving school, and was afforded time to develop his athletic prowess, even though his first sporting love had been rugby. He was soon entered into numerous Kenyan and all-African competitions and earned himself a place in the Commonwealth Games team to travel to Australia in 1962. However, it would take him a few years more to settle into the true heat of international competitive running.

His first Olympic Games came two years later, in Tokyo 1964. One of the most memorable races that summer was the 5,000m final, which featured a famous victory for America's Bob Schul. Behind Schul, tucked in the crowded second pack of runners, was Kenya's first champion in waiting: Keino, aged just 24, kept up with the best of the rest to finish in fifth place. He barely registered in the 1,500m as he quietly whispered on to the world stage.

Just a year later and he announced himself as the next long-distance runner to beat, clinching world records in the 5,000m and 3,000m, shattering the latter by six seconds.

An enormously successful four-year gap between Olympic Games meant Keino was Kenya's leading runner by a Nandi-country mile. Yet he was still not the favourite in any of his preferred events going to Mexico City in 1968.

Keino's most remarkable victory there came when he won gold in the 1,500m, having jogged over a mile to get to the stadium on time when the bus transporting him from the Athletes' Village got stuck in traffic. His first gold came with a helping hand, in a memorable example of team tactics. The 1,500m could easily have been handed to American Jim Ryun, who held the event's world record. However, between them, Keino and fellow countryman Ben Jipcho orchestrated a move that a Formula One pair would have been proud of.

Statistics
Born: 17 January 1940, Kipsamo, Kenya
Height: 6ft (1.83m)
Weight: 170lb (77kg)

Olympic Games Medals
Mexico City 1968
Men's 1,500m ....Gold
Men's 5,000m .... Silver

Munich 1972
Men's 3,000m Steeplechase...........Gold
Men's 1,500m .... Silver

Jipcho set a blistering pace over the first two laps in an attempt to tire Ryun, who was desperate to keep up. As the two tired, Keino took his cue and stormed past them, leaving the American with an impossible distance to recoup, and the Kenyans had their first gold medal in history. Keino's Olympic record was not broken until 1984.

Above: He lived to run, but retired from the sport the year after smiling his way to glory in this race in Munich 1972.

Right: Kip leads the field on his way to gold in the final of the 3,000m steeplechase in the Munich 1972 Olympic Games.

Even more remarkably, the race came only a week after Keino had collapsed during the 10,000m final, suffering from a severe gall-bladder infection. Despite being unable to eat, and with the dire warning that he risked his life by running ringing in his ears, he returned to the track to take silver in the 5,000m four days later. The 1,500m race followed but Keino again ignored the words of team-mates and officials, declaring: 'I must run for my country.' And how he did, with one of the greatest middle-distance performances ever.

Four years later and now 32 years old, Keino surprised many who thought him too old by qualifying for two events at the Munich 1972 Games. After narrowly missing out on gold but winning his second silver in the 1,500m, the veteran pipped his co-conspirator Jipcho to the gold medal in the new 3,000m Steeplechase event, and confirmed himself as not only the greatest Kenyan runner of all time, but also one of the greatest Olympians.

His reputation was further enhanced when, following retirement in 1973, he bought a farm with his wife and turned it into an orphanage, the Kip Keino Children's Home. Still close to athletics, he has chaired the Kenyan Olympic Committee and two of his children are promising young runners.

'I was thinking to myself, "This is the race of my life. If I die here, I die here."'

Kip Keino reflects on winning Kenya's first Olympic gold, having run against medical advice

DARREN **KENNY**
PARALYMPIC CYCLING – ROAD/TRACK

Despite suffering a potentially career-ending injury as a teenager, and then spending 12 years out of the saddle, Darren Kenny, OBE, defied the odds and returned to Cycling to become a star of the Athens 2004 Paralympic Games, and in the Beijing 2008 Paralympic Games established himself as one of the greatest Paralympic cyclists of all time.

In the case of many Paralympic athletes, taking up a sport is a way for them to overcome their disability, mentally at least. For Darren Kenny, however, it was the other way round. He first got into cycling at a young age but when he was just 18 years old, and was tipped for an extremely bright future, he was involved in an unfortunate cycling accident, in which he sustained a serious neck injury, cutting short his potential career.

For any athlete to resume competing in a sport that almost left them paralysed takes some bravery. Which is probably why it took Kenny 12 years, large parts of which were spent comfort eating, to get over his accident. But when he hit 30, Kenny decided to do something about his physical and mental state and get back in the saddle. His decision to take up cycling again was initially based on a desire to get fit and shed some weight from years of living the good life. However, it turned out to be the start of a

career as one of the most successful Paralympian cyclists of all time.

Kenny first appeared on the world stage at the Athens 2004 Paralympic Games, just four years after he had taken up the sport again. He seized his chance, and did so in some style. He honoured the Great Britain team with astonishing gold medal successes on the Track, winning the 1km Time Trial and the Individual Pursuit events. He also claimed a third medal, on the Road, clinching a silver medal for the combined Men's Road Race and Time Trial.

Because he had made a name for himself in Athens 2004, much was expected of the now veteran racer in the build-up to the Beijing 2008 Paralympic Games. Kenny certainly did not disappoint. In fact, he even surpassed himself, winning an outstanding four gold medals and a silver. His gold medal successes came in the 1km Time Trial, Team Sprint, Individual Pursuit and, lastly, Individual Road Race.

Statistics
Born: 17 March 1970, Salisbury, Dorset, England

Paralympic Games Medals
Athens 2004
Road: Men's Road Race/
Time Trial Bicycle CP Div 3............Silver
Track: Men's 1km Time Trial
Bicycle CP Div 3/4................Gold
Track: Men's Individual Pursuit
Bicycle CP Div 3.....................Gold

Beijing 2008
Road: Men's Individual
Road Race LC3-4/CP3.................Gold
Road: Men's Individual
Time Trial CP3.......................Silver
Track: Men's 1km Time Trial CP3......Gold
Track: Men's Individual
Pursuit CP3.............................Gold
Track: Men's Team Sprint
LC1-4 CP3/4...............................Gold

Left: Kenny proudly displays the five medals (four of them gold) that he won on two wheels at the Beijing 2008 Paralympic Games.

Right: Kenny heads for more golden glory for Great Britain as he leads Javier Ochoa of Spain in the Men's Individual Pursuit (CP3) at Beijing 2008.

Kenny's accomplishments are undoubtedly impressive, yet his worldwide fame and status are based more on quality than quantity, coming largely as a result of the style in which he won his many medals. He has broken numerous world records and holds all five of the track world records in his class. The undisputed best cyclist in the world in his category, the man from Dorset in the south-west of England has taken his Paralympic medal count to a grand total of eight, six of which are gold.

Although Sir Chris Hoy often grabs most of the headlines in the British press and the adulation of the British public when it comes to Cycling, Kenny should be regarded as just as important a figure in the nation's athletics circles, as he is currently the greatest Paralympic cyclist the world has to offer. His services on the track have been rewarded with honours off it too, and in 2009, for example, he was awarded an OBE for services to sport for athletes with a disability.

'I am going to catch up on four years of [no] sleep!'

Darren Kenny on his exhaustion after preparing for Beijing 2008

KIM SOO-NYUNG
ARCHERY

South Korean star Kim Soo-Nyung is often referred to as 'the Heavenly Archer', and looking at her Olympic Games record it is easy to see why. Her total of six medals makes her the most decorated woman in the sport's history, despite the fact that she spent between Barcelona 1992 and Sydney 2000 in retirement, missing the Atlanta 1996 Olympic Games.

Statistics

Born: 5 April 1971, Chungcheongbuk-do, South Korea
Height: 5ft 5in (1.65m)
Weight: 128lb (58kg)

Olympic Games Medals

Seoul 1988

Women's Individual Competition..Gold
Women's Team Competition ....Gold

Barcelona 1992

Women's Team Competition ....Gold
Women's Individual Competition.. Silver

Sydney 2000

Women's Team Competition ....Gold
Women's Individual Competition...................................... Bronze

Kim Soo-Nyung is widely recognised as the outstanding female archer of her generation, despite having spent the years between 1992 and 1999 in retirement. She already had four Olympic medals – three of them gold – by the time she decided to concentrate on raising a family at the age of 21, but her thirst for success was not fully sated, and she returned to win another gold medal and a bronze at the Sydney 2000 Olympic Games.

By then she was considered a veteran in her sport – a far cry from her exploits in Seoul 1988, when she was an unheralded 17-year-old going into the Games in her home country. By the end of the Seoul 1988 Games she had been christened

'The Viper' and her deadly accuracy had secured gold medals in both the Women's Individual and Team Competitions. In the Individual Competition Kim showed her true class. She had sailed into the final thanks to a series of remarkably consistent displays, but she saved her best until last as she recorded a final score of 344. It was her best tally in the entire competition and secured the gold medal in front of an adoring home crowd. That completed a clean sweep for the women's team, as Wang Hui-Gyeong and Yun Yeong-Suk, like Kim also teenagers, won silver and bronze medals respectively.

After the success of the South Korean women in the Individual Competition, it came as no surprise when they blew away the field to claim gold in the Women's Team Competition. Kim's golden run was only just beginning. She won gold in both the Individual and the Team Competitions in the 1989 and 1991 World Championships in Lausanne and Krakow respectively, as she kept hitting the bull's-eye with relentless accuracy. It was an era of unparalleled South Korean dominance in Women's Archery, and one that showed no signs of easing as the Barcelona 1992 Olympic Games loomed on the horizon.

Indeed, there was a feeling that if Kim was going to lose, then it would only be at the hands of a fellow countrywoman – and so it proved, as she lost the final of the Women's Individual Competition 112–105 to Cho Yun-Jeong. Two days later, Cho and Kim were competing alongside each other in the Women's Team Competition. Again they progressed to the final, where they faced China. And it was to be another gold medal for the South Koreans as they triumphed 236–228.

In the aftermath of claiming her fourth Olympic medal, Kim announced her retirement, deciding that at the age of 21 she had nothing left to prove; and her desire to start a family simply made the decision inevitable. But seven years and two

Left: Modern Archery's leading medalist, Kim Soo-Nyung was only 17 years old when she won gold medals in the Individual and Team Competitions on home soil in Seoul 1988.

Right: The South Korean draws her bow in her third and final Olympics, on the way to gold and bronze medals at the Sydney 2000 Games.

'It is much more difficult to win a national competition than to win a gold in the Olympics.'

Park Sung-Hyun reflects on the strength of Kim Soo-Nyung and her fellow South Korean archers

children later, the greatest female archer in history came out of retirement in a bid to compete in the Sydney 2000 Games. It was to prove a stunning comeback. Again, it was only a fellow South Korean who prevented her from winning gold in the Women's Individual Competition, as she lost in the semi-finals against Yun Mi-Jin, but the bronze medal was secured thanks to a 105–103 victory over Choe Ok-Sil of North Korea.

Kim has always been an outstanding team player, though, and this was proved once again as she joined forces with Yun Mi-Jin and Kim Nam-Soon for the Women's Team Competition. The result was a hugely comprehensive victory, as they beat Ukraine 251–239 in the final.

That was Kim's fourth gold medal and sixth Olympic medal overall, a record for a female archer that will be very hard to beat.

CAROLINA **KLUFT**
ATHLETICS

Carolina Kluft is regarded by many as the queen of Heptathlon. Not only did the Swedish star win gold in Athens 2004 but she also won nine consecutive gold medals in the event in major championships and was unbeaten in 22 Heptathlons and Pentathlons before opting to concentrate instead on the Long Jump and Triple Jump.

Statistics

Born: 2 February 1983, Sandhult, Sweden
Height: 5ft 10in (1.78m)
Weight: 143lb (65kg)

Olympic Games Medals

Athens 2004
Women's Heptathlon ....Gold

They say nice guys never win but Carolina Kluft certainly bucks the trend. How many athletes do you know who carry a fluffy mascot with them 'to remind me sport is meant to be fun'? Kluft's stuffed Eeyore toy, won at a fairground in Vienna, was with her in Athens 2004 when she won gold, having taken the lead after the High Jump and staying in front for the rest of the competition. She won by an Olympic record margin of 517 points, ahead of Lithuanian rival Austra Skujyte, and set a final total of 6,952 points.

Despite the intense competition of international athletics and the gruelling nature of the Heptathlon, which features seven events spread over two days, she has stuck to her philosophy of enjoying life both on and off the track. Her happy-go-lucky personality, not to mention her good looks and striking blonde hair, have made her a household name even beyond athletics, and have won her a horde of adoring fans.

in 2000 after her coach, Agne Bergvall, suggested she was well suited to the event. In fact she improved so rapidly that many experts believe she now has no weaknesses across the seven disciplines.

Her personal best of 7,032 points, a European record, ranks her second on the all-time Heptathlon points score list, just behind the legendary Jackie Joyner-Kersee, and she is also a member of the Swedish 4 x 100m Relay team in international competitions. Kluft won her first Heptathlon title at the World Championships in Paris in 2003 with a score of 7,001 points, becoming only the third woman ever to break the 7,000-point barrier, and within a year she was Olympic champion too.

Since then she has won two more world titles, in Helsinki in 2005 and Osaka in 2007, and such was her grip on the event that at one stage she was Olympic, World, European, World Indoor and European Indoor champion all at the same time. She chose not to defend her Olympic title in Beijing

Looking at her early life, it is easy to see that she was destined for the top. Kluft's mother, Ingalill, was a long jumper in the 1970s and her father, Johnny, played professional football for Swedish club Osters IF, and the genes clearly got passed down. Kluft first took up athletics at the age of 11 and proved a natural, eventually concentrating on the Heptathlon

2008, having opted in recent times to concentrate on the Long Jump and Triple Jump, only to struggle with injury. But her fans across the world are hoping she will return to the Heptathlon in the near future, which would make her a runaway favourite to win gold again at the London 2012 Olympic Games.

Above: Kluft prepares to throw the javelin in the Heptathlon at the Athens 2004 Games, which she went on to win by a record margin.

Right: Kluft extends her lead in the Heptathlon with the biggest Long Jump of the competition, recording a distance of 6.78m.

'The most important thing is that you're having fun. It's not about the results or being number one in the world, it's about feeling satisfied and enjoying it.'

OLGA **KORBUT**
GYMNASTICS – ARTISTIC

USSR

Olga Korbut is one of the most famous and important gymnasts of all time, credited with changing the face of her sport when she won the hearts of millions at the Munich 1972 Olympic Games, creating a media storm the likes of which had never been seen before.

Before Olga Korbut arrived at the Munich 1972 Games, the profile of women's Gymnastics was far lower than in the modern age, dominated by older athletes and with the emphasis on elegance rather than technique and acrobatics. But 17-year-old Korbut's performance changed all that. The little girl from Belarus won the hearts of the audience and the affection of millions of television viewers around the world with her daring tricks and willingness to show open emotion, in stark contrast to many Eastern bloc athletes at the time.

She amazed experts and fans alike with her flexibility and daring moves, becoming one of the first gymnasts ever to do a backward somersault on the bars and a back somersault to dismount from the Beam, a move which has now become known as the Korbut Flip. She also wiped tears from her eyes after a disastrous Uneven Bars routine in which she fell and ended her hopes of Individual All-Around gold. That one moment catapulted her to international fame as fans around the world wanted to reach out and help her. One supporter inside the arena even rushed to bring the weeping gymnast a bouquet of flowers in sympathy, and she won over the crowd again with her courage as she recovered from the setback to win three gold medals – two in the apparatus finals, in the Balance Beam and Floor Competition, and one in the Team Competition. Her Soviet Union team-mate Ludmilla Tourischeva took the Individual All-Around gold but there was no doubt Korbut was the star of the show and her performance had a huge effect on women's Gymnastics.

In the years that followed Munich 1972, the sport concentrated far more on technical brilliance, with the average age of competitors dropping dramatically.

In 1973 Korbut was named Athlete of the Year in America and she was accorded the same accolade in England the following year. She had quickly become the darling of the public around the world and although she went on to add to her medal tally – she won gold in the Team Competition and silver on the Balance Beam at the Montreal 1976 Olympic Games, despite going into the competition with injury problems – her legacy extended far beyond her winning record. The Soviet coaches and officials had designated Korbut as the woman who could beat the Romanian prodigy Nadia Comaneci in Montreal, but her lack of fitness led to under-par performances, and she was overshadowed not only by Comaneci but also by her own team-mate Nellie Kim.

Olga Korbut remains an iconic figure; her originality and courage changed the sport and, some would argue, even helped to ease the Cold War between East and West when she met US President Nixon at the White House.

Statistics
Born: 16 May 1955, Hrodna, Belarus
Height: 5ft (1.52m)
Weight: 86lb (39kg)

Olympic Games Medals
Munich 1972
Women's Floor Competition ....Gold
Women's Balance Beam
   Competition..Gold
Women's Team Competition ....Gold
Women's Uneven Bars
   Competition.. Silver

Montreal 1976
Women's Team Competition ....Gold
Women's Balance Beam
   Competition.. Silver

Below: Korbut's daring routines and engaging personality raised the profile of gymnastics across the globe.

Right: Overt, expressive emotion flowed throughout Korbut's performances at the Munich 1972 Games.

'I am not interested in medals or titles. I don't need
them. I need the love of the public and I fight for it.'

ALVIN 'AL' **KRAENZLEIN** USA
ATHLETICS

Apart from his historic haul of gold medals, one of the greatest compliments you could bestow upon Alvin 'Al' Kraenzlein is that he can be mentioned in the same breath as the indomitable Jesse Owens. His four golds at the Paris 1900 Olympic Games went unequalled until Owens' four in Berlin 1936, and his Athletics medal count remains a record in a single Games.

Statistics

Born: 12 December 1876, Milwaukee, USA

Died: 6 January 1928

Height: 6ft (1.83m)

Weight: 165lb (75kg)

Olympic Games Medals
Paris 1900

Men's 60m	Gold
Men's 110m Hurdles	Gold
Men's 200m Hurdles	Gold
Men's Long Jump	Gold

Alvin 'Al' Kraenzlein began competitive running and jumping at Milwaukee's East Side High School and, after enrolling at the University of Wisconsin in 1895, he was soon dominating his intercollegiate opponents in many speed events.

It was at the University of Pennsylvania that Kraenzlein really began to hone his skills and he set world records for the 120m high hurdles and the 220m low hurdles. While there are those who will point to his Olympic success later in his career, it can be argued that his legacy was greater even than what he achieved at the Games, for he revolutionised the way athletes negotiated the hurdles. The American athlete developed a never-before-seen technique which helped him glide over the obstacles – he cleared them with the lead leg extended. This method became standard for athletes in hurdling events. By the time Kraenzlein had graduated from Pennsylvania, he had won four straight intercollegiate championships, setting records along the way.

In the eyes of his contemporaries, nothing could surpass his exploits at the Paris 1900 Games. However, his achievements at state level, where he won the 120yd Hurdles, the 220yd Hurdles and the Long Jump between 1897 and 1899, were extremely impressive too. That pioneering straight-leg hurdling technique brought him two world records in addition to his five world records in the Long Jump, which were set in 1899.

But it was for his success at Paris 1900 that he should be remembered. He set a record by winning the four events he entered: the 60m, the 110m Hurdles, the 200m Hurdles and the Long Jump. It would be 36 years before another athlete matched him. His name? None other than Jesse Owens.

Kraenzlein's great rival in Paris was Meyer Prinstein. But before the duo went head to head in the Long Jump, Kraenzlein was picking up gold medals elsewhere: as well as his sprint victory, he set Olympic records in both hurdling events almost as a warm-up to his Prinstein showdown.

It was billed as the battle of the 'big three', featuring American duo Kraenzlein and Prinstein and the Irish athlete Peter O'Connor, though in reality the Irish competitor could not compete at the same level. The Americans had set six of the last seven world records during the previous three years and the Parisian crowd watched in eager anticipation as the Long Jump duel unfolded.

Prinstein led during the Saturday qualifying with a leap of 7.175m to Kraenzlein's 6.93m. Now for the controversy: it was claimed that the two men had reached a private agreement not to compete on the Sunday on religious grounds, but Kraenzlein did in fact jump a day after the qualifying – and edged out Prinstein by a centimetre to claim the gold.

It meant Kraenzlein had achieved a record-setting feat – four gold medals in individual events at a single Olympic Games – and one that remains unsurpassed to this day.

Left: Kraenzlein, who won four gold medals at Paris 1900, was a qualified dentist but later moved into coaching, training the German and Cuban national teams.

Right: At the Paris 1900 Games, Kraenzlein used his pioneering technique of straight-leg hurdling to win gold in the Men's 110m Hurdles.

'The country and national life, as a whole, can only be benefited from healthy enthusiasm and rivalry in the Olympic sports.'

Al Kraenzlein on what the Olympic Games mean to a country

LARISSA **LATYNINA**
GYMNASTICS – ARTISTIC

USSR

Larissa Latynina is unquestionably one of the greatest ever Olympians, having won 18 medals between Melbourne 1956 and Tokyo 1964. The record-breaking gymnast is the only female athlete to have won nine gold medals, and holds the record for the most individual medals in Olympic history.

The story behind the success of Larissa Latynina is as dramatic as her unrivalled Olympic success. She was born in the Ukraine in 1934, which was then part of the USSR, and was forced by hardship to mature quickly. Poverty affected her family when she was a child, then tragedy struck when she lost both parents and was orphaned in the aftermath of World War II. Sport was naturally far from her thoughts at that time; and, being more interested in dancing, she was intent on becoming a ballet dancer by the age of 11 years old.

Latynina did exercises with hoops and balls, which were performed to music, and she was so impressive that her teachers encouraged her to take up gymnastics. Her life changed irrevocably. By the age of 16 she had already become the National Schools Gymnastics Champion. Latynina graduated from high school with honours in 1953, and just a year later she was taking part in her first international tournament at the World Championships in Rome, Italy, where she finished 14th. She then went back to study at the Physical Training College in Kiev, where she met and married Ivan Latynina.

With her personal life secure for the first time, she was able to focus all her attentions on gymnastics, and stole the show at her first Olympic Games in Melbourne 1956, aged just 21. Though still a novice when it came to competing against the best athletes in the world, she quickly showed her ability when she fought off fierce opposition to win gold in the Individual All-Around Competition and on the Horse Vault. She also tied for another gold medal in the Floor Competition. Her success did not end there, as the Soviets won Team gold and a bronze in the Team Portable Apparatus Competition, and she clinched silver on the Uneven Bars. It helped the Soviet Union move past the USA when it came to the overall medal count.

There was no disputing her ability, and she proceeded to dominate once again at the European Gymnastics Championships in 1957, when she won every event. Latynina celebrated the birth of her daughter Tanya a year later, which forced her to spend some time away from competition. But she returned and made her mark once again at the Rome 1960 Olympic Games, where she starred by winning a medal in every

Left: The young Ukrainian pictured in Melbourne 1956, where she made her Olympic Games breakthrough at the age of 21.

Right: Latynina displays the gymnastic poise, strength and balance that contributed towards a record haul of Olympic Games medals.

Statistics

Born: 27 December 1934, Kherson, Ukraine
Height: 5ft 3in (1.6m)
Weight: 115lb (52kg)

Olympic Games Medals

Melbourne 1956
Women's Floor Competition............Gold
Women's Individual All-Around
   Competition..Gold
Women's Horse Vault
   Competition..Gold
Women's Team Competition ....Gold
Women's Uneven Bars
   Competition....................................... Silver
Women's Team Portable
   Apparatus Competition............. Bronze

Rome 1960
Women's Floor Competition............Gold
Women's Individual All-Around
   Competition..Gold
Women's Team Competition ....Gold
Women's Uneven Bars
   Competition....................................... Silver
Women's Balance Beam
   Competition....................................... Silver
Women's Horse Vault
   Competition..................................... Bronze

Tokyo 1964
Women's Floor Competition............Gold
Women's Team Competition ....Gold
Women's Horse Vault
   Competition....................................... Silver
Women's Individual All-Around
   Competition....................................... Silver
Women's Uneven Bars
   Competition..................................... Bronze
Women's Balance Beam
   Competition..................................... Bronze

event in which she took part. Latynina defended her Individual and Team Competition titles and also won gold in the Floor Competition. The medals just kept coming, and she picked up two more silvers and a bronze.

Back home in the Soviet Union, her achievements did not go unrewarded: she received numerous awards, such as the Order of

Lenin and the Soviet Badge of Honour. She is also one of an elite club of only four women ever to win four consecutive World Championship titles.

The Tokyo 1964 Olympic Games were to mark her final involvement in a major tournament, and she was determined to go out with a bang. She managed to win gold in the Floor Competition for the third straight time, and she also won her

third Olympic Team gold. There were also two more silvers and two bronze medals to add to her trophy cabinet. Words can hardly do justice to the amazing natural quality Latynina had at her disposal, but add to that her iron will and work ethic, and she will always go down in history as one of the greatest ever athletes to have participated in the Olympic Games.

'I repeat my old routine hundreds, sometimes thousands of times until I get it right. Monotonous? Not at all. I've been practising gymnastics for 16 years. I train five times a week in three-hour sessions, and I've never found it boring.'

CARL **LEWIS**
ATHLETICS

USA

Critically acclaimed as Sportsman of the Century by the International Olympic Committee in 1999, the American is one of only four Olympians in history to win nine gold medals. Such is his legacy that it took the might of the Jamaican Usain Bolt to finally take on his record of winning both the 100m and 200m in the same Olympic Games.

Carl Lewis may nowadays be enjoying acting roles as police officers and journalists in Hollywood movies, but his was never the career of a pretender. In the Seoul 1988 Olympic Games, Canadian athlete Ben Johnson's disqualification for doping only served to emphasise Carl Lewis's sincerity, as he shone through from second place to win gold and set a new world record.

There was no avoiding athletics as he grew up. His mother, Evelyn, was an Olympian, competing in the Helsinki 1952 Games in the 80m hurdles before establishing the Willingboro Track Club, in New Jersey, in 1969, with Lewis's father, William. At 15, he needed crutches to support his rapid growth, reportedly sprouting 2 $^1/_2$in (6.25cm) in just a month.

Despite the fact that it was still an amateur sport, Lewis was intent on succeeding in athletics, revelling in his obvious natural talent for jumping long distances. At the University of Houston, he developed a taste for sprinting too and caught the eye of Tom Tallez, the epitome of an all-

American 'coach'. Tallez would go on to train his greatest protégé to all major honours, the first being his famous quadruple gold haul at the Los Angeles 1984 Games, on home soil, a feat to match that of the great Jesse Owens. Lewis could never have imagined that, 11 years earlier, as the legendary Owens leant down to shake a little 12-year-old's hand at a small-town Athletics event in Philadelphia, he was staring up at an idol he would later emulate.

Lewis had been eager to compete in the Olympic Games since being drafted into the national team in 1980, but was denied the chance when the USA boycotted the Games in Moscow – a decision that would further erode the popularity of athletics in America. So it was in 1984 that the American public began to really become aware of Carl Lewis as he almost single-handedly re-established athletics as a major sport in his country. Having won the 100m, Lewis knew the Long Jump was his natural game and so he took just two of his allotted four jumps to avoid injury for later events. It worked. His first jump eased

Statistics
Born: 1 July 1961, Birmingham, Alabama, USA
Height: 6ft 2in (1.88m)
Weight: 176lb (80kg)

Olympic Games Medals
Los Angeles 1984
Men's 100m ....Gold
Men's 200m..Gold
Men's 4 x 100m Relay.........................Gold
Men's Long Jump................................Gold

Seoul 1988
Men's 100m ....Gold
Men's Long Jump................................Gold
Men's 200m......................................Silver

Barcelona 1992
Men's 4 x 100m Relay.........................Gold
Men's Long Jump................................Gold

Atlanta 1996
Men's Long Jump................................Gold

Left: Pictured just after winning gold in the Men's Long Jump at Los Angeles 1984, Lewis went on to equal Jesse Owens' record of four gold medals in one Olympic Games.

Right: Lewis raises his hands in jubilation after crossing the line first to win the gold medal in the Men's 200m at Los Angeles 1984.

him to gold and that enabled him to concentrate on bringing home the 200m and the 4 x 100m Relay golds as well.

In 1987, just over a year before his second Olympic Games, his father died of cancer. At the funeral, Lewis buried his 1984 100m gold medal with his father's body, proclaiming that it didn't matter because he was going to win more – and how he did. Despite needing the discovery of Johnson's cheating to win the 100m, Lewis flew

though the Long Jump again to earn his fifth and sixth gold medals in the Seoul 1988 Games.

Feeling the effects of age by 1992, the then 31-year-old still managed to out-do himself. After one of the most documented Long Jump duels in history, fought with fellow American Mike Powell at the 1991 World Championships, the two athletes locked horns again in Barcelona. Lewis had had to watch Powell beat him and break the world Long Jump record a year earlier, but

by pipping him to gold at the Olympic Games he cemented his place as an idol.

Age limited his pace four years later, but he defied the odds at 35 to scrape a place in the US team for Atlanta 1996. Again on home soil, Lewis capped off his career with another Long Jump gold medal and subsequently retired from sport to be named Olympian of the Century by the well-respected US magazine *Sports Illustrated*, as well as receiving numerous other lifetime accolades.

*'I want you to have this because it was your favourite event.
Don't worry, I'll get another one.'*

Carl Lewis on burying his first 100m gold medal with his father's body

JEANNIE **LONGO**
CYCLING

Jeannie Longo is considered to be the greatest female road cyclist of all time. Age has been no barrier for her as she has competed at the highest levels at the Olympic Games for over 20 years. The French cyclist, still competing at the top in her fifties, has also enjoyed considerable success away from the Olympic arena.

Longo, now known by her married name of Longo-Ciprelli, could easily have missed out on a remarkable sporting career if it had not been for her coach, and later husband, who convinced the young Frenchwoman to make a switch from skiing to cycling, aged 21. She won a major French title only months after the switch. Four years later Longo took part in her first Olympic Games, in Los Angeles 1984, aged 25, competing in the Women's Individual Road Race, but after a collision missed out on a medal, finishing sixth. Remarkably, she returned to compete in Seoul 1988 only a month after breaking her hip, just missing out on a top-20 finish.

At the Barcelona 1992 Games, Longo was back with a vengeance, picking up a silver medal in the Individual Road Race at the age of 33. Also that year in Barcelona, she finished fifth in the 3,000m Women's Individual Pursuit on the track.

Dominating her sport at all levels, the French cyclist also won a silver medal off-road, triumphing in the 1993 World Championships for mountain biking.

But her greatest glory came with gold and silver medals in the Atlanta 1996 Olympics in the Individual Road Race and Time Trial. By then, aged 37, Longo had also won 10 World Championship titles, including five World Championship road races – a feat that no other athlete, male or female, has managed to achieve.

Her fourth Olympic medal was awarded in Sydney 2000, when Longo grabbed the bronze in the Women's Individual Time Trial. Not content with a third-place finish, she also set the women's world record for the Hour race, leaving the mark at 45.094km.

At 49 years of age and as competitive as ever, she won her 55th French Championship title and also qualified for the Beijing 2008 Games. In the Individual Time Trial, Longo was ranked fourth, just missing out on an Olympic medal, 24 years after she first entered the Games. In total, she entered seven different Olympic Games – a record for a cyclist.

The French rider has accumulated more than 1,000 victories throughout her illustrious career and is still active. British Olympian Nicole Cooke, who won the Women's Individual Road Race in Beijing 2008, was only a year old when Longo took part in her first Games.

She has also won three consecutive Tour de France events, from 1987 to 1989, and has claimed second place a total of four times in 1985, 1986, 1992 and 1995, with a third position the following year.

Longo plans to train for the London 2012 Olympics, when she will be 53 years old. Besides her cycling, this remarkable athlete has also been awarded a degree in mathematics, an MBA and doctorate in sports management.

Statistics

Born: 31 October 1958, Annecy, Haute-Savoie, France
Height: 5ft 9in (1.74m)
Weight: 106lb (48kg)

Olympic Games Medals

Barcelona 1992
Women's Individual Road Race........Silver

Atlanta 1996
Women's Individual Road Race........Gold
Women's Individual Time Trial........Silver

Sydney 2000
Women's Individual Time Trial......Bronze

Below: Longo displays the gold medal she won for the Individual Road Race at the Atlanta 1996 Games. This was her fourth attempt at winnng gold in this event.

Right: Competing in her fifth Olympic Games, Longo races to win bronze in the Individual Time Trial at the Sydney 2000 Games.

'I am certainly like a diesel [engine]! My nickname used to be "the turbo-diesel" but the turbo part of it might be a bit tired!'

GREG **LOUGANIS**
AQUATICS – DIVING

USA

Greg Louganis is regarded as one of the greatest divers of all time, dominating his event at the Olympic Games and winning four gold medals.

Few, if any, can match the achievements of diver Greg Louganis at the Olympic Games. There have been other divers in the history of the sport who have recorded consecutive gold medals in the Platform and Springboard events, but it was the manner of his performances that made him stand out far above his fellow competitors. He was the first diver to amass 700 points in a diving competition under the current scoring system, and amazed audiences with his spectacular displays.

Louganis was adopted when still a baby after his birth parents were deemed too young to bring him up. He had a troubled childhood and was taunted at school for his dyslexia, his family background and his love of gymnastics. But he brushed aside the bullying and was fortunate in that his family had a swimming pool, where he constantly practised his diving skills. His father could see the passion Louganis had for the sport and decided to let him have diving classes.

Louganis never looked back and stunned his coaches when he scored a perfect 10 at the Junior Olympics national competition in Colorado Springs in 1971. In 1975 he made a big decision: to move away from his family and link up with diving coach Dr Sammy Lee, who was an Olympic gold medallist in London 1948. Lee was to be an inspirational force in Louganis's future success

and gave him the belief that he could go on to become one of the best in the world.

At just 16, Louganis made an immediate impact at his first Olympic Games, in Montreal 1976. Despite his lack of experience, he defied the odds to win silver for his performance in the 10m Platform, finishing runner-up behind Italian legend Klaus Dibiasi. Many said that Dibiasi was handing over the baton to the 16-year-old when he announced his retirement, and that certainly proved to be the case as Louganis won his first world Platform title in 1978.

It all seemed predestined for the American youngster to win his first major gold at the Moscow 1980 Olympics, but US President Jimmy Carter called for a boycott of the Games in protest at the Soviet Union's invasion of Afghanistan. Missing out on this opportunity did not derail his progress: Louganis maintained his position as one of the best divers in the world and stunned the crowds again at the World Championships in 1982 when he scored a 10 from all seven judges.

He did not have to wait much longer before clinching his first Olympic gold medals at the Los Angeles 1984 Games, and it was an occasion he will never forget as he became the first man in 56 years to clinch two Diving golds by winning the 10m Platform and 3m Springboard. He also passed 700 points in both events. His incredible

Statistics
Born: 29 January 1960, San Diego, California, USA
Height: 5ft 9in (1.75m)
Weight: 161lb (73kg)

Olympic Games Medals
Montreal 1976
Men's 10m Platform............................ Silver

Los Angeles 1984
Men's 10m Platform..............................Gold
Men's 3m Springboard ....Gold

Seoul 1988
Men's 10m Platform..............................Gold
Men's 3m Springboard ....Gold

Below: The smile of Louganis, a man who went from silver medallist at his first Olympic Games to win four gold medals before his career was over.

Right: The American's childhood training in dancing, tumbling and acrobatics contributed to his reputation as a graceful, effortless diver.

achievement did not go unrecognised elsewhere, and he was duly presented with the prestigious Sullivan Award in 1985 as the USA's most outstanding amateur athlete.

Just when he thought things could not get any better, he then wrote his name in the record books with his next foray into Olympic competition, at the Seoul 1988 Games. Up against divers who were half his age, Louganis managed to become only the second athlete to win double gold medals in two consecutive Olympic Games, winning the 3m Springboard and 10m Platform events. His success in the 3m Springboard was especially remarkable considering that he contrived to hit his head on the board and fall into the water as he attempted a reverse two-and-a-half-somersault pike in the preliminary rounds. Despite the head injury, he managed to carry on and finish his performance before being taken to hospital to have stitches put in the wound. He came back the next day, repeated the same dive, and came away with a gold medal in the finals.

Louganis announced his retirement in 1989, and he can look back at his career with pride after winning 47 National Championship titles and being a six-time World Champion. He faced an even bigger battle away from the sport after revealing in 1995 that he had tested positive for HIV, which he continues to fight.

'I don't want to be remembered as the greatest diver who ever lived. I want to be able to see the greatest diver. I hope I live to see the day when my records are broken.'

EDOARDO
MANGIAROTTI
FENCING

ITALY

The most decorated fencer in the history of the sport, Edoardo Mangiarotti won a record 13 Olympic medals in his 24-year Olympic Games career. Between 1936 and 1960, the Italian collected six gold, five silver and two bronze medals in the Team and Individual Epée and Foil. He was taught by his father, Giuseppe, who also schooled his brother Dario to become an Olympic gold medallist.

It was a bold decision by Giuseppe Mangiarotti when he decided to train his right-handed son to fence using his weaker left hand, believing it would give him a competitive advantage. The famous fencing master from Milan was carefully plotting the fledgling career of a young man who would eventually become the finest exponent of the sport in its history.

Swimming, cycling and running while he was growing up helped Mangiarotti develop strength and endurance – key conditioning for an Olympian who went on to compete at the highest level until the age of 41. His left-handed stance made him an awkward and unpredictable opponent, helping him to a string of impressive victories as a teenager. He competed in the 1935 World Championships a year before he was called up to the Italy Olympic team at the age of just 17.

Mangiarotti made quite an impact at the Berlin 1936 Games, becoming the youngest gold medallist in any sport as part of the triumphant Italian Epée team. World War II meant that there were no Games in either 1940 or 1944, and Mangiarotti was drafted into the army as an attack instructor, making use of his combat skills. He returned to Olympic competition at the London 1948 Games, where he won bronze in the Individual Epée and silver in the Team Epée and Team Foil. In the latter event, Mangiarotti was denied a second gold when the jury declared France to have won.

Helsinki 1952 was Mangiarotti's crowning glory, as he walked away with two gold and two silver medals. It was also here that he defeated his brother Dario in the final Individual Epée bout, taking sibling rivalry to the extreme as they thrust blades at one another. Edoardo

Statistics

Born: 7 April 1919, Renate, Italy
Height: 5ft 3in (1.6m)
Weight: 110lb (50kg)

Olympic Games Medals

Berlin 1936
Men's Team Epée.................................Gold

London 1948
Men's Team Foil...............................Silver
Men's Team Epée...............................Silver
Men's Individual Epée.................Bronze

Helsinki 1952
Men's Individual Epée......................Gold
Men's Team Epée...............................Gold
Men's Individual Foil......................Silver
Men's Team Foil................................Silver

Melbourne 1956
Men's Team Foil...............................Gold
Men's Team Epée...............................Gold
Men's Individual Epée.................Bronze

Rome 1960
Men's Team Epée...............................Gold
Men's Team Foil...............................Silver

Left: The Italian fencer won solo gold and as a team member in the Epée events in Helsinki 1952.

Right: Mangiarotti on the attack at Helsinki 1952, one of five Games he won medals at in a remarkable 24-year Olympic career.

became a master of picking up early points and building an insurmountable lead, earning golds in the Individual and Team Epées, his strongest discipline. The same strategy helped him to three more medals at the Melbourne 1956 Games.

Fittingly, his home Olympic Games in Rome 1960 were his last. Now 41 and the oldest member of the Italian team, Mangiarotti collected two more medals: gold in the Team Epée and bronze in the Individual Epée. It brought the curtain down on five Olympic Games over 24 years, including 13 medals, a tally that should have been greater, had two Games not been cancelled because of World War II. He also won 27 World Championship medals, 13 of them gold, in the nine competitions in which he took part.

Mangiarotti remains one of the most successful Olympians of all time, and the only fencer to have represented his country as standard bearer at the opening ceremony of an Olympic Games. Those achievements, not to mention his glittering Olympic career, were recognised by the IOC in 2003 when he was awarded the prestigious Olympic Order.

*'I was always called the child prodigy ... what was
my secret? Addressing every moment of life with the
complete desire to win.'*

ALAIN **MIMOUN**
ATHLETICS

FRANCE

Despite being born in Algeria, it was in France that Alain Mimoun became a hero. His Olympic escapades, resulting in three silver medals and one gold, earned him a place in the hearts of Olympic Games fans worldwide. His long rivalry with Emil Zátopek is well documented, and despite often finishing behind the Czech, Mimoun crowned his career by beating his great rival, in the Marathon at the Melbourne 1956 Games.

O n a blistering hot summer's day in Melbourne, at the 1956 Games, Alain Mimoun made himself a national hero. At 35, an age most runners have either hung up their boots or are striving to simply complete the race, Mimoun was awarded an Olympic medal, a gold medal.

Apparently destined to see out his career as a silver medallist, never a champion, his failure in the 10,000m seemed to seal his fate. The French press wrote him off after he came 12th, but Mimoun was determined to show he was not finished, begging the French Olympic bosses to let him run the Marathon. They initially declined as he had never run the distance before, but his determination paid off. He not only won the political battle but the race too, beating his great rival Emil Zátopek.

No wonder now that there are more than 30 gymnasiums and a stadium named after one of France's favourite sons. Mimoun began his Olympic career at London 1948, competing in the 5,000m and 10,000m. It was in the latter event that he won his first Olympic honour, picking up the silver medal. He lost out narrowly to Zátopek, and the Czech athlete would prove to be a thorn in the side of Mimoun's Olympic career. Despite their intense rivalry, the two running legends were great friends off the track.

Four years after London, Mimoun competed in his second Olympic Games in Helsinki 1952. Again he set himself the arduous task of competing in the same gruelling long-distance events, but this time had more success. He finished both finals with silver medals, taking his tally of Olympic gongs to three, although he was still chasing gold. As had been widely predicted, Mimoun finished second behind Zátopek in both races, and despite their great friendship, he was desperate to get one over on his foe.

The Frenchman's time finally came at the Melbourne 1956 Games. Both athletes were now considered to be veterans and neither was tipped to leave the Games with medals of any colour.

Mimoun defied the odds, however, and despite being at the tail end of his career he was victorious, finally beating his Czech nemesis, who finished sixth. His great success came in a Marathon raced in temperatures soaring to 40°C (over 104°F). His victory dealt a huge blow to Zátopek's pride, yet, as the Frenchman waited by the finish line for his great adversary to complete the race, the exhausted Czech fell into the arms of his waiting rival in a moment of genuine warmth. Mimoun later said the clinch meant more to him than the medal.

Following his long-awaited gold medal, the Algerian-born French runner defended his title at the Rome 1960 Games, but, at the age of 39, finished in 34th place. That he even attempted to retain his crown showed the competitive nature of one of the great characters in the history of the Olympic Games.

It marked the end of a remarkable journey for an athlete who was fortunate to be running at any level. Mimoun was enlisted in the French army at the age of 18, and very nearly had his foot blown off.

Fortunately for him and Olympic Games fans around the world, he survived the wounds and went on to become one of the greatest Olympians of all time. That said, it was in the army that he first discovered a talent for long-distance running, a hobby he was continuing for an hour every day even into his late eighties, according to reports in France.

Statistics
Born: 1 January 1921, Sidi Bel Abbes, Algeria
Height: 5ft 7in (1.7m)
Weight: 123lb (56kg)

Olympic Games Medals
London 1948
Men's 10,000m.....................................Silver

Helsinki 1952
Men's 5,000m...Silver
Men's 10,000m....................................Silver

Melbourne 1956
Men's Marathon...................................Gold

Above: Mimoun receives a hero's welcome on returning from his gold-medal-winning run in the Melbourne 1956 Olympic Games.

Right: Mimoun shows the strain on his way to winning silver behind arch-rival Czech runner Emil Zátopek in the 5,000m race in Helsinki 1952.

'They said I was Zátopek's shadow – now I was the sun.'

Alain Mimoun recalls his victory over arch-rival Emil Zátopek

111

EDWIN 'ED' **MOSES**
ATHLETICS

USA

Ed Moses is an American athlete who dominated the 400m Hurdles at the Olympic Games, winning gold medals at both Monteal 1976 and Los Angeles 1984. Remarkably, he went nine years, nine months and nine days undefeated, and managed to break the world record four times.

Ed Moses is regarded as one of the greatest ever track athletes. Over the course of his career he clocked up 26,000 miles (41,600km) and won 122 consecutive races. Aside from his natural grace and speed, he gained an advantage over his rivals by taking an unprecedented 13 steps between hurdles, instead of the normal 14.

Moses was born in Ohio in 1955 and was the second of three sons. As both his parents were involved in education, he took his schoolwork more seriously than most youngsters. But he also took a big interest in sporting activities and, after being turned down by the American Football and Basketball teams, focused his attentions on athletics and gymnastics. He turned down an athletics scholarship in favour of an academic scholarship to Morehouse College in Atlanta. Although the college did not have a running track, it still had a track team so Moses spent most of his spare time using the various public high-school facilities around the city to train.

Ironically, Moses only ran one 400m Hurdles race before March 1976, his first Olympic Games-winning year, and spent most of his time competing in the 110m Hurdles and 400m. But it was that one 400m Hurdles race that transformed his career. With a gigantic 9ft 9in (3m) running stride, he was unbeatable in the Olympic trials and stole the show with an American record of 48.30 seconds, sending him to his first Olympic Games in Montreal 1976.

Few would have guessed his lack of experience at a major international tournament, as he took the world by storm with one of the most impressive performances from a track athlete at the Olympics. The American not only secured his first gold medal, but he also set a new world record of 47.64 seconds. His success was to continue just a year later when he broke his own world record at the Pepsi Invitational, with a performance of 47.45.

Despite losing to German athlete Harald Schmidt in August 1977, this was to be his last defeat for nearly a decade as he went on an amazing unbeaten run of 122 straight victories. This winning streak has never been beaten, and stands in the *Guinness*

World Records. He would almost certainly have won a second consecutive gold medal had the USA not boycotted the Moscow 1980 Olympic Games. Instead he managed to break his own world record again in Milan, when he came away with a memorable time of 47.13 seconds.

Moses was determined to smash the record once more. In a birthday celebration to remember he registered a new mark of 47.02 in West Germany, when he turned 29. That time remained unbeaten until 1992. After winning a gold medal at the World Championships in Helsinki, Moses went into the Los Angeles 1984 Games brimming with confidence and received one of the biggest accolades of his career when he was asked to recite the Olympic Oath during the opening ceremony. It was a Games to savour as he won his second consecutive gold medal in the 400m Hurdles, on home soil.

Moses's amazing unbeaten run finally came to an end in 1987 when he was beaten by fellow American Danny Harris in Madrid, but he bounced back to

win another World Championships in Rome later that year. His last appearance at the Olympics came in 1988 and although he ran his fastest ever final, he had to settle for bronze after losing to American Andre Phillips. On retirement he became a global ambassador of the sport and was elected chairman of the Laureus World Sports Academy in 2000.

USA

Statistics
Born: 31 August 1955, Dayton, Ohio, USA
Height: 6ft 1in (1.85m)
Weight: 159lb (72kg)

Olympic Games Medals
Montreal 1976
Men's 400m Hurdles............................Gold

Los Angeles 1984
Men's 400m Hurdles............................Gold

Seoul 1988
Men's 400m Hurdles.....................Bronze

'Hopefully I will be remembered as the guy nobody could beat.'

Above: Moses dominated the 400m Hurdles like no other runner after winning gold at the Montreal 1976 Games with a world-record time.

Right: Moses leaps another hurdle at the Seoul 1988 Games, the only Olympic Games at which the American did not win a gold medal.

ALEXEI **NEMOV**
GYMNASTICS – ARTISTIC

Alexei Nemov has the medals to prove that he was an Olympic hero, but he was also the people's champion. Twelve medals over the Olympic Games of Atlanta 1996 and Sydney 2000 are a fitting tribute to the Russian gymnast, but his reputation was sealed when he quelled the crowd in Athens 2004 after they protested against the judges awarding him a low score in the Horizontal Bars.

It is rare that a four-time Olympic champion is remembered as much for an act away from the field of competition as they are for their performances on it, but Alexei Nemov's legacy was truly secured by his actions at the Athens 2004 Olympic Games. The Russian had already written his name in the record books with outstanding displays in both Atlanta 1996 and Sydney 2000, when in each Olympic Games he had won two gold, a silver and three bronze medals.

It was clear, though, that his best days were behind him by 2004, and he was not expected to challenge for the podium. Much the same had been said four years previously, however, and Nemov set about proving his critics wrong once again.

And, on the Horizontal Bars, he produced a fine display, complete with six release moves, including four in a row. Yet the judges' score of 9.725 put him last of the three competitors who had performed up to that point, and the crowd reacted furiously, booing the decision. The score was revised upwards slightly, but the uncharacteristic heckling continued for 15 minutes. The next competitor, American Paul Hamm, was unable to start his routine, and the crowd threatened to halt the Olympic Games. They only stopped when Nemov

took to the stage and pleaded with the fans for silence out of respect for the other gymnasts. Only then did they relent, and even though Nemov finished fifth, he was in many ways the true champion in Athens 2004.

Yet the Russian had never previously had much trouble when it came to picking up medals as a tangible reward for his exploits. Having started gymnastics at the age of five, he first competed in the World Championships as a 16-year-old, and was one of the leading world stars by the time of the Atlanta 1996 Games. By the end of that competition, his promise had been fulfilled. He claimed gold in the Vault and came close to winning the Individual All-Around Competition, only to stumble during a tumbling run, coming second to Li Xiaoshuang of China. His disappointment would certainly have been eased, though, by his performances in the other events, specifically in the Team Competition, which Russia won. He also claimed bronze medals in the Floor Competition, Horizontal Bars and Pommel Horse, to complete a superb Games.

But his star waned as he battled injury and struggled in the All-Around Competition. Yet the sign of a top-class athlete is the ability to save their best performances for when it matters, and that was the case with Nemov: he unleashed the best gymnastics of his career in the Sydney 2000 Games. A stunning performance in the Individual All-Around Competition saw him claim gold, and he was also on the top step of the podium after destroying the field in the Horizontal Bars. Another silver came his way in the Floor Competition, and again he claimed three bronze medals, this time in the Pommel Horse, Parallel Bars and Team Competition.

He was well liked and hugely respected for his achievements, but was denied what would have been a final medal in Athens 2004. Instead, he became one of the heroes of the Games, and a man who truly embodied the Olympic ideals.

Statistics

Born: 28 May 1976, Barashevo, Russia
Height: 5ft 9in (1.75m)
Weight: 165lb (75kg)

Olympic Games Medals

Atlanta 1996

Men's Vault Competition	Gold
Men's Team Competition	Gold
Men's Individual All-Around Competition	Silver
Men's Floor Competition	Bronze
Men's Horizontal Bars Competition	Bronze
Men's Pommel Horse Competition	Bronze

Sydney 2000

Men's Individual All-Around Competition	Gold
Men's Horizontal Bars Competition	Gold
Men's Floor Competition Competition	Silver
Men's Parallel Bars Competition	Bronze
Men's Pommel Horse Competition	Bronze
Men's Team Competition	Bronze

Left: Nemov had already won four gold medals from two Games by the time he competed at his final Olympic Games, in Athens 2004.

Right: Nemov shows off the combination of strength, skill and bravery on the Horizontal Bars that helped him to two Olympic medals in the event.

'It was a class act by Alexei. What he did was in the true Olympic spirit.'

USA Gymnastics President Bob Colarossi, after Alexei Nemov calmed crowd protests at Athens 2004

ISABEL **NEWSTEAD**

PARALYMPIC SWIMMING/ATHLETICS/SHOOTING

Isabel Newstead MBE was one of Britain's greatest ever Paralympians, with her record of 10 gold medals over five separate Paralympic Games nothing short of astonishing. Winning golds in Shooting, Swimming and Athletics, she was a shining star in the British Paralympic team until her death in 2007, aged just 51.

Isabel Newstead's success in the Paralympic Games was an inspirational example of triumph in the face of adversity. Newstead – who competed under her maiden name of Barr until 2000 – contracted a virus in her late teens that damaged her spinal cord, but she saw that as no obstacle to outstanding sporting achievement. And that fighting spirit was shown in the way she battled cancer until her premature death in 2007.

Newstead won a total of 10 gold medals and competed in five Paralympic Games, achieving success in a wide range of sports, from Swimming and Athletics to Shooting. She was

forced to give up Swimming in 1988 due to health issues, by which point she had already won six gold medals in the sport. But she continued with her other sports, and won a gold in the Discus Throw and two further Shooting golds in what was an illustrious career.

Yet it was Swimming that dominated Newstead's early sporting life, and certainly her first Paralympic Games in Arnhem 1980. There the Glasgow-born star entered three separate events, and left with three gold medals to her name. Victory in the 25m Backstroke, Breaststroke and Freestyle 1C categories saw Newstead complete a perfect Paralympic debut and announce herself as a force to be reckoned with. That impression was confirmed four years later in the New York/Stoke Mandeville Games. Having retained her 25m Breaststroke – although it was now in the 1B category – she also claimed gold in the Butterfly 1B and 3 x 25m Individual Medley 1B. A silver and two bronze medals were also secured in the pool as Newstead cemented her reputation in what was to be her last Paralympic Games as a swimmer.

Yet she showed that her time in the higher echelons of the sporting elite was far from over by winning her first gold medal in Shooting, standing on the top of the podium after the Women's Air Pistol 1A-1C. And her potential as an athlete was demonstrated when she won silver medals in both the Discus and Shot Put 1B, to complete an outstanding Games.

That promise was fulfilled in stunning fashion in the Seoul 1988 Paralympic Games, when Newstead was at her very best as she smashed the world record to win the Discus with a distance of 10.48m. A silver in the Shot Put and bronze medals in the Javelin and Air Pistol 2-6 were again testament to an outstanding and versatile talent.

Statistics

Born: 3 May 1955, Glasgow, Scotland
Died: 18 January 2007

Paralympic Games Medals

Arnhem 1980
Women's 25m Backstroke 1C...........Gold
Women's 25m Breaststroke 1C.......Gold
Women's 25m Freestyle 1C................Gold

New York/Stoke Mandeville 1984
Women's 25m Breaststroke 1B.......Gold
Women's 25m Butterfly 1B ....Gold
Women's 3 x 25m Individual
    Medley 1B................................Gold
Women's Air Pistol 1A-1C...................Gold
Women's Shot Put 1B........................ Silver
Women's Discus Throw 1B............. Silver
Women's 100m Freestyle 1B .... Silver
Women's 25m Freestyle 1B .... Bronze
Women's 25m Backstroke 1B .... Bronze

Seoul 1988
Women's Discus Throw 1B...............Gold
Women's Shot Put 1B........................ Silver
Women's Javelin Throw 1B.......... Bronze
Women's Air Pistol 2-6................... Bronze

Sydney 2000
Women's Air Pistol SH1.......................Gold

Athens 2004
Women's Air Pistol SH1.......................Gold

Left: Newstead was an almost unique athlete, winning Paralympic Games gold medals for Swimming, Athletics and Shooting.

Right: Seen here practising for the women's Air Pistol event, Newstead competed at the highest level for more than two decades.

Yet she had to wait until 2000 for her next medal – a gold in the Women's Air Pistol SH1, when both she and Chinese opponent Hai Yan Lin scored a world record total of 376 points, earning them joint top spot on the podium. And her astonishing career was rounded off in superb style when she retained her title four years later, although in Athens 2004 the glory was all hers as Newstead won by four points from Chin Mei Lin.

Indeed, when she died just three years later, she was the reigning Paralympic, World and European Champion, and few would have bet against her adding to her medal haul. The tributes that were paid to her talent and durability were truly heartfelt, and she stands as a shining example of what can be achieved in the world of Paralympic sport.

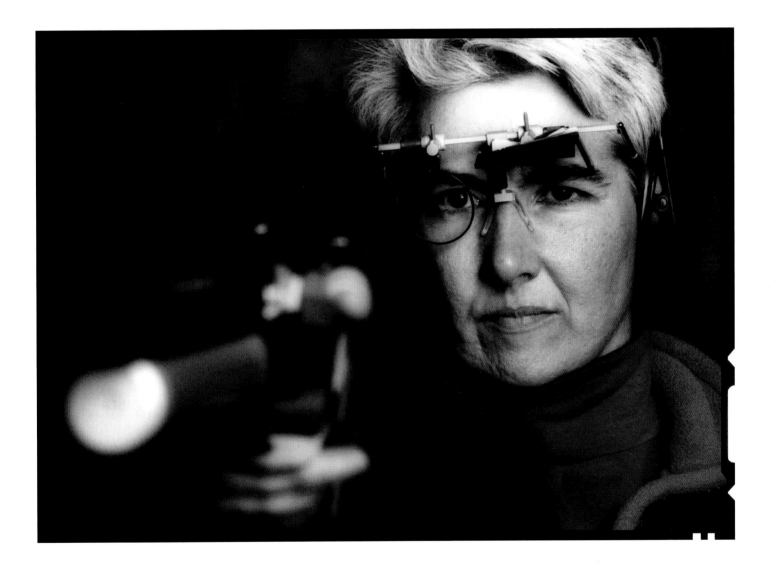

'Through Isabel's determination and effort she demonstrated all the outstanding qualities that we have come to recognise in elite athletes, and for that she will be remembered as one of Britain's great Paralympians.'

British Paralympic Association chief executive, Phil Lane

TADAHIRO **NOMURA**

JUDO

Japanese *judoka* Tadahiro Nomura burst on to the Olympic scene with gold at the Atlanta 1996 Games and went on to dominate Judo at the Olympics. An injury curtailed his career but his infectious enthusiasm for the sport – and his success – set him apart, as well as his record of being the first Olympic *judoka* to have won three consecutive gold medals.

I t is perhaps no wonder Tadahiro Nomura became such a successful *judoka*. His grandfather was a judo instructor in Japan and his father was the coach of Olympic icon Shinji Hosokawa, who won a gold medal in the Men's Extra Lightweight division at the Los Angeles 1984 Games, as well as a bronze in Seoul 1988. At the age of six, Nomura began lessons at his grandfather's martial arts school and it was not long before he was catching attention, winning several local and national competitions during his formative years. He entered Tenri University in 1993 and, having won the All-Japan Judo Championships three years later, gained a place in the Japanese Olympic team for the Atlanta 1996 Games.

Being relatively unknown outside his native Japan before the Olympic Games, Nomura's performances in Atlanta opened the eyes of the watching world, and his first gold medal hinted at the glory that was to follow him through two more Olympiads. After advancing to the final in the Men's Extra Lightweight category, Nomura fought Italian Girolamo Giovinazzo and defeated him by *seoi nage*, a throw developed by Jigoro Kano, the man many claim to be the founding father of the sport.

Gold in Atlanta 1996 marked the start of Nomura's reign as the man to beat, and he swiftly followed up that success with a brilliant performance at the All-Japan Judo Championships in 1997. This reinforced his supremacy in the Extra Lightweight category and, in 1998, he won the competition for the third consecutive year. It seemed nothing could stop him – except injury. And that is exactly what happened when he damaged his left knee in the Jigoro Kano Cup semi-finals in January 1999. His progress curtailed, Nomura was forced to retire from the competition and did not compete for the rest of the year. He concentrated on recovering from injury and on completing his degree in health education.

Nomura returned to judo in 2000 and won the All-Japan Judo Championships. That title also booked him a second trip to the Olympic Games.

Sydney was the destination in 2000 and, incredibly, Nomura won his gold-medal match against Jung Bu-Kyung by *sumo otoshi* – again developed by Jigoro Kano – after just 14 seconds. Nomura was the first 60kg *judoka* to win consecutive gold medals in that class. His third gold at Athens 2004 marked him as an all-time great. After beating Georgia's Nestor Khergiani, Nomura became the only Olympic *judoka* to have won three consecutive golds, and the first Olympic competitor from Asia to take three consecutive golds in any sport.

Nomura won the All-Japan Judo Championships for a sixth time in 2007 but, unfortunately for him, failed to clinch a place in the Japan squad for the Beijing 2008 Games, as he lost out to Daisuke Asano in the semi-finals of the Extra Lightweight category in an event that marked his final chance to reach a fourth successive Games.

Despite the setback, and a subsequent knee injury that seemingly brought an end to his career,

Nomura was always destined to go down in Olympic history as the yardstick by which all budding *judokas* should measure themselves.

But the story does not end there: after knee surgery in 2009, he announced a sensational comeback plan the following year with a view to taking on the world again at London 2012.

Statistics

Born: 10 December 1974, Nara, Japan
Height: 5ft 5in (1.65m)
Weight: 132lb (60kg)

Olympic Games Medals

Atlanta 1996
Men's Extra Lightweight.....................Gold

Sydney 2000
Men's Extra Lightweight.....................Gold

Athens 2004
Men's Extra Lightweight.....................Gold

Above: Nomura developed a taste for gold by winning three consecutive Olympic Games medals of that colour in the Men's Extra Lightweight class.

Right: Georgia's Nestor Khergiani is emphatically thrown to the mat during the gold-medal fight at the Athens 2004 Olympic Games.

*'My fellow 60kg competitors can wait and be
frightened, thinking, "Nomura might come back."'*

PAAVO **NURMI**
ATHLETICS

Known as 'The King of Runners', Paavo Nurmi was the best middle- and long-distance athlete of his generation, winning nine gold and three silver medals from the 12 events he competed in at three Olympic Games, between 1920 and 1928. His record 12 Olympic medals makes him one of the greatest track and field athletes ever.

Statistics

Born: 13 June 1897, Turku, Finland
Died: 2 October 1973
Height: 5ft 9in (1.75m)
Weight: 143lb (65kg)

Olympic Games Medals

Antwerp 1920

Men's 10,000m	Gold
Men's Individual Cross-Country	Gold
Men's Team Cross-Country	Gold
Men's 5,000m	Silver

Paris 1924

Men's 1,500m	Gold
Men's Team 3,000m	Gold
Men's 5,000m	Gold
Men's Individual Cross-Country	Gold
Men's Team Cross-Country	Gold

Amsterdam 1928

Men's 10,000m	Gold
Men's 5,000m	Silver
Men's 3,000m Steeplechase	Silver

It was the moment Paavo Nurmi decided he would become an Olympic champion. Aged 15, he watched his hero Hannes Kolehmainen, the original 'Flying Finn', win three gold medals in long-distance running events at the Stockholm Olympic Games in 1912. He soon owned his first pair of running shoes, and set about his pursuit of Olympic glory with a rigorous training schedule and complete dedication. As much as his natural athleticism, it was Nurmi's burning desire that turned him into a national icon in newly independent Finland.

A quiet and highly focused individual, he was driven by a craving for recognition of his success from his peers. And he commanded that attention by winning three golds and a silver at the Antwerp 1920 Games, five golds four years later in Paris 1924, and one gold and two silvers at the Amsterdam 1928 Games.

At his first Olympic Games, in Antwerp 1920, Nurmi announced himself to the world as he stormed to his three golds and one silver from four events. After a second-place finish in the 5,000m, he won the 10,000m before adding further golds in the Individual and Team Cross-Country events. His most successful Olympic Games, however, came in Paris 1924, bolstering his legacy with an incredible five gold medals in six days, highlighting his remarkable stamina and powers of recovery. Amazingly, he triumphed in the 5,000m final less than two hours after success in the 1,500m, which was to be possibly the most astonishing achievement of his glittering career.

By this time, Nurmi was smashing world records on a regular basis too, establishing himself as the master at distances ranging between 1,500m and 20km. His third individual gold in Paris 1924 came over 8,000m in the Individual Cross-Country, and he also went on to win Team golds in the Cross-Country and 3,000m. Such was his ambition that he was outraged when Finnish officials refused to let him defend his 10,000m title because of fears over his health. A furious Nurmi responded in typical fashion, returning to Finland and setting a world record for the distance that would last for the next 13 years.

Cross-Country events were discontinued after the 1924 Games and Nurmi's Olympic career ended after the Amsterdam 1928 Games, where he won gold in the 10,000m and silver in the 5,000m and 3,000m Steeplechase. He was desperate to win the Marathon at the Los Angeles

Left: Nurmi poses for a rare picture between events at the Paris 1924 Olympic Games, where he won a remarkable five gold medals.

Right: Nurmi at the back of the field behind Edvin Wide (746) of Sweden and Viho Ritola (329) of Finland during the Individual Cross-Country at Paris 1924.

1932 Olympic Games, and even travelled there to compete, but was banned on the grounds that he was a professional, because he'd been paid travel expenses for a meet in Germany earlier in the year. He had set his heart on finishing his career with a Marathon win, just as Kolehmainen had done in 1920, but nevertheless Nurmi had established himself as a more than worthy successor to his idol.

A statue of Nurmi stands outside the Finnish Olympic Stadium in Helsinki, while his status as a national hero was recognised when he was featured on Bank of Finland 10-mark notes in 1987, the first Olympian from any country to be honoured in such a fashion. After his death in 1973, Nurmi was fittingly accorded a state funeral, giving a whole nation the opportunity to say goodbye to their Flying Finn.

'All that I am, I am because of my mind.'

AL OERTER
ATHLETICS

USA

In the often unreported world of discus-throwing, Al Oerter established himself as a national hero and a giant among Olympians, becoming the first track-and-field athlete to win gold medals at the same event in four successive Olympic Games.

Born in New York, Al Oerter discovered a natural talent for throwing the discus at the age of 15, and won a scholarship to the University of Kansas. His first Olympic success came at the Melbourne 1956 Games when he had just turned 20. Oerter was not expected to win but his opening throw of 56.36m was huge and unassailable – a new Olympic record, a personal best and enough to claim gold by a margin of almost two metres.

The following year he was lucky to survive a serious car accident, and was able to resume his career and travel to the Rome 1960 Games as reigning Olympic champion. His friend and team-mate Rink Babka was expected to win, however, and was leading the field when Oerter asked for some advice on his technique. Babka graciously suggested a slight change in his throwing action, and Oerter then launched another huge throw, 59.18m, breaking his own Olympic record by three metres and claiming gold again.

Yet it was in Tokyo 1964 that he really caught the public's imagination as a sporting hero. Going for an unprecedented hat-trick, he tore the cartilage in his ribcage just days before the event, and was told to pull out of the competition and rest for six weeks.

But Oerter had other ideas. With a combination of pain-killing injections and heavy strapping keeping his body together, the American threw a massive 61m with his fifth and final throw – another Olympic record, another gold medal.

The indestructible American's final victory, and record-breaking fourth straight gold, came at the Mexico City 1968 Games, when again he overcame the odds. Considered too old by most observers, and well behind his rivals in terms of distance, he ignored a heavy rainstorm to continue his warm-up before propelling the discus a distance of 64.78m, shattering the field and setting yet another Olympic record. It also made him the first man to win the same event in four successive Games.

He decided to retire after the Mexico City 1968 Games to concentrate on his career in the fledgling computer industry, and on raising his young family. After all, he had set four Olympic and four world records in 12 years, and won four

Statistics

Born: 19 September 1936, New York City, USA
Died: 1 October 2007
Height: 6ft 4in (1.93m)
Weight: 280lb (127kg)

Olympic Games Medals

Melbourne 1956
Men's Discus Throw..............................Gold

Rome 1960
Men's Discus Throw..............................Gold

Tokyo 1964
Men's Discus Throw..............................Gold

Mexico City 1968
Men's Discus Throw..............................Gold

Left: A proud smile from the only athlete to win the same Olympic event four times in a row, while setting an Olympic record on each occasion.

Right: Oerter prepares to throw the discus on his Olympic debut at the Melbourne 1956 Games, en route to winning his first Olympic gold medal.

Olympic gold medals – what else was there to achieve in the sport?

But in 1976, aged 40, he took up training again, realising he could still compete with the best. Over the next seven years he recorded the best throws of his career, and in May 1980, shortly before the Moscow 1980 Olympic Games, threw a personal best of 69.46m. He never got the chance to go for a fifth gold, however, as he came fourth in the US Olympic trials, and his country also decided to boycott the 1980 Games. He could still throw huge distances well into his forties, once launching the discus almost 75m on a TV show, which, had it been in official competition, would have been a world record for years to come.

Oerter retained his interest and involvement in the Games by carrying the Olympic Flag for the USA team at the Los Angeles 1984 Games. He also conveyed the Olympic Flame for the 1996 Atlanta Games. Having retired to a successful life as a motivational speaker and fine artist, he died in 2007 of heart failure, at the age of 71.

Remarkably, he could have achieved even more Olympic glory had he continued to compete after his fourth gold medal, yet still there rested an Olympian whose feats very few, if any, will ever come close to matching.

'I don't compete with other discus throwers.
I compete with my own history.'

ELISABETA
OLENIUC-LIPA
ROWING

Elisabeta Oleniuc-Lipă is the embodiment of staying power. She won medals in six different Olympiads and is the only rower ever to win Olympic gold medals 20 years apart. Her unwavering desire explains her eight Olympic medals – a feat that not even legendary oarsman Sir Steve Redgrave could match.

Born in Siret, Romania, Elisabeta Oleniuc-Lipă possessed brains as well as brawn: she combined her rowing with working for the Romanian equivalent of the CIA, and her hard work and determination set her apart when it came to competing on the water. She began rowing at the tender age of 16, in 1980, and just two years later had begun her quest for stardom by winning a bronze medal in the Quadruple Sculls (4x) event with the Romanian team in the World Championships in Switzerland. The following year, she finished third in the Double Sculls (2x) as she prepared for the Los Angeles 1984 Olympic Games.

At 19, Oleniuc-Lipă was paired with Marioara Popescu in the Double Sculls (2x) event at Los Angeles 1984 and the duo stormed to success, with Oleniuc-Lipă claiming the first of her record medal haul. As the crowds saluted the victorious Romanian team down on the banks of Lake Casitas, there was an air of expectancy in the celebrations. In her next Olympic Games, at Seoul 1988, Oleniuc-Lipă justified the hype surrounding her and claimed more medals: silver in the Double Sculls (2x) and bronze in the Quadruple Sculls (4x). But despite her growing collection of medals, she was disappointed. The Seoul 1988 Games would prove to be the only time she failed to win an Olympic gold medal and, for someone with such lofty standards, the regret at not standing highest on the winners' podium was a situation that needed to be rectified. Oleniuc-Lipă need not have worried, however, as she would rediscover her top form in Barcelona 1992, four years later.

But before the golden girl's return to winning ways in Olympic competition, she was once again at the top of the list of competitors to beat in the World Championships. A year after her showing in Seoul, Oleniuc-Lipă won gold in the Single Sculls in Yugoslavia. While her Olympic record needs no introduction, her performances in the World Championships should not be overlooked either. She won no fewer than 12 World Championships medals, including nine silver gongs.

Statistics
Born: 26 October 1964, Siret, Romania
Height: 6ft (1.83m)
Weight: 176lb (80kg)

Olympic Games Medals
Los Angeles 1984
Women's Double Sculls (2x) ....Gold

Seoul 1988
Women's Double Sculls (2x)........... Silver
Women's Quadruple Sculls (4x) .. Bronze

Barcelona 1992
Women's Single Sculls (1x) ....Gold
Women's Double Sculls (2x) .... Silver

Atlanta 1996
Women's Eights (8+) ....Gold

Sydney 2000
Women's Eights (8+) ....Gold

Athens 2004
Women's Eights (8+) ....Gold

Left: Oleniuc-Lipă shows that gold-medal success is still to be keenly celebrated, even after winning medals in six different Oympic Games.

Right: The Romanian added a fifth and final gold medal to her collection as part of the winning Women's Eights (8+) – Coxed Eight – at the Athens 2004 Games.

The Barcelona 1992 Olympic Games established Oleniuc-Lipă as one of the leading rowers of her generation. Just one day after coming second in the Double Sculls (2x) event, she led the Single Sculls from start to finish to earn her second career gold medal – the 'CIA' agent had returned to her best. But she was not finished yet. At Atlanta 1996, she won another gold medal as a member of the Romanian Women's Eights (8+) team. With this race, she became the first rower in Olympic Games history to win six medals. Further golds were added with the Eights (8+) at Sydney 2000 and Athens 2004 – 20 years after her first gold medal.

Having competed at the highest level in three different decades, in a span that included six Olympic Games and yielded eight medals – five of them gold – Oleniuc-Lipă retired after the Athens 2004 Games, safe in the knowledge that it would take a Herculean effort to surpass her achievements.

'I am very happy because I won five gold medals in six different Olympic Games. I dedicate the medals to me.'

MERLENE **OTTEY**
ATHLETICS

While winning nine Olympic medals is amazing, the fact that Merlene Ottey's haul came between Moscow 1980 and Sydney 2000 (she also competed in Athens 2004) is a testament to her longevity as an athlete. Primarily a 200m runner, the Jamaican-born star – who later represented her new country of residence, Slovenia – holds the record for most successive appearances in the Olympic Games. That alone makes her one of the all-time greats.

Born in Hanover, Jamaica, in 1960, Merlene Ottey caught the athletics bug after her mother, Joan, bought her a book about the sport. Running barefoot through dirt tracks in rural Jamaica gave Ottey a sense of belonging and, from there, she was destined to turn her passion into her life. Having been amazed by the exploits of fellow Jamaican Don Quarrie at the Montreal 1976 Olympic Games, Ottey wanted desperately to join the ranks of her country's elite Olympians. The first step to realising her dream was achieved when she moved to America and attended the University of Nebraska.

She claimed the first of many non-Olympic medals – Ottey holds a record 14 World Championships medals – after taking bronze in the Pan American Games in 1979, a year before her Olympic Games debut. At the Moscow 1980 Games she won bronze, the first of her nine Olympic medals, finishing behind Natalya Bochina and the Olympic record-setting Barbel Eckert Wockel in the Women's 200m inside the Lenin Stadium. Ottey took bronze again in the 200m four years later at Los Angeles 1984, with Valerie Brisco-Hooks' Olympic record mark of 21.81 seconds required to beat the opposition this time. Ottey, who won gold in the event at the 1982 Commonwealth Games, also finished with bronze in the 100m in Los Angeles.

The Seoul 1988 Games were largely disappointing for Ottey as she failed to claim a medal, but her prowess in athletics remained undoubted, as her gold in the 200m at the World Championships in Budapest testified. Ottey went into the Barcelona 1992 Games in fine form, having won gold in the 200m at the Commonwealth Games and World Indoor Championships. But she did not quite have the Midas touch in Barcelona and had to settle for bronze again. At 32, Ottey had already been racing in the Olympics for 12 years, but her determination to compete at the top of her game seemed to strengthen with every medal she won.

Statistics

Born: 10 May 1960, Hanover, Jamaica
Height: 5ft 9in (1.75m)
Weight: 137lb (62kg)

Olympic Games Medals

Moscow 1980
Women's 200m .... Bronze

Los Angeles 1984
Women's 100m .... Bronze
Women's 200m .... Bronze

Barcelona 1992
Women's 200m .... Bronze

Atlanta 1996
Women's 100m .... Silver
Women's 200m .... Silver
Women's 4 × 100m Relay .... Bronze

Sydney 2000
Women's 100m .... Bronze
Women's 4 × 100m Relay .... Silver

Left: Always the competitor, Ottey posted a season best of 11.77 seconds in 2010 to become the proud holder of the over-50s 100m world record.

Right: Ottey (middle) came agonisingly close in the 100m final at the Atlanta 1996 Olympic Games, finishing just five-thousandths of a second off a gold medal.

Agonisingly for Ottey, her greatest chance of Olympic gold came four years later at Atlanta 1996, in the 100m final. She finished with silver, just five-thousandths of a second behind Gail Devers, after they both ran 10.94. Yet the Atlanta 1996 Games were her most successful: another silver, in the 200m, and bronze in the 4 x 100m Relay meant three medals in total.

Now for the crowning glory: at the Sydney 2000 Games, at the age of 40 and seasoned by six successive Olympiads, Ottey won a silver medal in the Women's 4 x 100m Relay. This was her ninth Olympic medal, more than any other female track-and-field athlete. That success by the evergreen Ottey had followed a bronze medal in the 100m.

After moving to Slovenia in 1998, she became a citizen of that country four years later. At the Athens 2004 Games she competed for Slovenia, her record seventh Olympiad. At 44, her legs couldn't quite carry her to more glory, but her presence in Athens 2004 underlined her dedication and, as reflected by the title of her authorised biography, she remained an *Unyielding Spirit*.

'I was the one always there, always trying and always doing my best – I would never quit.'

JAMES 'JESSE' OWENS USA
ATHLETICS

Jesse Owens was one of the greatest athletes of all time – and the man who destroyed Adolf Hitler's dream of using the Berlin 1936 Olympic Games as a showcase for the 'superiority of the Aryan race'. Owens won four gold medals, having set three world records in the space of a mere 45-minute spell a year earlier.

A great Olympic Games myth states that Jesse Owens was snubbed by Adolf Hitler after his success at the Berlin 1936 Games because he was black. The fact is that the dictator shook hands only with German winners on the opening day, and thereafter with no one at all. Owens himself felt that the biggest snub he received was from US President Franklin D. Roosevelt, who did not congratulate him or send a telegram, despite his phenomenal success on the Olympic track.

James Cleveland Owens was born in 1913 in Oakville, Alabama, but moved to Cleveland, Ohio, when he was nine, and it was there that a schoolmistress misheard his initials J.C. as 'Jesse' – and the name stayed with him. He discovered a talent for sprinting and was encouraged by coach Charles Riley, who allowed him to train before going to school in the mornings. By the time he was 20, he was making a name for himself, setting national college records in sprinting and Long Jump. He earned a place at the Ohio State University, although he had to stay off-campus, with other black students. Even when travelling with the college team, he had to eat and sleep separately from his white team-mates.

He really shot to fame in 1935, at the Big Ten meet in Ann Arbor, Michigan, when he set three world records and equalled a fourth – all in the space of 45 minutes. The feat was all the more remarkable because he had injured his back a week earlier, and was almost unable to compete. He ran the 100yd as a test for his injured back, and equalled the world record of 9.4 seconds, then went on to leap 8.13m, a world Long Jump record that was to stand for 25 years. He followed up with two new world records in the 220yd Sprint and Low Hurdles. It was an astonishing achievement, all in well under an hour, and no athlete has ever come close to matching it.

So when Owens went to the Berlin 1936 Games, he was favourite for his events, and did not disappoint. On three successive days he won the 100m, 200m and Long Jump, and a few days later was part of the successful 4 x 100m Relay team. It was the first time a track-and-field athlete had won four gold medals at an Olympic Games, and set a record that was not to be equalled until Carl Lewis' exploits almost 50 years later. But Owens' career effectively finished in Berlin. He chose to return to the US to discuss commercial offers from Adidas and others rather than join his team-mates for a post-Olympics tour of Sweden, and was stripped of his amateur status by the US administration, which meant he could never compete again. Instead, he was forced to eke out a living with a succession of 'stunt' races against horses and local sprinters, who were given a hefty head start. Owens did a series of mundane jobs and ran into severe financial difficulties.

But he finally received the recognition he deserved after the civil rights movement in the United States overturned many of the barriers that stood in the path of black people in the 1960s. He took on ambassadorial roles for major companies, travelling the world and becoming an accomplished public speaker before passing away at the age of 66, in 1980.

Statistics

Born: 12 September 1913, Oakville, Alabama, USA
Died: 31 March 1980
Height: 5ft 10in (1.78m)
Weight: 156lb (71kg)

Olympic Games Medals
Berlin 1936

Men's 100m	Gold
Men's 200m	Gold
Men's Long Jump	Gold
Men's 4 x 100m Relay	Gold

'Hitler didn't snub me – it was FDR who snubbed me. The President didn't even send me a telegram.'

Jesse Owens on US President Roosevelt after the Berlin 1936 Olympic Games

Above: Owens during the Berlin 1936 Games, where he won gold in all four events in which he competed.

Right: The American at the start of his 200m gold-medal win in Berlin, which he ran in a world-record time of 20.70 seconds.

LEE **PEARSON**
PARALYMPIC EQUESTRIAN

An unparalleled Equestrian king, Lee Pearson, OBE, CBE, has an astonishing nine gold medals in three successive Paralympic Games to his name. His inspirational story serves as a reminder to anyone that they can achieve their dreams if they have the heart.

Having regained consciousness after giving birth to the youngest of her three sons by Caesarean section, Lynda Pearson was wheeled down the hospital corridor, surrounded by a team of 10 doctors, nurses and psychologists.

In a scene more reminiscent of a Dickens novel, they arrived at a nondescript broom cupboard and there, the middle of a pile of mops and buckets, lay Lee Pearson in his crib with a cloth over the top. Born with arthrogryposis multiplex congenita, an extremely rare congenital disorder characterised by multiple joint contractures and severe muscle weakness, Pearson seemed to have been written off before he had even taken his first breaths. Lying there, in that dark and dingy cupboard was an Olympic champion in the waiting. With plastic splints that run from his buttocks to his heels, Pearson has won nine Paralympic Games Equestrian gold medals, five World Championships and three European titles, not to mention a notable victory in an able-bodied national championship event.

By the age of six Pearson had undergone 15 operations and was even carried up the stairs of 10 Downing Street by then Prime Minister Margaret Thatcher to receive a Children of Courage award. Then after being forbidden to play on bikes with his brothers, he decided to follow in his grandmother's footsteps and take up horse riding. Pearson was soon on ponies and displaying a natural technique that would have his competitors trailing in his wake.

He could not take his eyes off the Atlanta 1996 Paralympic Games, and was so inspired by watching riders Joanna Jackson and Anne Cecilie Ore that he was determined to add his name to the list of Equestrian gold medallists.

At his first Paralympic Games, in Sydney 2000, the speed-loving Pearson – who now also rides motorbikes, tractors and sports cars – was largely unknown, but the Games propelled him into the public spotlight. Having won gold in the Mixed Dressage, he went on to claim further golds in the Dressage Mixed Freestyle and Dressage Mixed Team events. Pearson had arrived.

Watching him astride the mighty Blue Circle Boy at Athens 2004 was to witness a true master at work. He controlled the horse with his hips and his fluid movement captivated the crowds and completed the first leg of a perfect hat-trick. If Sydney 2000 had made him a star, the Athens 2004 Paralympic Games four years later would make Pearson a man of the people. He claimed three gold medals in the same events and, following his Dressage Mixed victory, his humility and compassion won the hearts of a nation. Sliding off his horse and grabbing his crutches, Pearson presented his winner's flowers to Valerie Salles, whose mount Arestote had collapsed and died an hour earlier on entering the arena.

In Beijing 2008, Pearson completed his sensational hat-trick of three gold medals in three successive Games, reducing his competitors to mere also-rans. Pearson's inspirational tale is one of triumph over adversity, and of courage and a desire not to let his disability beat him. Competitors looking to London 2012 should be warned – this incomparable athlete may yet complete another astonishing clean sweep in his fourth Paralympic Games.

Statistics

Born: 4 February 1974, Cheddleton, Staffordshire, England

Paralympic Games Medals

Sydney 2000
Dressage Mixed, Grade 1.................Gold
Dressage Mixed Freestyle, Grade 1....Gold
Dressage Mixed Team, Open ....Gold

Athens 2004
Dressage Mixed, Grade 1.................Gold
Dressage Mixed Freestyle, Grade 1....Gold
Dressage Mixed Team, Open ....Gold

Beijing 2008
Dressage Mixed, Grade 1B...............Gold
Dressage Mixed Freestyle,
    Grade 1B....................................Gold
Dressage Mixed Team, Open ....Gold

Below: Pearson smiles after winning the Dressage Mixed Freestlye, Grade 1B at the Beijing 2008 Paralympic Games.

Right: Pearson rides Blue Circle Boy at Athens 2004. His other successes include winning the 2003 British National Championships, against able-bodied riders.

'I'm a nutter for speed but horses give you the freedom, movement and energy that pushing a wheelchair certainly can't.'

MARIE-JOSE **PEREC**
ATHLETICS

FRANCE

Described by some as the 'diva' of athletics, Marie-José Pérec is unfairly remembered for her extrovert character and an infamous disappearing act. She was the first athlete ever to win 400m gold medals at successive Olympic Games, and she beat the legendary Michael Johnson to the honour of a 200m and 400m sprint double at the same Games.

Marie-José Pérec's temperament has threatened to become her legacy throughout a seemingly unsettled career. Her reasons for fleeing the Sydney 2000 Olympic Games remain a mystery, but caused uproar, especially among the media, whom she blamed for her apparent anxiety and subsequent flight from Australia. Yet she brands her attitude as 'individualistic', and no other word could better describe both her illustrious career on the track and her antics off it.

Like many athletes, Pérec had little say in her early athletics career. She was spotted on her native West Indian island of Guadeloupe by a visiting French coach who, recognising her stupendous natural speed, encouraged her to move to Paris aged just 16. Only four years later, she competed in her first Olympic Games, in

trailing to defending champion Olha Bryzhina through every round, Pérec demolished her opponent by a clear two metres in the 400m final and announced her arrival on the Olympic stage. In admiration of her graceful long legs and elegance in triumph, her home nation bestowed on her the nickname of 'La Gazelle', and she would also skip through the 200m and 400m events at Atlanta 1966, leaving all other competitors in her wake.

She stormed the 400m, as expected, and became the first athlete of either sex to win two successive gold medals in this event. She was not finished there, however. Striving for personal greatness and distance from all other sprinters before her, Pérec became only the second athlete ever to win both the 200m and 400m events in the same Games and beat Michael Johnson to

Seoul 1988, where, despite setting a French 400m record shortly before, her inexperience and youth hindered her success.

It would be at the Barcelona 1992 Olympic Games that her potential was truly realised. She entered the competition as clear favourite after dominance in all events in the build-up. Despite

the feat by just 15 minutes and to considerably less acclaim than the American. Yet, regardless of a record that would see her labelled as, without doubt, one of the greatest Olympians of all time – and perhaps the most graceful and poised – it would be the frantic ups and downs of the next four years leading up to Sydney 2000

Statistics
Born: 9 May 1968, Basse-Terre, Guadeloupe
Height: 5ft 11in (1.8m)
Weight: 132lb (60kg)

Olympic Games Medals
Barcelona 1992
Women's 400m.......................................Gold

Atlanta 1996
Women's 200m ....Gold
Women's 400m......................................Gold

Above: Pérec on the podium at Atlanta 1996, where she became the first person to win a gold medal in the 400m race at consecutive Games.

Right: Pérec, pictured here crossing the line ahead of Merlene Ottey of Jamaica, added gold in the Women's 200m to her gold medal in the 400m at Atlanta 1996.

that would reshape her reputation. After Pérec had failed to show up at the European Indoor Championships in her adopted home city of Paris in 1994, she absconded to Los Angeles to train with renowned coach John Smith and his expanding stable of sprinters, which included the great Maurice Green. Despite coaching her to gold in 1996, he was subsequently ditched by Pérec and she returned to Europe, this time to Rostock

in Germany. After niggling injuries had allowed her only two professional races in the build-up to Sydney 2000, it was left to the great Wolfgang Meier, husband and coach to Marita Koch, who recorded an extraordinary time in the 400m dash in 1985, to coach her to more medals.

In the meantime, Australia's Cathy Freeman was emerging as the next 400m front-runner and was relishing the prospect of facing the French

'doe' on home soil – a mouth-watering prospect for spectators around the world too. Not long into the tournament, however, the unpredictable Pérec fled the country amid reports of intruders entering her apartment and hounding by the Australian press, allowing Freeman a clear track to the gold medal. But still, to this day, only 'La Gazelle' knows the real reason for her disappearance.

'It was a trauma, a real trauma. I had been prepared for the Olympics, not to fight an entire nation.'

Marie-José Pérec, commenting on her Sydney 2000 disappearance

CHANTAL
PETITCLERC
PARALYMPIC ATHLETICS

CANADA

Chantal Petitclerc is regarded as one of the best wheelchair athletes of all time after winning 21 medals at the Paralympic Games during her memorable career. The Canadian athlete won a clean sweep of five gold medals at both the Athens 2004 and Beijing 2008 Paralympic Games, and in 2010 she was the holder of the world records in the 100m, 200m, 400m, 800m and 1,500m.

Given the remarkable events surrounding her background, Chantal Petitclerc's is a truly amazing story. The Canadian was involved in an accident when she was aged just 13 and lost the use of both her legs. Petitclerc and a friend were building a bicycle ramp when the heavy barn door they were planning to use fell directly on her, breaking her spine and tragically confining her to a wheelchair.

Thankfully for Petitclerc, she met Gaston Jacques, a high school physical education teacher who played a decisive role in persuading her to train to start building up her stamina and strength through swimming. Up until that point Petitclerc had never seriously played a sport, and it must have taken some encouragement from Jacques to get her mind totally focused again following her life-changing accident.

Petitclerc was fortunate to have had so many helpful mentors at an early stage of her career and, at 18, was introduced to Pierre Pomerleau, who was a trainer at University Laval, in Quebec. Pomerleau introduced her to wheelchair sports

and she never looked back: she became a top-class athlete, dominating her sport for years to come. She has earned 21 Paralympic medals and even an Olympic Games gold, having won the 800m when it featured as a demonstration sport at the Athens 2004 Games.

And all this after an inauspicious start when she had to use a home-made wheelchair in her first race, in which she finished last, some considerable distance behind the other competitors. Despite her defeat, she was determined to bounce back and was desperate to achieve her goal of becoming a professional athlete. Petitclerc soon won medals competing in Canada, and started to believe she could become a real star on the international scene after holding the Canadian record in all categories of wheelchair racing.

It was at the Barcelona 1992 Paralympic Games that she first made a name for herself on the world stage, winning bronze in both the 200m and 800m. Her success here was just the beginning, though, and within four years she established herself as the most dominant female wheelchair

Statistics
Born: 15 December 1969, Saint-Marc-des-Carrières, Quebec, Canada

Paralympic Games Medals
Barcelona 1992

Women's 200m TW4	Bronze
Women's 800m TW4	Bronze

Atlanta 1996

Women's 100m T53	Gold
Women's 200m T53	Gold
Women's 400m T53	Silver
Women's 800m T53	Silver
Women's 1,500m T52-53	Silver

Sydney 2000

Women's 200m T54	Gold
Women's 800m T54	Gold
Women's 100m T54	Silver
Women's 400m T54	Silver

Athens 2004

Women's 100m T54	Gold
Women's 200m T54	Gold
Women's 400m T54	Gold
Women's 800m T54	Gold
Women's 1,500m T54	Gold

Beijing 2008

Women's 100m T54	Gold
Women's 200m T54	Gold
Women's 400m T54	Gold
Women's 800m T54	Gold
Women's 1,500m T54	Gold

Left: Petitclerc celebrates winning one of her five gold medals at the Beijing 2008 Paralympic Games.

Right: Victory in the 1,500m T54 wheelchair race in Beijing brought a fitting end to Petitclerc's Paralympic career.

racer in the world at the Atlanta 1996 Paralympic Games. Petitclerc won gold in both the 100m and 200m and also picked up silver medals in the 400m, 800m and 1,500m.

It was a pattern that continued at the 2000 Games in Sydney, where she won gold in the 200m and 800m, and also collected silver in the 100m and 400m. The 800m final was one of high drama as half the field crashed during the race. Petitclerc's gold medal was not secured until

her team successfully appealed for the race not to be re-run.

Refusing to relax and be content with her amazing success, Petitclerc went on to record one of the biggest achievements of her career and make history within her sport at the Manchester 2002 Commonwealth Games, when she won gold in the 800m in a world-record 1:52.92. The records just kept coming at the Athens 2004 Paralympic Games as she picked up an unprecedented five

gold medals, setting three world records in the process and taking the sport to a whole new level.

Despite having told reporters at the Beijing 2008 Paralympic Games that they could be witnessing her last involvement in an international race meeting, Petitclerc defied all the odds once again when she struck gold and recorded a second consecutive sweep in all five of her races. As one of the all-time great athletes of the Paralympic Games, it is hard to think of a better role model.

*'I knew I wanted to be the best wheelchair racer in history.
I just didn't think Canadians would cheer so loudly for me
and be one of the best parts of the dream.'*

MICHAEL **PHELPS**
AQUATICS – SWIMMING

When Michael Phelps entered eight events at the Beijing 2008 Olympic Games and won eight gold medals – the only Olympian ever to achieve that feat – he ensured his place in history as possibly the greatest swimmer of all time.

Who would have thought a boy from Baltimore County who was diagnosed with attention-deficit hyperactivity disorder (ADHD) as a youngster would go on to become such a swimming legend? His sisters, Whitney and Hilary, are also accomplished swimmers, however, and Phelps first took to the pool as a seven-year-old, setting national age group records within three years.

By adulthood it was clear he had the perfect physique for the sport, not least because of his incredible arm span of 6ft 7in (2.01m) and his size 14 feet. And he has used those attributes to good measure. He idolised Australian swimming legend Ian Thorpe in his youth and has certainly joined his hero in swimming's pantheon of greats. Phelps' domination of the sport began four years before the Beijing 2008 Games, in Athens 2004, when he also won eight medals – six golds and two bronzes – to become only the second athlete in Olympic history after Soviet gymnast Alexander Dityatin to do so.

His aim in Beijing was to achieve a clean sweep in each of his eight events and eclipse the performance of Olympic legend Mark Spitz, who won seven golds in Munich 1972, and that ambition placed huge pressure on Phelps going into the Games. Remarkably, however, he achieved his dream, winning every race he entered, including Freestyle, Butterfly, Relay and Individual Medley titles – setting seven new world records in the process.

In all he took part in 17 races over a period of just nine days and perhaps the closest of them all was the 100m Butterfly final, in which he beat Milorad Cavic by just one-hundredth of a second. The record-breaking eighth gold came in the 4 x 100m Medley Relay on 17 August 2008 – and in some style. Phelps joined team-mates Brendan Hansen, Aaron Perisol and Jason Lezak to win in a new world record of 3:29.34, 0.7 seconds ahead of the Australian quartet.

His total of 14 Olympic gold medals surpasses the previous best of 10 set by Ray Ewry, and his overall total of 16 medals makes him the most decorated man in Olympic history, only two behind Soviet gymnast Larissa Latynina. Considering that he has pledged to swim at the London 2012 Games, there is potential for him to shatter the Olympic medals record and establish a mark that could last for a long, long time.

Phelps has been named World Swimmer of the Year six times, giving an indication of the extent of his domination, and won seven golds at the 2007 World Championships, not to mention five golds and a silver at the same event in 2005 and 2009.

Statistics
Born: 30 June 1985, Baltimore, Maryland, USA
Height: 6ft 4in (1.93m)
Weight: 201lb (91kg)

Olympic Games Medals
Athens 2004
Men's 4 x 200m Freestyle Relay........Gold
Men's 100m Butterfly...........................Gold
Men's 200m Butterfly...........................Gold
Men's 200m Individual Medley.......Gold
Men's 400m Individual Medley.......Gold
Men's 4 x 100m Medley Relay.........Gold
Men's 200m Freestyle.................... Bronze
Men's 4 x 100m Freestyle Relay.... Bronze

Beijing 2008
Men's 200m Freestyle.........................Gold
Men's 4 x 100m Freestyle Relay.......Gold
Men's 4 x 200m Freestyle Relay.......Gold
Men's 100m Butterfly...........................Gold
Men's 200m Butterfly...........................Gold
Men's 200m Individual Medley.......Gold
Men's 400m Individual Medley.......Gold
Men's 4 x 100m Medley Relay.........Gold

'Dream as big as you can dream, and anything is possible ... I am sort of in a dream world. Sometimes I have to pinch myself to make sure it is real.'

Michael Phelps celebrates his record-breaking performance in Beijing 2008

Left: Phelps has the distinction of setting a world or Olympic record time in each of the 14 gold- and two bronze-medal winning finals he has swum at the Olympic Games.

Right: Phelps on the way to winning gold in the Men's 200m Individual Medley at the Beijing 2008 Olympic Games, with a world-record time of 1:54.23.

MATTHEW **PINSENT**
ROWING

Sir Matthew Pinsent's partnership with Sir Steve Redgrave will forever be remembered as one of the greatest in rowing history, but after winning four consecutive gold medals between Barcelona 1992 and Athens 2004 and dominating the water with different partners, he undoubtedly deserves his own special place in the Olympic pantheon.

Statistics

Born: 10 October 1970, Holt, Norfolk, England
Height: 6ft 5in (1.95m)
Weight: 242lb (110kg)

Olympic Games Medals

Barcelona 1992

Men's Pairs (2-)..Gold

Atlanta 1996

Men's Pairs (2-)..Gold

Sydney 2000

Men's Fours (4-)..Gold

Athens 2004

Men's Fours (4-)..Gold

Matthew Pinsent's greatest moment came on Saturday, 21 August at the Athens 2004 Games when he led Great Britain's Men's Fours (4-) – or coxless four – to one of the most dramatic victories ever seen in an Olympic final, beating the Canadian team by only eight 100ths of a second. The British crew of Pinsent, James Cracknell, Ed Coode and Steve Williams were under intense pressure to repeat the heroics of four years earlier, when legendary oarsman Steve Redgrave was in the boat as he won a record fifth Olympic gold in Sydney 2000. But with 200 metres to go the Canadians took the lead and it needed an astonishing last, agonisingly painful burst of strength, with Pinsent increasing the stroke rate, to claw back in front and win the race by inches.

Races, winning both. He claimed his first Olympic gold at the age of 21, sitting in front of Redgrave in Barcelona 1992, having already gone an entire season unbeaten in the Men's Pairs (2-) – coxless pairs.

The Pinsent–Redgrave combination triumphed again in Atlanta 1996 and in all they won seven World Championship golds in a remarkable tale of success, culminating in an emotional gold in Sydney 2000 in the Men's Fours (4-) in Redgrave's final race of a distinguished career.

Following Redgrave's retirement, Pinsent went on to prove he deserves legendary status in his own right, forging an equally successful partnership with Cracknell. In 2001 they completed a unique feat in the history of rowing, by winning the Men's Pairs (2-) at the World Championships in Lucerne, a mere two hours after taking gold in

The result meant that he became only the fifth athlete in history to win four consecutive gold medals at an Olympic Games after a career spanning more than a dozen years.

It all began for Pinsent at St Catherine's College, Oxford, where he was president of the Oxford Rowing Club, taking part in two Oxford and Cambridge Boat

the Men's Pairs (2+) – coxed pair. They returned to defend their Men's Pairs (2-) title a year later, breaking the world record by four seconds on the way to victory.

Pinsent was awarded the MBE in 1993, made a CBE in 2000 and knighted in 2004, the year that he also announced his retirement.

Above: Pinsent celebrates gold in the Men's coxless Four (4-) at the Sydney 2000 Games, after beating the Italian crew by 0.38 of a second.

Right: On the way to gold at Sydney 2000, Pinsent demonstrates the power and technical nous that made him an ideal 'stroke', setting the pace for his crew-mates.

'I haven't stopped smiling since we won and even if I'd found out my house had burnt down when I got home I would still be smiling.'

Matthew Pinsent, after winning a fourth Olympic gold medal

OSCAR **PISTORIUS**

PARALYMPIC ATHLETICS

Oscar Pistorius has fought battles on and off the racetrack, having won a landmark case against the International Association of Athletics Federations (IAAF) in 2008 that has allowed him to race against able-bodied competitors. The 'Blade Runner' is a treble world record-holder – now he's ready to compete in both the London 2012 Paralympic and Olympic Games.

In a little over three years, Oscar Pistorius went from never having stepped on to a racetrack, let alone running a race, to dominating the athletics world and claiming three world records. His story is as inspirational as it is enthralling, with many more challenges awaiting him.

When Pistorius was 11 months old he was diagnosed with a congenital condition that meant he was missing the fibula in both legs, which resulted in amputation halfway between his knees and ankles. But this did not disturb the champion-in-waiting's quest for sporting greatness. After starring for his high school rugby team, as well as playing water polo and tennis at state level, he was introduced to running in 2004 while undergoing rehabilitation on a knee injury.

And he never looked back. At 17, and having trained for only two months, he ran the 100m in 11.51 seconds in an open competition in his home town of Pretoria. The world record was 12.20. At that moment, it was clear Pistorius was destined for stardom and in the next eight months he had the whole world amazed at his exploits.

The 'fastest man with no legs' raced alongside Marlon Shirley and Brian Frasure at the Athens 2004 Paralympic Games and took the bronze medal in the 100m T44, but it was in the 200m T44 that he really shone, winning gold and breaking the world record with a time of 21.97 seconds – the previous world record of 23.42 was the mark he had set in the heats. The startling result made him the first amputee ever to run the 200m in under 22 seconds and Pistorius eventually left the Games with an incredible four world records and two medals.

In 2005, he won gold in both the 100m and 200m T44 at the Paralympic World Cup in Manchester, following on from his commendable sixth-place finish in the 400m final of the open/able-bodied category at the South African Championships. His efforts away from the track

are just as awe-inspiring: he took on the IAAF to win a landmark ruling regarding his bid to race against able-bodied competitors in Olympic competition in 2008. The sport's governing body argued that his carbon-fibre blades would give him an unfair advantage over able-bodied contestants. Undeterred, he fought on and ultimately secured the result he wanted. But, by his own admission, the strenuous legal battle compromised his training, which led to his failure to qualify for the South African team for the Beijing 2008 Games.

As is the Pistorius way, he smiled in the face of adversity and settled for a place in the Paralympic Games, blowing the competition out of the water in the 100m T44, 200m T44 and 400m T44 and becoming the first-ever Paralympian to win gold in all three events. Currently the world record holder in the 100m T44, 200m T44 and 400m T44 events, Pistorius will have the world running scared at the London 2012 Paralympic and maybe Olympic Games too – just as long as they can keep up with him.

Statistics

Born: 22 November 1986, Johannesburg, South Africa
Weight: 177lb (80.5kg)

Paralympic Games Medals

Athens 2004

Men's 200m T44	Gold
Men's 100m T44	Bronze

Beijing 2008

Men's 100m T44	Gold
Men's 200m T44	Gold
Men's 400m T44	Gold

'You're not disabled by the disabilities you have, you are able by the abilities you have.'

Above: Pistorius celebrates after winning the the Men's 400m T44 final at the Beijing 2008 Paralympic Games.

Right: Pistorius wears the prosthetics that lent him the nickname 'Blade Runner' at Beijing 2008.

STANISLAV
POZDNIAKOV
FENCING

RUSSIA

Stanislav Pozdniakov only took up fencing while at university, but the trainee teacher has certainly handed out a few lessons to his rivals since then. The Russian Sabre champion has won more individual gold medals than anyone else in the history of the sport, including the four Olympic golds that sealed his reputation.

Statistics

Born: 27 September 1973,
Novosibirsk, Russia
Height: 5ft 10in (1.78m)
Weight: 165lb (75kg)

Olympic Games Medals

Barcelona 1992

Men's Team Sabre................................Gold

Atlanta 1996

Men's Individual Sabre.......................Gold
Men's Team Sabre................................Gold

Sydney 2000

Men's Team Sabre................................Gold

Athens 2004

Men's Team Sabre.......................... Bronze

Stanislav Pozdniakov's place at the top of the Sabre-fencing hierarchy is unlikely ever to be challenged. The winner of five Olympic medals, including four golds, the Russian's dominance of his sport is almost unparalleled. He won his fifth World Championships crown in 2007 in St Petersburg to take his individual gold-medal tally to 11, with five European Championships victories to add to his Atlanta 1996 Games gold.

Yet it is his superb Team performances that have helped make him a true legend: an incredible 15 Team golds, including three Olympic Games titles, mean that his 26 major tournament victories may never be beaten.

He was a natural talent, even though he came to the sport relatively late after a childhood spent dreaming of becoming a professional footballer. But under the guidance of Boris Pisetsky, who was his coach throughout his stellar career, he simply destroyed his opponents, thanks in part to an unusual training regime that included time spent playing ice hockey and football, as well as stints on the ski slopes. And at the age of 18 he qualified for the Barcelona 1992 Olympic Games as part of the Unified Team, which was composed of 12 of the 15 former Soviet Republics. Alongside Aleksander Chirchov, Vadym Huttsait, Grigory Kiriyenko and Georgy Pogosov, the Unified Team went on to win the Team Sabre gold medal, defeating Hungary 9–5 in the final.

Two Individual World Cup crowns followed before what was to be Pozdniakov's most successful Olympic Games, in Atlanta 1996. He eased into the final, where he met fellow Russian Sergey Sharikov. It was a tight contest, but Pozdniakov won 15–12 thanks to two late hits, helping him to claim his only Individual Olympic title. Sharikov was forced to put his disappointment behind him three days later, however, when the pair were joined by Grigory Kiriyenko for the Team event. Russia were too good for the competition as they won every fight with ease, thrashing Hungary 45–25 in the final.

Aged just 22, Pozdniakov now had three Olympic gold medals to his name, yet his golden run was to come to a premature end at the Sydney 2000 Olympic Games. Widely tipped to win gold, he was unfortunate to come up against the in-form Mathieu Gourdain of France in the third round. A shock 15–11 defeat to the eventual silver medallist meant that for the first time in his career, the Russian had entered an Olympic competition and might not win a gold. His

Left: Pozdniakov had already won more fencing gold medals than any other swordsman, even before the Beijing 2008 Olympic Games.

Right: The Russian is fierce in combat, displaying the guile that earned him the right to compete for medals in five successive Olympiads.

disappointment was to be short-lived, though, as he teamed up once again with Sharikov for the Team event. Alongside Alexei Frossine, the team's third member, the Russians were again the dominant force. With Hungary defeated in the quarter-finals, the Russian team swept past France in their final bout, a 45–32 victory securing a third successive Team Sabre gold.

Pozdniakov was again the favourite when Athens 2004 came around, but for the second Olympic Games in succession he fell to a shock defeat, this time losing out to Dmitri Lapkes of Belarus in the quarter-finals of the Men's Individual Sabre. The Men's Team Sabre was also a relative disappointment, as Russia narrowly lost to Italy in the semi-finals, although they

claimed the bronze medal by winning the play-off match against the USA.

Pozdniakov tried to raise his game for one final Games, in Beijing 2008, but he came 17th in the Individual Sabre and the Russians could only finish fourth in the Team event. But despite that letdown his legacy was assured, and his record is set to stand the test of time.

'It's only natural for a human being to strive to achieve more and, for an athlete, to try to have more wins … Now that some time has elapsed since I left competitive sports, I feel I did no less than I wanted.'

STEVE **REDGRAVE**
ROWING

GREAT BRITAIN

Having won gold medals at five consecutive Olympic Games, rowing legend Sir Steve Redgrave can rightfully claim to be one of the greatest Olympians of all. His illustrious career lasted nearly 20 years and his Olympic reign spanned three decades, beginning in Los Angeles in 1984 and continuing all the way through to Sydney in 2000.

Statistics
Born: 23 March 1962, Marlow, Buckinghamshire, England
Height: 6ft 5in (1.95m)
Weight: 227lb (103kg)

Olympic Games Medals
Los Angeles 1984
Men's Fours (4+) ....Gold

Seoul 1988
Men's Pairs (2-) ....Gold
Men's Pairs (2+) .... Bronze

Barcelona 1992
Men's Pairs (2-) ....Gold

Atlanta 1996
Men's Pairs (2-) ....Gold

Sydney 2000
Men's Fours (4-) ....Gold

When Stephen Geoffrey Redgrave, face etched with pain and gasping for breath, famously said, 'Anyone who sees me go anywhere near a boat again, ever, you've got my permission to shoot me,' following his victory in the Men's Pairs (2-) – or coxless pairs – in Atlanta 1996, the public were given a glimpse of just how much it takes to reach the top in one of the most demanding Olympic sports. Early mornings on the river in freezing conditions, almost 24-hour training schedules, the strictest of fitness regimes and a willingness to go through the pain barrier are par for the course for anyone who wants to be a medal contender on the water. But Redgrave was a match for anyone he faced and arguably the greatest rower of all time.

His Olympic success began as early as the Los Angeles 1984 Games when he won gold in the Men's Fours (4+) – coxed – at the tender age of just 22 and, despite the notable outburst in Atlanta, he was still going strong when he won a fifth and final gold meal in Sydney 2000 at the age of 38. In between those performances he triumphed with partner Andy Holmes in the Men's Pairs (2-) in Seoul 1988 Olympics, before teaming up with Matthew Pinsent for the 1990 World Championships in Tasmania in what became one of the greatest partnerships rowing has ever seen – they won seven world titles and three Olympic gold medals together.

The pair triumphed in Barcelona 1992, setting an Olympic record that still stands to this day, and went on to triumph again four years later in Atlanta 1996. They also hold a world record in the Pairs (2-), set in Vienna in 1991, and rowed together again in Sydney 2000 as part of Britain's triumphant Fours (4-) – coxless fours. It was that final, historic, Olympic gold medal that sealed his position as Great Britain's greatest Olympian and a darling of the British public.

Images of the dramatic finale, which saw Great Britain's team of Redgrave, Matthew Pinsent, James Cracknell and Tim Foster beat Italy by just 0.38 of a second, have gone down in Olympic history, especially the post-race celebrations when Matthew somehow found the energy to clamber down the boat and embrace his long-time colleague. Redgrave's achievements are all the more remarkable when you consider that he had to deal with health problems during his career, including diabetes and ulcerative colitis. He was diagnosed as diabetic at the age of 35 but still continued his training to be ready for the Olympic Games in Sydney three years later.

His successes were by no means limited to the Olympic Games, either. Redgrave enjoyed four unbeaten seasons between 1993 and 1996, won nine World Championship gold medals, 23 titles at Henley and a hat-trick of Commonwealth gold medals, and was awarded an MBE in 1996, a CBE in 1998 and a knighthood in 2001.

Born close to the River Thames in Marlow, Buckinghamshire, he has been a giant of rowing in so many ways – not least because of his 6ft 5in frame. And even after retirement he played a major part in helping London win the Olympic Games for 2012, ensuring that his legacy continues.

Above: Redgrave celebrates after being awarded his gold medal for winning the Men's Pairs (2-) with Matthew Pinsent at the Atlanta 1996 Olympic Games.

Right: Redgrave's last hurrah was a record-breaking fifth consecutive gold medal, won in the Men's Fours (4-) at Sydney 2000.

*'He is an athlete who is really in the golden book of
the history of the Olympic Games.'*

Former International Olympic Committee president Juan Antonio Samaranch, speaking
after watching Redgrave win in Sydney 2000

VILLE **RITOLA**
ATHLETICS

'Flying Finn' Ville Ritola possessed an unwavering desire for success in long-distance running and his duels with legendary countryman Paavo Nurmi captivated the crowds during the Olympic Games of Paris 1924 and Amsterdam 1928. He won eight Olympic medals, including five golds, and his exploits at the Paris Games in 1924 had to be seen to be believed.

Number 14 of 20 children, Ville Ritola left his native Finland in 1913 at the age of 17 and emigrated to the USA to join seven other siblings, who had moved there previously. The move to the States invigorated his desire to run and when he joined the Finnish-American Athletic Club, he met Hannes Kolehmainen, who had moved to America following the Stockholm 1912 Olympic Games. Kolehmainen wanted the young Ritola to join the Finnish squad for the Antwerp 1920 Olympic Games, but Ritola selflessly turned down the offer because he believed he was not prepared for such a big step. However, by the time the Paris 1924 Games came around, he felt he was ready – ready to take on the world.

In his first ever race in Olympic competition, the 10,000m, he absolutely stormed into the record books, winning a gold medal and breaking his own world record by an astonishing 12 seconds. He completed the race in a time of 30:23.2, setting the tone for a remarkable Olympic Games for himself. Just three days after his world record-breaking exploits, Ritola was at it again. This time, he tackled the 3,000m Steeplechase and finished a full 11 seconds ahead of fellow Finn Elias Katz. His time of 9:33.6 set a new Olympic Games record – not bad for an athlete who had never previously run in that event.

With two golds behind him – both achieved by claiming world and Olympic records – Ritola turned his attention to the 5,000m, billed as a showdown between himself and fellow 'Flying Finn' Paavo Nurmi. Ritola failed to claim another gold as Nurmi reigned supreme, running home in an Olympic record time of 14:31.2 – the incomparable Finn would go on to claim 12 Olympic medals during his career, nine of them gold.

The 5,000m was the first time that Ritola and Nurmi had done battle on the track in Olympic competition, but for the Men's 3,000m Team race they combined to claim a gold medal each as the Flying Finns lived up to their names to beat Great Britain into second place. Ritola and Nurmi also did battle in the Individual Cross-Country, the latter once again claiming the gold medal as he reaffirmed his status as the leviathan of long-distance running.

The two Finnish runners, racing against each other and for each other, were one of the abiding memories from the Paris 1924 Olympic Games, but the role of other athletes, such as Heikki Liimatainen should not be overlooked. Liimatainen, just as Elias Katz did in the 3,000m Team event, formed the third prong of the fearsome Finnish triumvirate that secured another gold medal, this time in the Team Cross-Country event.

At 32, Ritola still had the capacity to dominate four years later as he beat his rival Nurmi in the 5,000m to win gold in Amsterdam 1928, although Nurmi once again gained revenge by claiming gold in the 10,000m. While he could not quite hit the heights achieved by Nurmi during his Olympic Games career, Ritola retired after the Amsterdam 1928 Games safe in the knowledge that he had become a marathon man for all occasions.

Statistics

Born: 18 January 1896, Peraseinajoki, Finland
Died: 24 April 1982
Height: 5ft 9in (1.75m)
Weight: 145lb (66kg)

Olympic Games Medals
Paris 1924

Men's 10,000m	Gold
Men's 3,000m Steeplechase	Gold
Men's 3,000m Team	Gold
Men's Team Cross-Country	Gold
Men's 5,000m	Silver
Men's Individual Cross-Country	Silver

Amsterdam 1928

Men's 5,000m	Gold
Men's 10,000m	Silver

Left: Ritola was the 14th of 20 children, but usually finished first on the track, where he won five gold and three silver Olympic medals.

Right: 'Flying Finns' do battle once again: Ritola leads fellow countryman Paavo Nurmi at the Amsterdam 1928 Olympic Games.

'Ottaa Ritolat'

Ville Ritola's speed inspired a new Finnish expression – 'To make a swift exit'

DAVID **ROBERTS**
PARALYMPIC SWIMMING

One of Great Britain's most successful Paralympic athletes of all time, alongside Baroness Tanni Grey-Thompson, David Roberts CBE is a swimmer like no other. Diagnosed with cerebral palsy at a young age, he took up swimming on his doctor's advice. He has since become the greatest Paralympian swimmer in his country's history.

David Roberts was just 11 years old when his condition was diagnosed, and a doctor recommended that he take up swimming, to help with his muscle strength and overall fitness. However, what was simply proposed as a form of physiotherapy soon turned out to be the stage on which he became the star of the show.

Roberts began his Paralympic career at the Sydney 2000 Games. As a young competitor, at just 20 years of age, he was not expected to have much success, and certainly not win much in the way of medals. But the Welshman was an over-achiever and left Australia with his first seven Paralympic medals, three of which were gold. Against all the odds, his gold medal successes came in the 50m Freestyle, the 100m Freestyle and the 4 x 100m Freestyle.

Four years on, by the Athens 2004 Paralympic Games, the pressure had mounted on him to succeed once more. This time he had a target in mind and he was expected to emulate his achievements of four years previously. And he did not fail to deliver. Despite winning two fewer medals, four of the five that he did bag were gold.

Almost repeating his feats in Sydney 2000, he won gold in the 50m and 100m Freestyle and 4 x 100m Freestyle Relay events. But this time he added the 400m Freestyle gold to his repertoire, having won silver four years earlier.

By this point Roberts was considered one of the greatest Paralympians in the world, and the Welsh athlete was just four gold medals short of equalling Tanni Grey-Thompson's record of 11 Paralympic golds. When the Paralympic Games journeyed to Beijing in 2008, he accomplished all that was expected of him, if not more. Even his biggest fans were concerned he might buckle under the weight of expectation, but he showed the cool of a true sporting champion. He won yet another four gold medals, taking his overall tally to 11 golds in just three Paralympic Games. By matching the legendary Grey-Thompson's record, he became the most successful male British Paralympian of all time. The four events in which he claimed gold were exactly the same four events that he had won in Athens 2004, making him the greatest Paralympic swimmer in the world.

His achievements in the Games led to many awards in his personal life away from the pool.

Statistics
Born: 25 May 1980, Pontypridd, Wales

Paralympic Games Medals
Sydney 2000
Men's 50m Freestyle S7 ....Gold
Men's 100m Freestyle S7...................Gold
Men's 4 x 100m Freestyle
   Relay 34 Points.............................Gold
Men's 100m Backstroke S7............ Silver
Men's 400m Freestyle S7.............. Silver
Men's 4 x 100m Medley
   Relay 34 Points................................. Silver
Men's 4 x 50m Freestyle
   Relay 20 Points...............................Bronze

Athens 2004
Men's 50m Freestyle S7 ....Gold
Men's 100m Freestyle S7...................Gold
Men's 400m Freestyle S7..................Gold
Men's 4 x 100m Freestyle
   Relay 34 Points.............................Gold
Men's 200m Individual
   Medley SM7 ....Silver

Beijing 2008
Men's 50m Freestyle S7 ....Gold
Men's 100m Freestyle S7...................Gold
Men's 400m Freestyle S7..................Gold
Men's 4 x 100m Medley
   Relay 34 Points..................................Gold

Left: Roberts celebrates in the pool at the Beijing 2008 Paralympic Games, where he set a new world record on the way to winning the 400m Freestyle.

Right: The Welshman in action at the Athens 2004 Paralympic Games, where he bagged himself four gold medals and one silver.

After the Athens 2004 Paralympics Games, he was awarded an MBE for services to disabled sport; and following his wonderful success in Beijing 2008, he was upgraded to a CBE. He was also bestowed with the great honour of being standard bearer of the Union Jack and leading the Great Britain team at the Paralympic closing ceremony after the Beijing 2008 Games. Following his much deserved accolades he was also inducted into the Welsh Sports Hall of Fame in 2009.

Roberts will be only 32 by London 2012, so he will certainly have the opportunity to break Tanni Grey-Thompson's record in front of his own home fans. If he does become Britain's most successful Paralympian of all time, there will be calls for a knighthood – and Roberts will surely have the chance of parading the flag at the closing ceremony once more.

'At the end of the day I am a small-town bloke from a small valley, but I've got a big heart.'

WILMA **RUDOLPH**
ATHLETICS

Wilma Rudolph's story is one of the most emotional and uplifting in sporting history, and her legacy far exceeds the memory of three gold medals at the Rome 1960 Olympic Games. She battled adversity with grace and humility to become not only an Olympic champion, but also a darling of her nation, inspiring in particular a string of African-American athletes to follow in her footsteps.

Statistics

Born: 23 June 1940, St Bethlehem, Tennessee, USA
Died: 12 November 1994
Height: 5ft 11in (1.8m)
Weight: 130lb (59kg)

Olympic Games Medals

Melbourne 1956

Women's 4 x 100m Relay............. Bronze

Rome 1960

Women's 100m ....Gold
Women's 200m ....Gold
Women's 4 x 100m Relay...................Gold

Wilma Rudolph's Olympic medals on their own are enough for the sprinter to be regarded as one of the greatest female athletes of all time, but when you consider the obstacles she had to overcome her achievements take on a new meaning. Rudolph spent the early years of her life just fighting to stay alive and was fitted with metal leg braces at the age of six after contracting polio. But somehow she came through it all with remarkable fortitude. It is hardly surprising that Rudolph's life story has already been turned into a movie, an adaptation of her autobiography written in 1977. Sadly, for Rudolph and her followers, it ended tragically in November 1994 when she died of cancer at the age of just 54. But America will never forget her and neither will the world of athletics.

As a runner she was smooth, graceful and lightning quick – fans in the 1950s and 60s were told: 'Don't blink – you might miss her. And that would be a shame.' She hit the peak of her fame in Rome 1960 when she officially became the fastest woman in the world and the first American woman to claim three gold medals on the track. She won the 100m in a remarkable time of 11 seconds (only denied a world record because of the wind speed) and the 200m in 23.2 seconds, having broken the Olympic record in an earlier heat. With the world watching, including 80,000 fans in a packed stadium, she then anchored the USA in the 4 x 100m Relay, combining with Tennessee State team-mates Martha Hudson, Lucinda Williams and Barbara Jones before overtaking her German opponent on the final leg to win gold in 44.5 seconds. Add in the bronze medal she won in the 4 x 100m Relay in Melbourne 1956 when she was only 16 years old, and it's fair to say Rudolph – believed to be inspired by Jesse Owens – was a true Olympian.

But it was the way the public took her to their hearts that made her stand out. Some called her 'The Tornado', others 'The Black Gazelle' or 'The Black Pearl', but to everyone she was special, particularly in her home country, where she raised the profile of Athletics to a new high and played a major part in racial integration.

The story of her childhood charmed everyone. Tales of her premature birth in a poor family of 22 children; the years spent ill in bed suffering from a succession of illnesses including pneumonia, scarlet fever, whooping cough, chickenpox and polio; not to mention the metal braces and revelations that her brothers and sisters took turns massaging her crippled leg every day to bring her back to health. After three years in braces she became a budding all-state basketball star before being spotted by Tennessee State track coach Ed Temple, who transformed her into a sprinter.

Even after her career had ended, the softly spoken athlete won admirers through her charity work and constant efforts to encourage others, setting up the Wilma Rudolph Foundation, a not-for-profit sports programme. Whether it is as a spectacular athlete, a graceful human being or an inspiration to others, she will never be forgotten.

Below: Rudolph went from being a child with polio to being the world's fastest woman.

Right: The Italian press came up with the name 'La Gazzella' after Rudolph gracefully sprinted to gold in the 100m at the Rome 1960 Games.

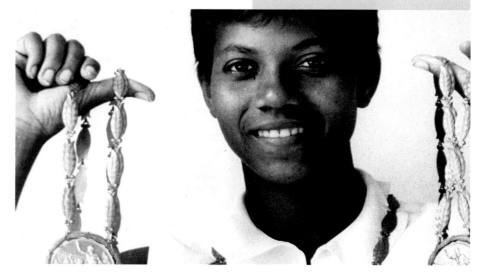

'She was beautiful, she was nice, and she was the best.'

Wilma Rudolph's Rome 1960 team-mate Bill Mulliken remembers what made her special

RICARDO **SANTOS**
VOLLEYBALL – BEACH

Some Olympic athletes have won medals by raising their levels of performance for a two-week period, but the sign of a truly class act is when a competitor performs at the highest level over a long period of time. So it is with Ricardo Santos, the Brazilian Beach Volleyball star. He has won gold, silver and bronze medals – more than anyone else in his event – marking him out as a true star of the Olympic Games.

If Olympic sports could be invented for Brazilians to excel at, surely Beach Volleyball would be at the top of the list. Ricardo Santos has never even played the indoor version of the sport; for him, the beach is his second home.

Three Olympic Games and three medals are the tangible reward for a special talent. Nicknamed either 'The Wall' or 'The Block Machine' due to his skills at the net, Santos has been at the top of his powers for a decade. He only took up the sport in 1994, aged 19, yet within six years had an Olympic silver medal to his name. In Athens 2004, the colour of the gong around his neck was gold, and in Beijing 2008 he returned home with a bronze, giving him the full set of medals.

His first partner was Ze Marco de Melo, and despite having just become full-time members of the international Beach Volleyball tour, the duo were ranked as one of the best two teams going into the Sydney 2000 Games. It was a billing they lived up to as Sweden, Austria, Canada and Germany were all defeated en route to the final. There they faced the American pair Dain Blanton and Eric Fonoimoana, to whom they had never lost in their four previous meetings. Yet despite being just a point away from taking the first set, Santos and Ze Marco stumbled, with the Americans breaking their duck and taking victory in two sets.

After that Olympic Games, Santos switched partners, first of all pairing up with Jose Geraldo Loiola, before in 2002 deciding to partner Emanuel Rego in what would prove a match made in heaven. They served notice of their intent by winning the 2003 World Championships in front of their home fans in Rio de Janeiro, and stormed through to the semi-finals in Athens the following year. There they were pushed to the limit by Patrick Heuscher and Stefan Kobel of Switzerland, who were leading 10–9 in the deciding set before the Brazilians came back to claim victory 15–12. Yet if the semi-final was a struggle, the final itself was a breeze. Santos and Emanuel were never behind, defeating Spanish pairing Javier Bosma and Pablo Herrera 21–16, 21–15 to claim gold.

The dominance of the Brazilian duo did not stop there, though. The Fédération Internationale de Volleyball (FIVB) voted them Team of the Year in 2005, 2006 and 2007, while Santos was named best offensive player in all three of those years, as well as most outstanding player in both 2005 and 2007. Appropriately for a man who lists boxing, jiujitsu and paintball as his hobbies, no one was willing to take Santos on when he was paired with Emanuel. But their aura of invincibility was punctured at the Beijing 2008 Games. Aged 33, they lost in the semi-finals to their fellow countrymen Fabio Magalhaes and Marcio Araujo.

The defeat was bitterly disappointing for them, but Santos and Emanuel picked themselves up to thrash Georgian pair Jorge Terceiro and Renato Gomes 21–15, 21–10 to take bronze.

That makes the full set of Olympic medals: Santos has tasted glory in three consecutive Olympic Games and he shows no signs of slowing down just yet. Some things simply make sense: a Brazilian dominating the Beach Volleyball circuit is certainly one of them.

Statistics
Born: 6 January 1975, Salvador, Brazil
Height: 6ft 7in (2m)
Weight: 230lb (103kg)

Olympic Games Medals
Sydney 2000
Men's Beach Volleyball.................... Silver

Athens 2004
Men's Beach Volleyball.......................Gold

Beijing 2008
Men's Beach Volleyball................. Bronze

Above: Santos celebrates winning a point during the gold-medal match at the Athens 2004 Games, when the Brazilian pair defeated Spaniards Bosma and Herrera.

Right: Despite his strength and skill at the net, Santos could only come home with a bronze medal from the Beijing 2008 Games.

'For me, personally, Ricardo and Emanuel are the best.'

Georgian Beach Volleyball player Renato Gomes gives his opinion

LOUISE **SAUVAGE**
PARALYMPIC ATHLETICS

AUSTRALIA

Louise Sauvage is one of Australia's most celebrated athletes, with an incredible haul of 13 Paralympic medals to her name. Born with a severe spinal disability, the wheelchair racer went on to dominate four Paralympiads with an unwavering spirit.

Being born with the bone disease myelodysplasia, which inhibits the lower half of the body, would be enough to halt the career of most Olympic hopefuls before they'd even begun. Not so Louise Sauvage. The Australian athlete's resolve was only strengthened by the hand that fate had dealt her. She was involved in sport from the age of three when her mother, Rita, would take her to the local swimming pool in Perth to give her exercise. Sauvage underwent no fewer than 20 operations under the age of 10.

Before she dominated in the Paralympic Games, Sauvage had to endure yet more adversity. At the age of 14 she was told that metal rods were to be inserted in her back to combat the worsening curvature of her spine and, lying for months in a hospital bed in Australia, gold medals seemed a distant prospect. Happily, she made a full recovery – the only downside was that the rods in her back curtailed her swimming career, and she turned her focus to her wheelchair and the track. By 1990, aged just 17, she was taking part in her first international competition, the World Championships in Assen, Holland, where she claimed gold in the 100m and set a new world record in the process.

Sauvage then opted to make sport her full-time career, and she reaped the rewards. In the Barcelona 1992 Paralympic Games she took gold in the 100m TW4 as well as the 200m and 400m events, while claiming silver in the 800m race. Having once again blitzed the competition four years later in Atlanta 1996, where she won four gold medals, Sauvage turned her attentions to the prestigious Boston Marathon and she managed to break the stranglehold 'The Queen of Boston', US racer Jean O'Driscoll, had on the competition.

But Sauvage's exploits at the Atlanta 1996 Games did not garner the respect she believed they warranted. In America, she was appalled by the lack of coverage athletes received and felt they were treated as an afterthought following the Olympic Games. But she received the adulation she deserved at the Sydney 2000 Paralympic Games. As she approached the final stages of the Women's 5,000m T54, her hands red raw from pushing her wheelchair towards the finish line, Sauvage was met with a ferocious wall of noise, willing her on to gold.

Statistics
Born: 18 September 1973, Perth, Australia

Paralympic Games Medals
Barcelona 1992
Women's 100m TW4 .... Gold
Women's 200m TW4 .... Gold
Women's 400m TW4 .... Gold
Women's 800m TW4 .... Silver

Atlanta 1996
Women's 1,500m T52-53 .... Gold
Women's 400m T53 .... Gold
Women's 5,000m T52-53 .... Gold
Women's 800m T53 .... Gold

Sydney 2000
Women's 1,500m T54 .... Gold
Women's 5,000m T54 .... Gold
Women's 800m T54 .... Silver

Athens 2004
Women's 400m T54 .... Silver
Women's 800m T54 .... Silver

Left: Sauvage shows off to the home crowd one of the two gold medals she won at the Sydney 2000 Paralympic Games.

Right: With nine gold medals already to her name, Sauvage made it to second place on the podium with this display in the 800m T54 at the Athens 2004 Paralympic Games.

'I felt as if I was almost picked up and bowled along by the roar of the crowd, the breath of the crowd. Almost literally, they propelled me to the line [and] to the gold,' she said. Unfortunately for her, Sauvage was denied gold in the final of the 800m T54 event, when half the field in the

final crashed and the Canadian team successfully appealed against the decision to re-run the race. Sauvage came second to her arch-rival, Chantal Petitclerc.

Once more, four years on at the Athens 2004 Paralympic Games, Petitclerc had the measure

of Sauvage and won the same event again. Nevertheless, the silver medal – and another in the 400m – were still ample reward for an athlete who fully deserved the slogan that adorns the Sydney Harbour Bridge in her name: 'You'll never know what you can do or achieve until you try.'

'I never thought of myself as being different, or disadvantaged. I'm just me – the way I am. The circumstances of my life put me in a wheelchair – but it has been my own efforts that have taken me around the world, and to the successes I have had.'

BORIS **SHAKHLIN**
GYMNASTICS – ARTISTIC

Boris Shakhlin, more commonly known as 'Man of Iron', is regarded by some as the best ever Olympic gymnast to have participated in the sport. The Russian athlete won 13 medals during his memorable career and is tied at third among all-time Olympic medal holders in all sports.

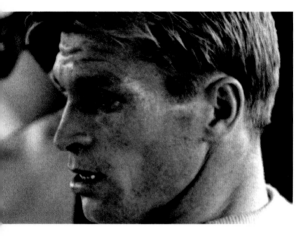

Boris Shakhlin can boast the best ever record for a male Olympian in Gymnastics, having won six gold medals in separate events. The talented Russian won 13 Olympic medals during his career, which was a record for a male athlete until Soviet gymnast Nikolai Andrianov overtook him.

The story behind Shakhlin's success is remarkable considering his tough upbringing in Siberia, where he was orphaned at the age of 12. His father was killed in a railway accident and he and his elder brother were subsequently raised by his grandmother. Although he was unusually tall and well built for an aspiring gymnast, Shakhlin decided to take a keen interest in the sport and later settled in Kiev, where he was coached by Alexander Mishakov. He was fortunate in that his training partner Viktor Chukarin had already progressed to the very top and made an immediate impact at the Helsinki 1952 Olympic Games when he won Team Competition and Individual All-Around gold medals. These achievements gave Shakhlin the impetus to try and emulate his partner and attempt even bigger things on the world stage.

He made his first major appearance at the 1954 World Championships, where he finished fourth and started to really believe he had the potential to compete against the best gymnasts in the world. It was at his first Olympic Games in 1956 that he made a real name for himself when he picked up gold medals in the Pommel Horse and Team Competitions. This seemed to spur him on to even greater heights and, although much was expected of him, Shakhlin still shocked gymnastics just two years later at the World Championships in Moscow when he picked up a record five of the eight titles available.

His dominance of the sport continued at the Rome 1960 Olympic Games, where he won four gold medals in the Vault, Parallel Bars, Pommel Horse and Individual All-Around Competitions. Add to that tally two more silver medals and a bronze and it became a tournament for the Russian athlete to remember. One might think that his gold medal success would rate as his biggest achievement, but he personally rated his bronze in the Horizontal Bars event as his most memorable feat. Shakhlin was up against two Japanese competitors when he hurt his hand and it looked as if he would have to pull out of the final, as blood was pouring from a wound. But he somehow defied all the odds and the pain to complete his routine and managed to come away with a bronze medal.

He had already been dubbed 'Man of Iron' for his amazing strength and stamina, and his reputation was massively enhanced by that bloodied display in Rome. His indomitable aura helped him intimidate opponents, forcing them to strive beyond their best, and he continued to dominate his sport in a number of different events. His success continued at the Tokyo 1964 Olympic Games, where he picked up gold in the Horizontal Bars as well as clinching two silver medals and a bronze.

Shakhlin suffered a heart attack at 35, which forced him to retire from the sport in 1966. He put it down to smoking and suffered a further attack 11 years later. A ferociously proud Siberian, he received numerous accolades from the Soviet regime and maintained close links to gymnastics as a coach, serving on the men's technical committee of the International Gymnastics Federation for 24 years. He died in 2008.

Statistics

Born: 27 January 1932, Tyumen, Russia
Died: 30 May 2008
Height: 5ft 7in (1.7m)
Weight: 156lb (71kg)

Olympic Games Medals

Melbourne 1956
Men's Team Competition....................Gold
Men's Pommel Horse
  Competition..Gold

Rome 1960
Men's Individual All-Around
  Competition..Gold
Men's Vault Competition ....Gold
Men's Parallel Bars
  Competition..Gold
Men's Pommel Horse
  Competition..Gold
Men's Team Competition............... Silver
Men's Rings Competition .... Silver
Men's Horizontal Bars
  Competition..................................... Bronze

Tokyo 1964
Men's Horizontal Bars
  Competition..Gold
Men's Individual All-Around
  Competition..................................... Silver
Men's Team Competition............... Silver
Men's Rings Competition .... Bronze

Left: Shakhlin prepares to talk to the press during the Tokyo 1964 Games.

Right: Shakhlin shows his control and strength on his way to winning one of four gold medals at the Rome 1960 Olympic Games.

'Having reached all possible heights [in his own career], he always remained devoted to the Olympic Movement. To the last gasp, Boris shared his experience with the youngest generation.'

Ukrainian Olympic Committee President, Sergei Bubka

UDHAM **SINGH**
HOCKEY

Arguably the finest hockey player ever to come out of India, Udham Singh amassed four medals in Olympic competition, a record-setting feat matched only by his fellow countryman, the indomitable Leslie Claudius. On his day, the half-back was virtually unplayable.

Born in a small village near the Jallandhar region of Punjab, Udham Singh studied at the Victor High School and DAV College, where, despite his slight frame, India's star-in-waiting regularly out-muscled his competitors on the hockey field. That determined, battling approach was a sign of things to come. Singh quickly emerged as a force to be reckoned with and was promptly named captain of his college hockey team. In the same year, 1947, he was recruited as a physical trainer by the Punjab police force – an organisation with a rich history in producing formidable hockey teams.

The London 1948 Olympic Games would have been his first, but he sustained a finger injury in the build-up to the event and was subsequently ruled out. Such a blow did not deter him, however, as he responded to the disappointment by playing a pivotal role in India's international series victory over Afghanistan in 1949. He finally got his taste of Olympic competition at the Helsinki 1952 Games as India swept all before them en route to a final showdown with the Netherlands. Marshalled by the irrepressible Balbir Singh – another member of the Punjab police force – India thrashed the Netherlands 6–1, with Balbir Singh scoring nine of India's 13 goals in the tournament.

Singh secured his second gold medal at the Melbourne 1956 Olympic Games as India successfully defended their title. By this time, he was a key member of the Indian side and his part in their 14–0 win over Afghanistan and 16–0 win over the United States underlined his credentials as a powerhouse in Hockey. The final was a tense affair, though, and India held out to beat bitter rivals Pakistan 1–0, with Singh winning another gold to add to his growing collection.

It seemed as though nothing could stop Singh and the team – by the time they reached the final at the Rome 1960 Olympic Games they were on a 30-match winning run, having scored 197 goals and conceded a meagre eight. But he was surprisingly denied a third gold medal as Pakistan avenged their defeat from the previous Games to beat India.

Back home, the result was considered a national tragedy, and plans were immediately put in place to reclaim the gold medal in Tokyo 1964. The early stages of the Hockey tournament at the Tokyo 1964 Olympic Games left a lot to be desired for India and Singh, as the team only scraped through to the final – and a rematch against Pakistan – following 1–1 draws with East Germany and Spain. Pakistan, on the other hand, won seven matches in a row going into the final; but Singh and India reigned supreme once again as Mohinder Lal scored the only goal of the game.

Singh's four Olympic Games Hockey medals remain a record but his prowess off the pitch was just as laudable, as he successfully coached the Indian side and masterminded their run to the final of the Asian Games in 1970, where they finished runners-up to their nemesis, Pakistan.

Statistics

Born: 4 August 1928, Punjab, India
Died: 23 March 2000
Height: 5ft 6in (1.68m)
Weight: 128lb (58kg)

Olympic Games Medals

Helsinki 1952
Men's Team Tournament....................Gold

Melbourne 1956
Men's Team Tournament....................Gold

Rome 1960
Men's Team Tournament.................Silver

Tokyo 1964
Men's Team Tournament....................Gold

Below: Singh in action in a sport that he – as part of the highly successful Indian team in which he played – came to dominate.

Right: Singh's record-breaking medal tally of three golds and one silver could have been more if injury had not stopped him participating in the London 1948 Games.

'I believe achievement has no ending.'

PETER SNELL
ATHLETICS

NEW ZEALAND

Peter Snell, the man of steel with enormous lungs, displayed an unwavering desire and determination to reach the pinnacle of middle- and long-distance running. He won three gold medals during his Olympic career – a reward for the excruciating pain he would put himself through in training.

During his formative years it was clear that Peter Snell had a talent for sport – he was his school's tennis champion and he also played to a high level at cricket and rugby. But at 19, it was a chance meeting with running coach Bill Bailey that introduced him to the world of athletics.

Snell also met the influential New Zealand athletics coach Arthur Lydiard through Bailey and initially he failed to keep up with the pair during the long-distance training, often asking if he could complete the distances by car. At that time, he just saw running as a supplement to his main love, tennis. As Lydiard nurtured his young protégé, it was obvious that Snell had a talent for lung-bursting runs and it was a good job he did, too, as the New Zealander was urged to run 100 miles (160km) a week as part of his training. Running in the searing heat in Auckland meant Snell would lose around 7lb (3.17kg) a day in sweat alone. It was worth it, though, as he would soon reap the rewards.

He was an unknown quantity going into the Rome 1960 Olympic Games, but his performances in the 800m soon had the world paying attention. He claimed gold in the 800m with an Olympic record time of 1:46.3 in what was the first step on his ascent to greatness. In January 1962, with all those weeks of 100-mile runs behind him, Snell stunned the world again as he broke the world record for running the mile, before a huge crowd at Crook's Gardens in Wanganui. His time of 3:54.4 was remarkable, but Snell was by no means finished. Amazingly, just a week later he set a new world record for the half-mile as he trounced a visiting United States team at Christchurch.

By the Tokyo 1964 Games, he was the big draw. Crowds had flocked to see him run in New Zealand, his competitors feared him, and records, when Snell was in town, were at his mercy. He was the defending champion, back in competition looking to claim a seemingly impossible 800m/1,500m double and, since his surprise victory in Rome, he had broken the 800m world record with

1:44.3 during that masterclass against the USA in Christchurch.

Snell, predictably, was not concerned by the weight of expectation being heaped on him, and he lived up to his tag as the man of the moment and set an Olympic record of 1:45.1 on his way to claiming his second Games gold in the 800m. All that was left was the 1,500m a few days later to complete the double. He did not disappoint. Having hung back to conserve his energy, Snell timed his late burst to perfection and won his third Olympic Games gold, beating Czech opponent Josef Odlozil with a time of 3:38.1. The rare double feat would not be achieved again by a male athlete in any open global championship until Rashid Ramzi won both gold medals for Bahrain at the 2005 World Championships.

While his retirement was frustratingly premature, athletics' loss was orienteering's gain as the New Zealander won his category, men aged 65 and older, in the 2003 United States Orienteering Championship. Winning was in his blood.

Statistics
Born: 17 December 1938, Opunake,
    New Zealand
Height: 5ft 10in (1.78m)
Weight: 176lb (80kg)

Olympic Games Medals
Rome 1960
Men's 800m .... Gold

Tokyo 1964
Men's 800m .... Gold
Men's 1,500m .... Gold

Below: Snell acknowledges the applause of the crowd after adding 1,500m gold to the gold medal he had already won in the 800m at Tokyo 1964.

Right: Surging away from the rest of the field on the fourth and final lap, Snell finished 1.4 seconds ahead of his nearest rival in the 1,500m at Tokyo 1964.

*'As a teenager I had no idea that I had the potential to win
an Olympic gold medal and my athletics career developed
only by lucky circumstances.'*

MARK **SPITZ**
AQUATICS – SWIMMING

Mark Spitz was one of the greatest swimmers of all time, roaring into the record books at the Munich 1972 Olympic Games with an astonishing haul of seven gold medals, each in a world-record time, a feat not bettered until fellow American Michael Phelps won eight golds in Beijing 2008. Spitz already had two golds from Mexico City 1968, and finished with a total of nine gold medals, one of only five Olympians to have achieved this medal feat.

Mark Spitz was known as 'Mark the Shark', as much for his single-minded ambition as his speed through the water. Having won countless titles as one of America's top young swimmers, he confidently predicted he would bring back six gold medals – only he made his bold statement four years too early. With 10 world records, Spitz expected to clean up at the Mexico City 1968 Games, but won only two golds, in the 4 x 100m and 4 x 200m Freestyle Relays.

It would be another four years before he hit the jackpot, at Munich 1972. By now 22, he again predicted he would win six golds but actually came home with seven. He came home with the 100m and 200m Freestyle and Butterfly, as well as the 4 x 100m and 4 x 200m Freestyle Relays and the 4 x 100m Medley Relay. All of these were achieved in world-record times, as he underlined his reputation as the best swimmer on the planet.

It was hardly surprising. Spitz had begun swimming almost as soon as he could walk, and after daily sessions in the sea during his early childhood years in Hawaii, he swam under leading coach Sherm Chavoor when his family returned to the mainland United States to live in California. By the age of 10 he held 17 US records for his age group, and one world record. His family even moved to Santa Clara when he was 14 so he could work under the leading coach, George Haines, at the Santa Clara Swim Club. At one point he held National High School records in every stroke and at every distance. By the age of 17 he had set his first senior world record, in the 400m Freestyle, and went on to break more records by the time the Mexico City 1968 Olympic Games came around. But his boasts rebounded on him, as he lost out in all his individual events – though he did win two team gold medals.

However, four years later it all came good for him. Spitz was one of the stars of Munich 1972 with his record-breaking haul, although his Games were touched by tragedy. The kidnap and murder of Israeli athletes and officials by Palestinian terrorists meant he had to leave early: as a prominent Jewish athlete, Spitz was considered a potential target and taken away from the Athletes' Village, even though he had finished competing at this stage. After the Munich 1972 Games, Spitz retired from competition and also gave up his plans to be a dentist, instead capitalising on his fame and becoming a successful businessman, specialising in property.

Such was his undeniable self-belief and competitive nature that he tried a brief comeback to swimming 20 years later in a bid to compete at the Barcelona 1992 Olympic Games at the age of 41. He failed, almost inevitably, to make the times required in the US Olympic trials, as the sport had changed beyond recognition and he was now approaching middle age.

Statistics
Born: 10 February 1950, Modesto, California, USA
Height: 6ft (1.83m)
Weight: 161lb (73kg)

Olympic Games Medals
Mexico City 1968
Men's 4 x 100m Freestyle Relay	Gold
Men's 4 x 200m Freestyle Relay	Gold
Men's 100m Butterfly	Silver
Men's 100m Freestyle	Bronze

Munich 1972
Men's 100m Freestyle	Gold
Men's 200m Freestyle	Gold
Men's 100m Butterfly	Gold
Men's 200m Butterfly	Gold
Men's 4 x 100m Freestyle Relay	Gold
Men's 4 x 200m Freestyle Relay	Gold
Men's 4 x 100m Medley Relay	Gold

Below: The American swimmer set 26 world records, including one before he was even 10 years old, and was named World Swimmer of the Year three times.

Right: Spitz made the pool his own at the Munich 1972 Olympic Games, winning seven gold medals, all in world-record times.

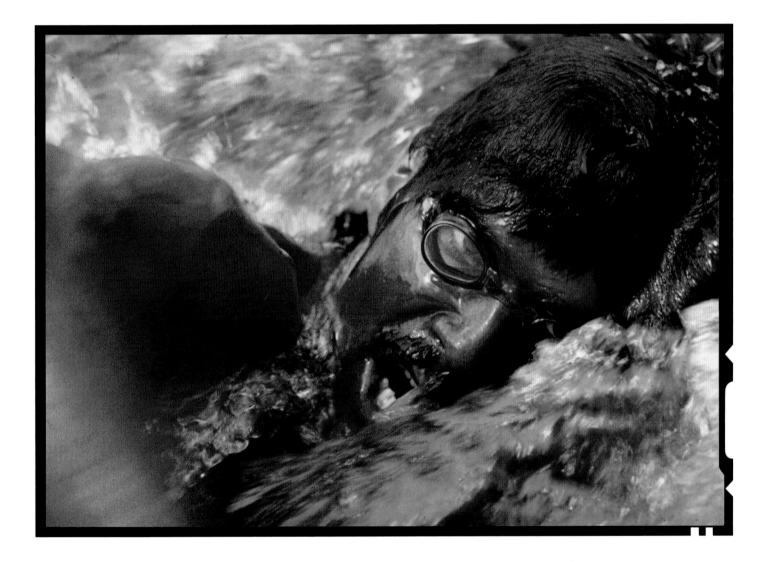

*'The memories of the Munich Games for me
are of triumph and tragedy.'*

TEOFILO **STEVENSON** CUBA
BOXING

One of only three men to win three Olympic Games Boxing gold medals, Teofilo Stevenson is the greatest Heavyweight boxer never to be a World Champion. He won Olympic Heavyweight golds in Munich 1972, Montreal 1976 and Moscow 1980, but turned down vast sums of money to turn professional in favour of continuing to proudly represent Cuba as an amateur.

For Teofilo Stevenson, the pursuit of glory for his country was far more important than money. His stunning performances as an amateur prompted multi-million-dollar offers for him to turn professional, with promoters desperate to encourage him to defect to America and pundits enthusiastic about the prospect of a fight against the great Muhammad Ali. With his chiselled good looks and charisma, Stevenson was a promoter's dream.

He was also, however, a proud Cuban, and a 1974 headline from *Sports Illustrated* magazine succinctly summarised his attitude: 'He'd Rather Be Red Than Rich,' it proclaimed. A complete athlete, with an all-action style of combination punching that drew comparisons with Muhammed Ali, Stevenson was the first boxer to win a gold medal three times in the same weight division, and is ranked alongside Laszlo Papp as the best boxer in Olympic Games history.

He started boxing at an open-air gym in his home town of Camaguey under the tutelage of former national Light Heavyweight champion John Herrera, refusing to tell his mother that he was learning to fight in the ring. He won junior titles in the mid-1960s and was then taken under the wing of Soviet trainer Andrei Chervonenko, a former boxer from Moscow. Impressive victories over the likes of German Bernd Andern meant that Stevenson headed to his first Olympic Games, at Munich 1972, with a growing reputation as an extremely skilled and dangerous fighter.

Those who had not seen him before soon found out about Stevenson's skill, as the 20-year-old Cuban knocked down Ludwik Denderys of Poland within 30 seconds of his first Olympic bout. In the quarter-finals, he produced his most memorable performance, one for which he will forever be revered by his compatriots. Stevenson beat American Duane Bobick, favourite to win the competition, by knocking him down three times in the third round, to the delight of the Cuban

nation. He went on to win gold with ease as the Cuban team entered a period of dominance that would last for many years. Before the Munich 1972 Games they had never won a Boxing gold – they returned from Germany with three.

It was during the aftermath of Munich 1972 that Stevenson started to turn down countless offers to turn professional. He then won the World Championships in 1974 and arrived at the Montreal 1976 Games as a national hero, and indisputably the world's best Heavyweight amateur by some distance. He consolidated his supremacy by comfortably retaining his title, beating Romanian Mircea Simon in the final with seemingly plenty of energy still in reserve. At the Moscow 1980 Olympics Stevenson became the second boxer ever, after Papp, to win three Olympic Boxing gold medals.

In 1982, defeat by Francesco Damiani ended an extraordinary 11 years unbeaten, and was the only time he failed to win a World Championships that he contested. Stevenson would probably have achieved an unprecedented fourth straight gold medal in Los Angeles 1984, but he was denied the chance by the Cuban boycott of the Games. In any case, he retired a national hero and one of the greatest boxers of his – or any – generation.

Statistics
Born: 23 March 1952, Puerto Padre, Las Tunas, Cuba
Height: 6ft 3in (1.9m)
Weight: 209lb (95kg)

Olympic Games Medals
Munich 1972
Men's Heavyweight..............................Gold

Montreal 1976
Men's Heavyweight..............................Gold

Moscow 1980
Men's Heavyweight..............................Gold

Left: At the Moscow 1980 Olympic Games, Stevenson became one of only three boxers ever to have won three Olympic gold medals.

Right: Stevenson pictured making his mark against Nigeria's Solomon Ataga in the first round of the Moscow 1980 Olympic Games Heavyweight Boxing competition.

'What is a million dollars compared to the love of my people? I wouldn't exchange my piece of Cuba for all the money they could give me.'

SARAH **STOREY**
PARALYMPIC SWIMMING/CYCLING

Sarah Storey is Great Britain's most successful currently competing Paralympic athlete, and a multiple gold-medallist in both Swimming and Cycling. She began her Olympic career as a 14-year-old in Barcelona 1992 and won 16 Swimming medals over four Games, before switching to Cycling for Beijing 2008, where she won a further two gold medals.

To win a Paralympic gold medal is a special achievement that few people manage. To taste success several times in one sport, then change to another and do it again is momentous, and a sign of greatness. That is what Sarah Storey did. A world-class swimmer with a plethora of medals to prove it, she turned to Cycling and immediately became a champion. She has taken to the cycling track with such success that she is aiming to become the first Briton to compete in both the London 2012 Olympic Games and Paralympic Games.

Storey was born without a left hand due to a congenital defect, but always pursued her Olympic dream. She is now considered one of the strongest competitors in the world: her personal best in the LC1 3km Individual Pursuit of 3:34.26 would have earned her a top-eight place at the Beijing 2008 Olympic Games, and a bronze medal at the World Championships.

Storey made her international debut as a schoolgirl at the Barcelona 1992 Paralympic Games, and defied the odds and her age to return home to Manchester with two golds, three silvers and a bronze. Then known by her maiden name of Bailey and aged just 14, Storey produced stunning swims to triumph in the 100m Backstroke S10 and the 200m Individual Medley SM10. She continued swimming at the next three Paralympic Games with great aplomb. At the Atlanta 1996 Paralympic Games, she retained her 100m Backstroke S10 and 200m Individual Medley SM10 titles, while adding her third gold in the 100m Breaststroke SB10. After winning five medals at Atlanta 1996, Storey collected two silver medals at the Sydney 2000 Paralympic Games, and then added to that two silvers and a bronze at the Athens 2004 Paralympic Games.

However, after two Paralympic Games without a gold medal, Storey decided on a change of direction and committed herself to Cycling, reasoning that it required many of the same attributes as Swimming, which she insists will always remain her main sport. So utterly

Left: Storey holds her gold medal in the Velodrome at the Beijing 2008 Paralympic Games – 16 years after winning gold in the swimming pool at Barcelona 1992.

Right: Great Britain's leading Paralympic swimmer switched to Cycling in 2005 after developing an ear infection that forced her out of the water.

Statistics
Born: 26 October 1977, Manchester, England

Paralympic Games Medals
Barcelona 1992
Women's 100m Backstroke S10.....Gold
Women's 200m Individual
   Medley SM10 ....Gold
Women's 400m Freestyle S10...... Silver
Women's 4 x 100m Freestyle
   Relay S7-10... Silver
Women's 4 x 100m Medley
   Relay S7-10... Silver
Women's 100m Freestyle S10.... Bronze

Atlanta 1996
Women's 100m Backstroke S10......Gold
Women's 100m Breaststroke SB10...Gold
Women's 200m Individual
   Medley SM10 ....Gold
Women's 400m Freestyle S10...... Silver
Women's 100m Freestyle S10.... Bronze

Sydney 2000
Women's 100m Backstroke S10... Silver
Women's 4 x 100m Medley
   Relay 34 points.................................. Silver

Athens 2004
Women's 100m Breaststroke
   SB9.. Silver
Women's 200m Individual
   Medley SM10 .... Silver
Women's 100m Freestyle S10.......Bronze

Beijing 2008
Road: Women's Individual
   Time Trial LC1–2/CP4 ....Gold
Track: Women's Individual
   Pursuit LC1–2/CP4...............................Gold

'There is a disadvantage, but that's not to say that, with good technique, you cannot get the same end product as an able-bodied athlete. I would never have believed when I went to my first Games [as a swimmer] in 1992 that this time I would be looking forward to my fifth Games, and as a cyclist.'

single-minded was Storey that she never even contemplated the idea that her switch might not be a success. Nevertheless, even she did not expect to perform with such distinction at her first Cycling World Championships in 2006, where she won a gold, two silvers and a bronze. In the same year, Storey broke the 3,000m Individual Pursuit world record for her LC1 class

three times, underlining a dominance that she would carry into her fifth Paralympic Games, the first she had contested on a bicycle.

The Beijing 2008 Paralympic Games got off to a perfect start for Storey, as she won her first Cycling gold on the track in the Women's Individual Pursuit by beating American rider Jennifer Schuble with a world-record time of

3:36.637. Storey has set world records more than 70 times in her career in the pool and on the track. A second Olympic gold medal followed on the road, in the Women's Individual Time Trial, making her the second most successful British Paralympian ever, behind Dame Tanni Grey-Thompson. That could soon change if Storey gets her way at the London 2012 Paralympic Games.

SHIRLEY **STRICKLAND** AUSTRALIA
ATHLETICS

Shirley Strickland, the woman with the Midas touch, claimed three golds in her haul of seven medals in Olympic track and field events, a record that remained unsurpassed until Sydney 2000. The Australian sprinter-hurdler was equally accomplished away from athletics, and later became a physics teacher, track and field coach and politician.

Shirley Strickland was raised next to the wheat fields of Western Australia and her father, David, became a professional runner after being denied a place in the Paris 1900 Olympic Games because he could not pay his own fare there. The anguish at not being able to compete would one day be offset by his daughter's domination of the Olympic Games.

It was at the London 1948 Olympic Games that her illustrious Olympic career was launched and in many ways she was a pathfinder for future Australian athletes, who – whether it be a Louise Sauvage or an Ian Thorpe – will forever remember Strickland's trailblazing exploits. After the 1948 national championships, she was selected for all the women's track events at the London 1948 Games and claimed medals in three of them. She won bronze in the 100m – finishing behind the irrepressible Fanny Blankers-Koen, which was no disgrace considering that year's Olympic Games were all about the Dutch star, who won gold in all the events Strickland entered, including the 200m, 80m Hurdles and the 4 x 100m Relay.

Strickland managed bronze in the 80m Hurdles and silver in the 4 x 100m Relay as she began to establish herself as a major player in Athletics, and in the lead-up to the Helsinki 1952 Olympic Games she was unstoppable, winning five medals in the Australian Track and Field Championships as well as three golds at the British Empire Games, which were held in Auckland.

Helsinki 1952 would further elevate Strickland into the pantheon of greats: Australia finished with six gold medals, the best in their history, and she contributed one of them. She got her revenge over Blankers-Koen in the 80m Hurdles and claimed her first Olympic Games gold with a world record time of 11.01. To cap it all, the victory meant she became the first woman to win five Olympic medals.

Defending her 80m Hurdles crown in her home country four years later would be Strickland's finest hour. By then she was 31, a mother and a physics teacher, yet she still found the determination to beat the best the world had to offer. Not only did she defend the 80m Hurdles title that she had won at Helsinki, she did so by beating Germany's Gisela Kohler with an Olympic record time of 10.7, and became the first woman to win gold at successive Olympic Games.

The unstoppable force of Betty Cuthbert and Strickland, combined with Australian team-mates June Foulds-Paul and Heather Armitage, went on to claim another gold in the 4 x 100m Relay. That gave Strickland an unprecedented seven Olympic track and field medals, a tally that remained unequalled until Poland's Irena Szewinska reached the same landmark 20 years later. Jamaican Merlene Ottey reached her seventh in Atlanta 1996 before winning an eighth and ninth in the Sydney 2000 Olympic Games.

After athletics Strickland became a politician and a keen environmentalist, selling her Olympic medals to raise £150,000 to help save forestry. She was accorded a state funeral on her death.

Statistics
Born: 18 July 1925, Northam, Western Australia, Australia
Died: 11 February 2004
Height: 5ft 8in (1.73m)
Weight: 126lb (57kg)

Olympic Games Medals
London 1948
Women's 4 x 100m Relay................ Silver
Women's 100m.................................. Bronze
Women's 80m Hurdles.................. Bronze

Helsinki 1952
Women's 80m Hurdles.......................Gold
Women's 100m.................................. Bronze

Melbourne 1956
Women's 80m Hurdles.......................Gold
Women's 4 x 100m Relay...................Gold

Left: Strickland at the Helsinki 1952 Games. Forty-eight years later, she was chosen by her country to bear the Olympic Torch at the opening ceremony of the Sydney 2000 Games.

Right: Strickland possessed natural speed and athleticism, which was reflected in the fact that two of her three Olympic gold medals came in the 80m Hurdles.

'She stood for hard work and self-discipline. She was talented enough to be anything.'

Australian athlete Ron Clarke on Strickland

NAIM **SULEYMANOGLU** TURKEY
WEIGHTLIFTING

Few Olympic Games fans would expect a man standing just 4ft 11in (1.5m) tall to be a giant of his sport, but Turkish weightlifter Naim Süleymanoğlu is no ordinary athlete. Nicknamed 'The Pocket Hercules', Süleymanoğlu won gold medals at three successive Olympic Games between Seoul 1988 and Atlanta 1996, and is considered pound-for-pound one of the strongest weightlifters who ever lived.

It is hard to put a price on success, but in the case of weightlifter Naim Süleymanoğlu, Turkey made an exception. Born in Bulgaria of Turkish descent, the diminutive star was recognised as an astonishing athlete early in his career, with his first world record coming at the age of 15. Yet he defected to Turkey in 1986 after the Bulgarian authorities sought to change his name to Naum Shalamanov as part of a bid to limit Turkish culture and identities within their borders. The rules stated that Süleymanoğlu would have to wait three years before he could compete for his adopted country; with the Seoul 1988 Olympic Games just two years away, the Turkish authorities were not willing to wait. Thus the Bulgarian government received $1m in compensation, allowing the weightlifter to compete for Turkey in Seoul 1988.

It proved a sound investment as Süleymanoğlu tore up the record books and embarked on a period of dominance that marks him out as a true Olympic legend. He had set 32 world records by the age of 22, going on to set 46 in total, and was World Champion on seven occasions. Yet he saved his best for the Olympic Games – his career reached the heights his family had always hoped for when they sent him away to a training camp at the age of just 10. He was 21 by the time of the Seoul 1988 Olympic Games, and he more than lived up to his tag of favourite. His winning total of 342.5kg in the 62kg class – a category in which he broke six world records – was good enough to have also won gold in the weight category above his own.

He retained his world title a year later, but instead of steeling himself for a period of dominance, Süleymanoğlu stunned the world of weightlifting by retiring. Thankfully for fans of the sport, his time away from competition was short-lived as he reversed his decision in time to compete in the Barcelona 1992 Olympic Games. Again, there was to be no questioning his supremacy. Another gold medal was his reward, although he needed

to lift 'only' 320kg to seal a second successive Olympic Games victory by 15kg from Bulgarian Nikolay Pechalov.

However, it was to be much tougher for Süleymanoğlu when the Atlanta 1996 Games came around. The 62kg competition quickly developed into a classic, as Süleymanoğlu and Valerios Leonidis of Greece matched each other lift for lift. World records were broken, with few expecting Leonidis to beat his rival's lift of 185kg. Yet the Greek was not to be deterred, and raised the world-record mark by 2.5kg. That put the pressure squarely back on Süleymanoğlu, who knew he had to match that total of 187.5kg if he was to become the first weightlifter ever to win

three successive golds. It was a chance to make history and Süleymanoğlu was not prepared to let it pass him by – he tied the world record to claim victory once more.

He retired again shortly afterwards and, despite an unsuccessful comeback for the Sydney 2000 Games at 33, he will be remembered as a legend of his sport. Süleymanoğlu was awarded the Olympic Order in 2001. If he was not so strong, he might have struggled under the weight of all his medals.

Statistics
Born: 23 January 1967, Ptichar, Bulgaria
Height: 4ft 11in (1.5m)
Weight: 141lb (64kg)

Olympic Games Medals
Seoul 1988
Men's 56kg ....Gold

Barcelona 1992
Men's 56kg ....Gold

Atlanta 1996
Men's 64kg ....Gold

Above: Standing only 1.5m tall, yet able to lift almost three times his body weight, Süleymanoğlu became the first weightlifter to win gold in three consecutive Olympic Games.

Right: The Bulgaria-born Turk on his way to another world record and another gold medal in the Men's 62kg category, this time at the Atlanta 1996 Olympic Games.

*'Silver or bronze is nothing for me. I am only
satisfied with gold.'*

SUSI **SUSANTI**
BADMINTON

INDONESIA

Susi Susanti wrote her name into the record books at the Barcelona 1992 Games, when she became the first ever female Badminton champion. It was the sport's debut in the Olympic Games, and the Indonesian maestro had the perfect tournament as she progressed without dropping a game en route to glory. She then followed up that success with a bronze medal four years later in Atlanta 1996.

Statistics

Born: 11 February 1971, Tsikmalaya, Indonesia
Height: 5ft 3in (1.6m)
Weight: 115lb (52kg)

Olympic Games Medals

Barcelona 1992
Women's Singles.....................................Gold

Atlanta 1996
Women's Singles..............................Bronze

When Badminton made its Olympic debut back in 1992, it needed a champion who could prove that the sport was there to stay. In Susi Susanti, it got exactly that.

The Indonesian was only 5ft 3in (1.6m), but her superb footwork and elegant style won her a host of new admirers, including the winner of the Men's Singles, Alan Budikusuma, who is now her husband and father of her three children.

Susanti was the dominant player of her era, winning virtually every tournament on offer in the early to mid-1990s, with the Olympic Games being the icing on the cake. She won the All England Singles title in 1990, 1991, 1993 and 1994, and was also crowned World Champion in 1993. Having won the Olympic Games gold a year previously, that World Championship victory ensured she was the first woman to hold the titles of Olympic, World and All England champion at the same time.

And her superiority was superbly demonstrated in Barcelona 1992. After being given a bye through the first round she beat Harumi Kohara, Wong Chun Fan and Jaroensiri Somhasurthai to reach the semi-finals. She had been playing at her very best, and Huang Hua, her great Chinese rival, was simply unable to compete. Susanti won 2–0 for the fourth successive time as she eased into the final, where she faced Bang Su-Hyeon. The Korean was to become a mainstay at the top table of women's badminton players, and four years later she went on to win Olympic gold. But Susanti was simply unstoppable in Barcelona, and another 2–0 victory completed the perfect competition. She had played five matches and had not lost a game on her way to becoming the first female Olympic champion in Badminton history. It was now beyond question that she was the best in the world, possibly ever.

And Susanti set about maintaining her position in the years after 1992. It could indeed be argued that 1993 was her finest year, with her victories in the All England and World Championships, and she was again the woman to beat as the Olympic Flame headed to the United States and Atlanta in 1996. Her first two ties, against Doris Piche and Katarzyna Krasowska, saw her extend her perfect Olympic record to seven matches without dropping a set, and although Han Jingna pushed her to the limit in the quarter-finals, Susanti still won 2–1. Yet her perfect record went up in smoke in the semi-finals as Bang had her revenge. Susanti was well below her best, and it was her turn to be on the wrong end of a 2–0 defeat as Bang breezed into the final, which she won. There was still to be a medal for Susanti, though, as she beat Kim Ji-Hyeon of South Korea to take the bronze.

The 1996 Games were to be her last, however. In 1997 Susanti married Budikusuma and announced her retirement from badminton. It was perhaps a premature end to her sporting career, but Susanti had done more than enough to secure her place in the pantheon of Olympic greats, and her achievements were rewarded when she was given a place in the International Badminton Federation Hall of Fame in 2004.

Below: Susanti retired in 1997 and married Alan Budikusuma, who also won gold at the 1992 Games. They run a badminton club in north Jakarta.

Right: Widely regarded as the finest female badminton player Indonesia has ever produced, Susanti dominated women's Singles from the early to mid-1990s.

'I was happy to accept the award and thanked all the Indonesian people who have made it possible for me to receive it.'

Susi Susanti after being inducted into the International Badminton Federation's Hall of Fame

IRENA **SZEWINSKA**
ATHLETICS

Irena Szewińska is undoubtedly one of the greatest female athletes of all time, winning medals in four consecutive Olympic Games, a feat never accomplished before by any runner – male or female. In 1998, her status was upgraded in Olympic circles when she was named a member of the International Olympic Committee.

Born to Polish-Jewish parents in the Soviet city of Leningrad (now St Petersburg), Irena Szewińska returned to Poland at an early age and it was clear that her parents had a prodigious talent on their hands – but it was not clear how far she would go. But as the years passed, it became obvious the track and field genius possessed the ability to dominate as a sprinter and a jumper. Her first Olympic Games gave everyone a glimpse of what was to come.

While mere mortals can only dream of conquering the world as a teenager, Szewińska was no normal athlete. At just 18, she stormed to success at the Tokyo 1964 Games, securing her first gold medal as a member of Poland's world-record-setting women's 4 x 100m Relay team, with a time of 43.6 seconds.

The result in the Women's 4 x 100m Relay final stunned spectators, with the much-fancied United States beaten into second place, despite fielding the intimidating Wyomia Tyus and Edith McGuire, who had won the Women's 100m and 200m events respectively. However, they could not compete with Szewińska's team – a star had been born. In the same Olympic Games, she secured a silver medal in the 200m and her time of 23.10 seconds set a European record.

But Szewińska was just as prolific in the field. In a remarkable Olympic Games debut, she claimed a silver medal in the Long Jump and was only denied gold by a world-record set by Great Britain's Mary Rand. That aside, this was still the start of Szewińska's era of dominance – a spell that would span five Olympic Games.

At the Mexico City 1968 Games, four years after her debut, and now competing under her married name of Kirszenstein-Szewińska, she once again blew away her sprint competitors. She won the 200m event and set a new world record of 22.5 seconds, breaking her own record set three years earlier. Her ever-increasing medal haul grew with a bronze in the 100m event, although this time the American sprinter Tyus had the final say, winning the gold to avenge her 4 x 100m Relay defeat in Tokyo 1964.

Szewińska's athletic prowess was not entirely restricted to the Olympic Games; as well as her

Statistics
Born: 24 May 1946, St Petersburg, Russia
Height: 5ft 9in (1.75m)
Weight: 132lb (60kg)

Olympic Games Medals
Tokyo 1964
Women's 4 x 100m Relay...................Gold
Women's Long Jump..........................Silver
Women's 200m ....Silver

Mexico City 1968
Women's 200m ....Gold
Women's 100m................................. Bronze

Munich 1972
Women's 200m .... Bronze

Montreal 1976
Women's 400m.......................................Gold

Left: Szewińska established and maintained an outstanding all-round record at the highest level, including competing at five Olympic Games between Tokyo 1964 and Moscow 1980.

Right: The Soviet-born Pole first came to international attention as an 18-year-old at the Tokyo 1964 Games, competing under her maiden name of Kirszenstein.

'I have often been asked whether I was bored with Athletics. I have always replied "no". Sport is my passion. Together with my family, it has brought me all the joys of the world.'

three gold, two silvers and two bronzes, she won five European Championships gold medals, but it was thanks to her showings on the grandest stage that she became a household name.

The defending 200m champion lost her title at the Munich 1972 Olympic Games but, as per usual, she picked up a medal, finishing in the bronze position. It was, however, in Montreal 1976 that her performances would define her as one of the greatest athletes ever to have graced the Olympic Games.

She might have started out as a 100m, 200m and Long Jump specialist, but having decided to focus on the 400m, Szewińska showed, by her performance in the Montreal 1976 Games, that she was right to make the switch. Already the first woman to run 400m in under 50 seconds, with a time of 49.90 at Warsaw's Kusociski Memorial athletics meet earlier in the year, in the 400m in the 1976 Games, she won by around 10 metres with another world-record time of 49.29, justifying her billing as one of the all-time greats.

RYOKO **TANI**
JUDO

To win medals at five Olympic Games is an astonishing achievement, but Japanese *judoka* Ryoko Tani has had no ordinary career. Standing at just 4ft 9in (1.45m), Tani has dominated the world of Women's Extra Lightweight judo for a generation, winning seven World Championships between 1993 and 2007 to go with her two Olympic golds.

If you are going to carry the hopes of a nation at the Olympic Games you need to be a person of stature – and despite being under five feet tall, Ryoko Tani has always risen to the big occasion. A huge celebrity in Japan, Tani – who went under her maiden name of Tamura until her high-profile wedding to Japanese baseball star Yoshitomo Tani in 2003 – went 12 years without losing in a major competition between 1996 and 2008. Her only regrets may be that her defeats at either end of that run both came in the Olympic Games, but having become the first female Judo wrestler to win consecutive gold medals, at Sydney 2000 and Athens 2004, she has still proved her pre-eminence in the sport.

Tani has certainly come a long way since she burst on to the scene aged just 16 in 1992. She stormed to the final in Barcelona 1992 before coming up short against reigning World Champion Cecile Nowak of France. Her response to that defeat was unequivocal, as she went on an incredible 84-match winning streak, claiming the 1993 and 1995 World Championship titles. Yet to her immense frustration, that astonishing record came to an end in the most crucial bout of all – the Atlanta 1996 Olympic Games final.

While Tani had been the unheralded youngster who made an impact four years previously, this time it was the turn of North Korean 16-year-old Kye Sun-Hui, who came from nowhere to take the world of judo by storm. Tani was a huge favourite going into the gold-medal match, but she was surprised by her opponent's aggressive tactics and was unable to establish any sort of rhythm as she saw gold slip away.

With two silver medals to her name, the pressure on Tani was huge as the Sydney 2000 Games approached at the end of another unbeaten four-year period. Her dreams nearly came crashing down in the semi-finals as she narrowly beat Cha Hyon-Hyang, but she progressed to her third consecutive Olympic final. Her performance left no argument as to who was the best *judoka* in the world, as she crushed Lyubov Bruletova of Russia, winning after scoring *ippon* thanks to an *uchimata* (inner thigh throw) after just 36 seconds.

In 2003 Tani's profile was raised even further thanks to her wedding, but a year later it was more Olympic glory, this time in the shape of Athens 2004, that dominated her thoughts. Tani's adoring public were not to be disappointed as

Statistics

Born: 6 September 1975, Fukuoka, Japan
Height: 4ft 9in (1.45m)
Weight: 106lb (48kg)

Olympic Games Medals

Barcelona 1992
Women's Extra Lightweight .... Silver

Atlanta 1996
Women's Extra Lightweight .... Silver

Sydney 2000
Women's Extra Lightweight .... Gold

Athens 2004
Women's Extra Lightweight .... Gold

Beijing 2008
Women's Extra Lightweight .... Bronze

Below: Tani's bronze medal in Beijing 2008 placed her in a group of only six female athletes in Olympic history to win medals in five different Olympic Games.

Right: After her bronze medal at Beijing 2008, Tani said: 'The Olympic Games are held once every four years. I have taken part ... five times and now I want to be a good mother.'

she beat Frenchwoman Frédérique Jossinet in the final, becoming the first female *judoka* to retain an Olympic title. It was to be Tani's last taste of glory for three years, however, as she took two years out of competition following the birth of her son. That ended her run of six successive World Championship victories, but she returned in 2007 to claim her seventh title.

She was fit enough to compete in her fifth Olympic Games in Beijing 2008 the following year. Yet her hopes of a third consecutive gold medal disappeared in the semi-finals, when she lost to Romanian Alina Dumitru. Tani did manage to secure the bronze, however, as she beat Lyudmila Bogdanova from Moldova to complete her set of Olympic medals. Her place in the pantheon of Olympic greats is assured, whether or not she competes again in the Olympic Games.

'My goal at Sydney? At best a gold, at worst a gold.'

DALEY **THOMPSON**
ATHLETICS

With his cheeky smile, incredible determination and unquenchable competitive spirit, Daley Thompson CBE is often credited as the man who took the Decathlon to the masses, and after winning Olympic gold medals in Moscow 1980 and Los Angeles 1984 and setting four world records during an illustrious career, he can justly claim to be one of the Olympic Games' greats.

The Decathlon, which features 10 separate track and field disciplines, has to be the greatest test of athletic ability in any sport anywhere in the world, so it is no exaggeration to describe Daley Thompson as one of the most remarkable sportsmen in history.

To say he was a natural athlete would be an understatement, especially when you consider that he won the first two Decathlons he entered in 1975 at the tender age of 17, and finished 18th in the Montreal 1976 Olympic Games a year later having already been crowned Amateur Athletic Association (AAA) champion. By 1979 he had won the first of his three Commonwealth Games gold medals and was well on his way to becoming a serious rival for even the world's very best decathletes, good enough to represent his country in the long jump and sprint relays too.

But it was the Olympic Games that really defined his career and provided the most memorable highlights. His first victory came in Moscow 1980, and within three years he had also added World Championship gold to become the first decathlete to hold the European, World and Olympic titles simultaneously. By this stage of his career the rivalry with German decathlete Jurgen Hingsen had also developed, the competition between them fascinating fans and commentators alike.

The two men seemed to take it in turns to set new world records, each inspiring the other ahead of the Los Angeles 1984 Olympic Games, but once they had arrived in LA, there was only one winner. Thompson went ahead after the opening 100m and never looked back, leading all the way to the end, matching his rival's world record despite easing up in the final event of the competition, the 1,500m.

His victory gripped viewers back home in the UK, where supporters were drawn not only to his competitive spirit but also to his irreverent personality, which made him a natural for

television interviews. Pictures of him holding his medal aloft and sending a message home to friends and colleagues, saying, 'I've got the Big G, boys – the Big G!', only endeared him further and his fame reached an all-time peak.

When the Decathlon's updated scoring tables were introduced and officially backdated Thompson became the sole world record holder ahead of Hingsen with a score of 8,847 – a mark that stood for eight years before it was beaten by American Dan O'Brien, who raised it to 8,891 in 1992. In fact, Thompson's score still stands as a UK record more than a quarter of a century later.

Thompson never quite recreated the heights of Los Angeles 1984 in his later career, although he remained unbeaten in the Decathlon until 1987, which in itself was a prodigious achievement. He missed out on the medals in Seoul 1988, finishing fourth in his fourth Olympic Games, and eventually retired in 1992 due to a persistent hamstring injury. Off the track he was awarded an MBE in 1982, the OBE in 1986 and the CBE in 2000 for his contribution to sport, and he is an ambassador for the London 2012 Games.

Statistics
Born: 30 July 1958, London, England
Height: 6ft (1.83m)
Weight: 203lb (92kg)

Olympic Games Medals
Moscow 1980
Men's Decathlon....................................Gold

Los Angeles 1984
Men's Decathlon....................................Gold

'Being a decathlete is like having ten girlfriends. You have to love them all, and you can't afford losing one.'

Daley Thompson, in his irreverent style, sums up the appeal of the Decathlon

Above: Thompson prepares for the Javelin event at Los Angeles 1984. His eventual gold medal came amidst a run of 12 successive Decathlon victories.

Right: Thompson balances as he prepares for a throw in the Shot Put event of the Decathlon, en route to overall victory in the Los Angeles 1984 Games.

JENNY **THOMPSON**
AQUATICS – SWIMMING

Her 12 medals, including eight golds, make Jenny Thompson the most successful female Olympian ever to compete in the pool. She appeared in four Olympic Games between 1992 and 2004, winning all eight of her golds in Relay events, never quite managing to clinch an individual title.

Jenny Thompson once said she could swim before she could walk. Those who watched her dominate swimming during the 1990s and become the most decorated female American Olympian ever could well believe that. Thompson's was a dramatic career, full of highs and lows, from her race-winning performances in the Relays to her failure to win an individual gold even when she was the best in the world. Gymnast Larissa Latynina, with nine gold medals, is the only woman to have come first more times in Olympic history.

Thompson's exceptional talent was evident by the age of 14, when she competed for her country for the first time. In fact, she became the youngest American gold-medal swimmer when she won the 50m Freestyle at the 1987 Pan-American Games. She earned a reputation for being fast, strong and fiercely competitive, and soon Thompson was lining up at the Barcelona 1992 Games as race favourite. She went into those Olympic Games in the form of her life after breaking the world record for the 100m Freestyle with a time of 54.48 seconds at the USA trials.

However, Thompson had to settle for silver in her best event, the 100m Freestyle, after she was placed second to China's Zhuang Yong with a time of 54.84. Thompson's frustration and disappointment grew as she could only finish fifth in the 50m and did not even reach the 200m final, two events she was expected to win medals in. But in typically defiant fashion she responded by winning two gold medals as part of the 4 x 100m Freestyle Relay and 4 x 100m Medley Relay teams.

Thompson always kept her swimming in perspective, and she had other interests that compelled her to enrol at Stanford University to study for a degree in human biology. Since her retirement she has qualified as a doctor and now works as an anaesthetist.

While at Stanford, Thompson was part of a dominant college swimming team, but of course it was at the Olympic Games where it really counts. She went into the Atlanta 1996 Games seemingly past her best, with the career span of swimmers considered to be much shorter than in most other sports. A poor showing in the trials

Statistics
Born: 26 February 1973, Danvers, Massachusetts, USA
Height: 5ft 10in (1.78m)
Weight: 152lb (69kg)

Olympic Games Medals
Barcelona 1992
Women's 4 x 100m Freestyle Relay.....Gold
Women's 4 x 100m Medley Relay ....Gold
Women's 100m Freestyle.........................Silver

Atlanta 1996
Women's 4 x 100m Freestyle Relay.....Gold
Women's 4 x 200m Freestyle Relay....Gold
Women's 4 x 100m Medley Relay ....Gold

Sydney 2000
Women's 4 x 100m Freestyle Relay.....Gold
Women's 4 x 200m Freestyle Relay....Gold
Women's 4 x 100m Medley Relay ....Gold
Women's 100m Freestyle.................... Bronze

Athens 2004
Women's 4 x 100m Freestyle Relay.....Silver
Women's 4 x 100m Medley Relay ....Silver

Left: Thompson waves to her supporters at the Athens 2004 Games, where she bowed out of Olympic competition with two silver medals.

Right: No one said it was going to get any easier – Thompson displays her trademark determination as she swims for Olympic glory.

meant that Thompson was not able to enter any Individual swimming events in Atlanta, but despite this she competed in three gold-medal-winning Relay teams: the 4 x 100m Freestyle, the 4 x 100m Medley and the 4 x 200m Freestyle. Thompson's form picked up and she won three World Championships in a row in the 100m Freestyle heading into the Sydney 2000 Games.

Once again, she could not win that elusive Individual gold and had to settle for bronze in the 100m Freestyle, but she swam the anchor leg to take gold and help the USA team defend their titles in the 4 x 100m and 4 x 200m Freestyle Relays, while swimming the Butterfly leg in the winning 4 x 100m Medley Relay team.

She retired after Sydney 2000 to concentrate on her studies, but Thompson made a comeback for Athens 2004. At the age of 31, she was the oldest member of the USA Swimming and Diving team. To cap her career she earned silvers in the 4 x 100m Freestyle and 4 x 100m Medley Relays, taking her total medals tally to 12 and cementing her status as an Olympic superstar.

'What keeps me going is finding out how far I can push myself. How fast can I be? How long can I stay on top? That striving for excellence, that feeling of knowing you have trained till you don't have one drop of energy left, that's what keeps me happy.'

IAN **THORPE**
AQUATICS – SWIMMING

AUSTRALIA

Ian Thorpe would have been hailed as one of the finest swimmers in history no matter where or when he won his five gold medals. But the fact that the Australian thrived under the pressure of competing in front of his home crowd in the Sydney 2000 Games, where he won three of those golds, marks him out as a special talent and guarantees him a place in the annals of the sport.

One of the great ironies about Ian Thorpe's success as a swimmer is that when he took up the sport aged just eight he was diagnosed with an allergy to chlorine. The condition faded over time, but many of 'Thorpedo's' rivals would have been left praying that it resurfaced, such was his dominance over two successive Olympic Games.

An astonishing physical specimen, Thorpe burst on to the scene at an early age. He won the 400m Freestyle in the World Championships in Perth in 1998 when he was just 15. That was not his only gold medal of those championships, though, as he was part of the 4 x 200m Relay team. Thorpe was making waves, yet just in case anyone had missed him he then won four golds in that year's Commonwealth Games in Malaysia.

Medals were stacking up, but the one thing Thorpe had yet to do was break any world records. That all changed in 1999, when he claimed the Short Course 200m Freestyle world record in a time of 1:43.28. As the Sydney 2000

Olympic Games approached, the pressure grew on the youngster, who was then aged just 17. The front-page headline of Sydney's *Daily Telegraph* labelled him 'Invincible', and on the first day of the competition it seemed that was the case. First up was the 400m Freestyle, and despite a challenge from Italian Massimiliano Rosolino, Thorpe was always in control. The Australian came home in a time of 3:40.59 – setting yet another world record. Later the same evening he was part of the victorious 4 x 100m Freestyle team, but those celebrations were cut short the following day when Thorpe could only finish second to Pieter van den Hoogenband in the 200m Freestyle, although his pain was eased when he picked up gold in the 4 x 200m Relay.

By the time the Athens 2004 Olympic Games rolled around, Thorpe had amassed another 15 gold medals over two World Championships and the Commonwealth Games. But personal disaster struck when he false-started in the heats for selection for the 400m, and he was fortunate

Statistics
Born: 13 October 1982, Sydney, Australia
Height: 6ft 5in (1.95m)
Weight: 229lb (104kg)

Olympic Games Medals
Sydney 2000
Men's 400m Freestyle ....Gold
Men's 4 x 100m Freestyle Relay .....Gold
Men's 4 x 200m Freestyle Relay.....Gold
Men's 200m Freestyle .... Silver
Men's 4 x 100m Medley Relay ...... Silver

Athens 2004
Men's 200m Freestyle ....Gold
Men's 400m Freestyle ....Gold
Men's 4 x 200m Freestyle Relay ... Silver
Men's 100m Freestyle .... Bronze

Below: Ian Thorpe holds up yet another medal, this time from the Men's 100m Freestyle final in Athens 2004. His amazing swimming career turned him into a superstar.

Right: The 'Thorpedo' powers through the water on his way to the finals of the Men's 100m Freestyle in Athens 2004.

enough to be reprieved when Craig Stevens, who had finished second, relinquished his place, allowing Thorpe to compete in Athens. When it came to it, Thorpe was worth the fuss. He was not at his best in the 400m but held off the challenge of fellow Australian Grant Hackett, before his crowning glory in the 200m. Billed as 'The Race of the Century', Thorpe held off the challenge of van den Hoogenband, Hackett and Michael Phelps to take gold in a new Olympic record time of 1:44.71. Silver in the 4 x 200m Freestyle and a bronze in the 100m Freestyle ended another stunning Olympic Games for the Australian swimmer.

Yet that was to be Thorpe's final impact. Glandular fever and a broken hand forced him to withdraw from the 2006 Melbourne Commonwealth Games, and he announced his retirement on 21 November 2006. With five Olympic gold medals, three silvers and a bronze, Ian's career marks him out as a true legend.

'For myself, losing is not coming second. It's getting out of the water knowing you could have done better. For myself, I have won every race I've been in.'

JIM **THORPE**
ATHLETICS

USA

The half Native American, half Irish-American is widely hailed as the greatest athlete of the 20th century, an all-round sportsman and champion of many. Yet, after winning gold in the very first genuine Olympic Games Pentathlon and Decathlon events, he was wrongly stripped of his medals just a year later.

His Native American name, Wa-tho-huck, meaning 'Bright Path', was given to him by the Sac and Fox tribe on the Indian reservation in Oklahoma where he was born. Little did they know then how brightly the light at the end of this road would shine, as he went on to be declared the 'Greatest Athlete of the First Half-Century' in an American press award in 1950.

But, with an Irish-American father, he was also christened Jacobus Franciscus Thorpe, to give him the best chance of success in the American-Indian schools set up by the US government, two of which he attended, most famously the Carlisle Industrial Indian School in Pennsylvania. To say that he achieved success there would be an understatement, as the man the sporting world came to know as Jim Thorpe defined what it meant to be an all-round sportsman – a master, not a jack, of all trades.

After becoming his school's best American football and track and field star, the stocky yet agile man progressed to become his country's greatest American football player before World War I, and would later be inducted into the sport's Hall of Fame.

On the football field he was said to be accomplished in any position, and those attributes led to an invitation to take his versatility, determination and natural athletic gift on to the track. He sailed with the US team to Europe for the Stockholm 1912 Olympic Games, training hard on board the ship as it made the long Atlantic crossing, and was drafted in as the United States' main Pentathlon prospect after dominating their trials.

In the first Modern Pentathlon event on 7 July, he demolished the field in four of the five sports, easily winning the 200m and 1,500m, the Discus Throw and the Long Jump, and finishing third in the Javelin Throw. He also found time to come fourth in the individual High Jump and seventh

in the Long Jump, impressing US team officials to such an extent that they quickly put him up for the Decathlon too. He did not let them down either, winning four of the events outright and finishing in the top four of every single one. He won the gold medal with an unprecedented 8,413 points – a record that would stand for nearly 20 years and would have earned him a silver medal at the London 1948 Olympic Games.

After handing out his medals, the king of Sweden pulled Thorpe aside for a second to say, 'Sir, you are the greatest athlete in the world.' 'Thank you, King,' he responded before returning to America to throngs of people at his very own ticker-tape parade in New York City – the most heroic of all-American welcomes. 'I heard people yelling my name,' he said, 'and I couldn't realise how one fellow could have so many friends.'

Statistics

Born: 28 May 1888, Bellemont, Oklahoma, USA
Died: 28 March 1953
Height: 6ft (1.83m)
Weight: 190lb (86kg)

Olympic Games Medals
Stockholm 1912
Men's Pentathlon.................................Gold
Men's Decathlon.................................Gold

Below: A professional American footballer and baseball player later in life, Thorpe is regarded by some as America's greatest all-round athlete ever.

Right: Thorpe set world records in the Pentathlon and Decathlon, both of which included the Discus Throw, at the 1912 Stockholm Olympic Games.

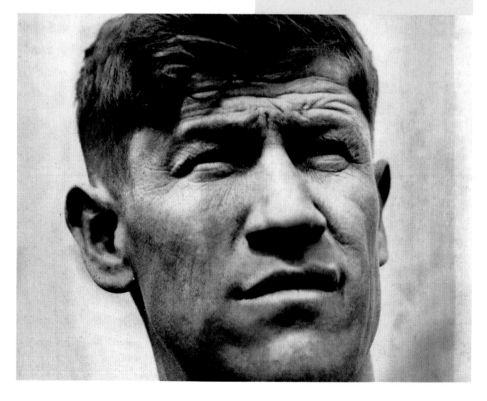

However, the tears of joy would soon turn bitter. Thorpe was painfully stripped of his medals just a year later, but not his dignity. The Olympic Committee declared his successes illegitimate after it was found he had violated amateur rules, having competed at semi-professional level for a minor-league baseball team. Clearly hurt by this very public removal of his status, he never competed in another Olympic trial, let alone event, claiming he had played baseball 'for the love of the game, not the money'. In a display of defiance, he concentrated the rest of his sporting career on playing baseball and American football for the New York Giants. He is one of only two men ever to have played for the Giants in two different sports.

Meanwhile, his family campaigned to have his 1912 records and medals reinstated. They eventually succeeded, but not until 1982, almost 30 years after the death of possibly America's greatest ever all-round athlete.

'Sir, you are the greatest athlete in the world.'

King Gustav V of Sweden, upon awarding Thorpe his second gold medal of the Stockholm 1912 Games

GWEN **TORRENCE**
ATHLETICS

USA

Undoubtedly one of the most versatile sprinters of all time, the American athlete was lightning fast on all counts, winning Olympic medals at 100m, 200m and 400m and ranking first in all three disciplines. Gwen Torrence is also remembered for her strong opinions, becoming something of a heroine for speaking out against doping in athletics.

It's a shame Gwen Torrence has never expressed a desire to become a television pundit, as it is for her forthright opinions and blunt delivery that she will be remembered – that and her adaptability and brilliance at every sprint event on the track. Torrence, more than most, felt she had the right to articulate her feelings about every opponent when she was inducted into the USA Track and Field Hall of Fame after a career that has marked her as possibly the fastest all-rounder of the last quarter-century.

Spending her first days in an incubator after complications at birth was possibly the only time Torrence kept still, with her career constantly moving forward. She was spotted first by high school coach Ray Bonner, as she chased down and caught the fastest member of the school's American football team after he'd stolen her notebook. Bonner would train her to become first High School champion, next the State's best, then University and All-American champion, winning an array of track and field honours before storming the trials for the Seoul 1988 Olympic Games by which time she would turn 23.

Torrence went into Seoul 1988 already labelled as 'the girl to beat' but came away tagged a 'sore loser' as she was defeated by her compatriot Florence Griffith-Joyner, who set a world record for the 200m. Of this Torrence said: 'There's no way! A 21.9 to a 21.3? It doesn't happen that way.' But she refused to let any controversies dampen her resolve and returned for the Barcelona 1992 Olympic Games even stronger.

After more questionable performances at the World Championships a year earlier, with Torrence denied gold from second place after Katrin Krabbe's disqualification for failing a drugs test, she was determined to emerge as the 'pure' victor. She did so, bounding to Olympic gold in the 200m and 4 x 100m Relay and picking up silver in the 4 x 400m Relay along the way. But after finishing just outside the medals in the

100m, she labelled two of the top three 'dirty', and lit the touchpaper. Torrence, though, proudly defended her stance: 'I was going to try to get control of the drug problem some kind of way,' she explained.

She would continue her pursuit of fair competition while becoming number one in the world at all three of her chosen running events: 100m, 200m and 400m. For her outspoken defiance, however, she would become an isolated figure, criticised by fellow competitors at each championship, and by the press too.

It was perhaps the personal attack from her idol, Jamaican Merlene Ottey, that finally broke her resolve. Despite still heading the rankings in all three sprint disciplines she admitted Ottey's comments 'hurt', and only managed a solitary bronze medal by herself, despite winning gold in the 4 x 100m Relay at the Atlanta 1996 Games.

Torrence has now fulfilled another lifelong dream, that of becoming a hair stylist, and is said to deny being 'the three-time Olympic gold medallist Gwen Torrence' when stopped by fans in the street. But, however fast she moves, Torrence can never avoid being recognised as one of the fastest and most genuinely competitive women ever to take part in the Olympic Games.

Statistics
Born: 12 June 1965, Decatur, Georgia, USA
Height: 5ft 7in (1.7m)
Weight: 126lb (57kg)

Olympic Games Medals
Barcelona 1992
Women's 200m ....Gold
Women's 4 x 100m Relay...................Gold
Women's 4 x 400m Relay............... Silver

Atlanta 1996
Women's 4 x 100m Relay...................Gold
Women's 100m.................................. Bronze

Below: Torrence celebrates on the podium with the bronze medal she won in the Women's 100m at the Atlanta 1996 Olympic Games.

Right: Torrence sprinting to third place at Atlanta 1996. It was to be her last Olympic Games, as she retired from competitive sport a year later.

'I'm not afraid to say what I think. I'm not like
Jackie Joyner-Kersee, nice to everyone.'

DARA **TORRES**
AQUATICS – SWIMMING

USA

Dara Torres has won 12 medals over five Olympic Games, but the simple statistics barely do justice to the legendary American swimmer. Some 24 years after winning her first Olympic Games medal, the 41-year-old mother claimed three silver medals in Beijing 2008, becoming not only the oldest ever swimmer to win a medal but also only the seventh woman to stand on the podium at five different Games.

Records are there to be broken, but there is a sense that Dara Torres' astonishing Olympic achievements may never be surpassed. She had already won four Olympic medals by the time she came out of retirement for the Sydney 2000 Olympic Games, but, despite being the oldest member of the US team at 33, she claimed a further five, including two golds. Seemingly satisfied with her haul she retired again – only to return eight years later for the Beijing 2008 Games.

The 41-year-old was now the oldest swimmer in Olympic history, but she swiftly became the oldest ever medallist, winning three silver medals as she set about proving single-handedly that age is just a number. Yet the boot was firmly on the other foot when Torres started her Olympic career in her home town of Los Angeles in 1984. Aged just 17, she had started swimming a decade before and had been competing in international competitions at the age of 14. She was entered in

the 4 x 100m Freestyle Relay – an event in which she has now won five medals – and swam her individual split in 55.92 seconds, as the American team beat the Netherlands and West Germany to take the gold medal.

Four years later, at the Seoul 1988 Games, there was to be no gold, but by the time the competition was over she had a full set of medals, taking silver in the 4 x 100m Medley Relay and bronze in the 4 x 100m Freestyle Relay. Torres also entered the individual 100m Freestyle, but came seventh – the only time she has entered an Olympic event and not won a medal.

By the time the Barcelona 1992 Games came around, she had decided to concentrate on the 4 x 100m Freestyle Relay. It was to prove a fine choice, as she swam a time of 55.33 seconds to help America to gold in a world-record time. Torres announced her retirement after the Games, deciding that she had nothing left to prove. After embarking on a successful modelling career, as well as promoting a fitness training method, she stunned the world of swimming by announcing her comeback in time for the Sydney 2000 Olympic Games.

She began her comeback in 1998, giving herself little time to get up to speed, but was virtually unstoppable in Sydney 2000. She won her first ever individual medals, claiming bronze in the 50m and 100m Freestyle and another bronze in the 100m Butterfly. But it was in the team events that Torres was again at her best, as she led the US women's squads to gold in both the 4 x 100m Freestyle Relay and the 4 x 100m Medley Relay – setting world-record times in both events.

Torres decided that now she really had achieved all she could in the sport, retiring for a second time and becoming a mother after giving birth to her daughter, Tessa. But in 2006 she made her second comeback. It was again to

Statistics
Born: 15 April 1967, Beverly Hills, California, USA
Height: 6ft (1.83m)
Weight: 150lb (68kg)

Olympic Games Medals
Los Angeles 1984
Women's 4 x 100m Freestyle Relay...Gold

Seoul 1988
Women's 4 x 100m Medley Relay ... Silver
Women's 4 x 100m Freestyle
Relay...Bronze

Barcelona 1992
Women's 4 x 100m Freestyle Relay...Gold

Sydney 2000
Women's 4 x 100m Freestyle Relay...Gold
Women's 4 x 100m Medley Relay ......Gold
Women's 100m Freestyle................ Bronze
Women's 50m Freestyle .... Bronze
Women's 100m Butterfly................ Bronze

Beijing 2008
Women's 4 x 100m Freestyle Relay .. Silver
Women's 4 x 100m Medley Relay ... Silver
Women's 50m Freestyle .... Silver

Left: Only silver this time, but still a smile from the popular American at the Beijing 2008 Games.

Right: Torres in action in the 100m Butterfly in Sydney 2000, where she added bronze to her amazing medal tally.

prove hugely successful. Winning the US heats for both the 50m and 100m Freestyle, she chose to concentrate on the 50m and 4 x 100m Freestyle and Medley Relays.

Aged 41, she was the oldest ever Olympic swimmer, and she came agonisingly close to winning her first individual gold at Beijing 2008.

Her time of 24.07 seconds would have been a new Olympic record, but German Britta Steffen beat her by one-hundredth of a second. That medal was Torres' third silver of the Games, after the US team's performances in the 4 x 100m Freestyle Relay and 4 x 100m Medley Relay, giving her an astonishing list of records.

She is now one of just three Olympians to hold four medals of each colour, and is tied with swimmer Jenny Thompson for the most medals ever won by an American woman. And with Torres still not officially announcing her retirement, there is a chance she might make another amazing reappearance on the world scene.

'If it helps anyone else out there who ... put off something they thought they couldn't do because they were too old, or maybe thought that because they have children they can't balance what they want to do and be a parent, then I'm absolutely thrilled.'

Dara Torres after the Beijing 2008 Games

HUBERT **VAN INNIS**
ARCHERY

An astonishing 20 years passed between Hubert Van Innis' first and second Olympic Games, but from just two Olympic appearances the Belgian carved out a reputation as the ultimate archer. Six of his nine Olympic medals were gold, and he might well have become the most successful Olympian ever had he been able to compete in the intervening Games.

As an architect in his professional life, Hubert Van Innis relied on absolute precision. It was with similar unerring accuracy that he fired arrows into targets. Stronger over the shorter distances, he won two golds at the Paris 1900 Games and four more in Antwerp 1920, as well as adding three silvers in the process. Van Innis' medal count certainly benefited from the exceptional number of Archery events held at those Games, but he still established himself as one of the most successful Olympians in history, despite missing the St Louis 1904 and London 1908 Games and Archery not being held in Stockholm 1912.

At the first Games of the 20th century in Paris and the inaugural Olympic Archery competition, Van Innis competed in four events, winning the Men's 33m Au Cordon Doré and Au Chapelet while coming second in the 50m Au Cordon Doré. The era in which Van Innis competed was very different from today and times have certainly changed since his heyday. When Van Innis started his Olympic career, the prize for coming first was not a gold medal but silver, while second place was rewarded with bronze. The IOC had retrospectively to reassign Van Innis gold medals for his two victories in 1900, where only French and Belgian competitors advanced to the final round.

While Van Innis dominated at 33m, the chasing pack was closer to him over the longer distances. He finished only a disappointing fourth in the 50m Au Chapelet event of 1900 and came second in the 50m Au Cordon Doré, just two points behind Henri Herouin. An incredible 20-year hiatus followed and by the time he next appeared at a Games, Van Innis was aged 54 and arguably beyond his best. In his prime years, Van Innis had missed the St Louis 1904 Games, where only competitors from the host nation took part in the Archery events; nor did he make the trip to the UK for the 1908 London Games. The Stockholm 1912 Games did not include Archery and the 1916 Games were cancelled because of World War I. All of which meant that two decades had passed before Van Innis next picked up his arrows in Olympic competition.

It was due to great Belgian interest that Archery was reinstated for the Antwerp 1920 Olympic Games. But records and descriptions of the Archery competition at these Games are very obscure, perhaps due to the fact that only three countries – Belgium, France and the Netherlands – participated. In an insight to just how far the Modern Olympic Games have developed since their inception, the Archery competition was simply held in a park in Antwerp.

The structure of the competition was very different to the event we are familiar with today. There were two types of contest: the 'fixed bird' events, for which contestants shot at small birds attached to crossbeams on a long pole; and the so-called 'moving bird target' events, which – despite the name – were actually a lot closer to the target Archery events that make up the modern-day Olympic programme.

The host country dominated and Van Innis was their star Olympian, taking his overall medal haul to six golds and three silvers. He secured Individual golds in the 28m and 33m Moving Bird Target competition. He scored 144 and 139 points in the two events respectively, but was beaten to silver in the 50m competition, only managing 106 points. In the Team contests, Van Innis benefited from the strength in depth of Belgian archery, as the host country won two of the three Team Moving Bird Target events, with Van Innis leading the way.

After his success in 1920, Archery was not seen again as an Olympic sport during Van Innis' lifetime, but he was still winning World Championships in team competitions in 1933, at the age of 67.

Although the format of Archery at the modern Olympic Games has moved on significantly since his day, Van Innis will always be regarded as one of the best ever in his sport.

Statistics
Born: 24 February 1866, Elewijt, Vlaams-Brabant, Belgium
Died: 25 November 1961

Olympic Games Medals
Paris 1900
Men's Au Chapelet, 33m..............Gold
Men's Au Cordon Doré, 33m ....Gold
Men's Au Cordon Doré, 50m ...... Silver

Antwerp 1920
Men's Individual Moving
    Bird Target, 28m ....Gold
Men's Individual Moving
    Bird Target, 33m ....Gold
Men's Team Moving
    Bird Target, 33m ....Gold
Men's Team Moving
    Bird Target, 50m ....Gold
Men's Team Moving
    Bird Target, 28m .... Silver
Men's Individual Moving
    Bird Target, 50m................... Silver

Right: Van Innis had to wait 20 years between appearances at Olympic Games. This didn't bother him though. His extraordinary ability was born from a lifelong passion for the sport.

'*Kim Soo-Nyung was to women's archery what Belgian Hubert van Innis was to the men's.*'

Hubert Van Innis is compared favourably to the best archer ever

ESTHER **VERGEER**
WHEELCHAIR TENNIS

NETHERLANDS

Forget Roger Federer or the Williams sisters, this Dutch Paralympian could well be regarded as the most dominant tennis player of all time. Esther Vergeer has been world number one longer than any other tennis player in history – for over 10 years – and did not lose a Singles match in any competition from 2003 going into the summer of 2010, winning gold after gold at the last three Paralympic Games.

E sther Vergeer is an outstanding example of a paraplegic sportsperson, refusing to let disability inhibit her ambitions and taking pride in being a role model to those confined to a wheelchair.

An operation to remove haemorrhaging blood vessels from her spine left her without the use of her legs at just eight years old, but within three years she was playing wheelchair basketball and wheelchair tennis, the latter to a level previously thought impossible. Vergeer had one significant source of help early in her career: namely, the Dutch government's policy of providing aspiring paraplegics with a free sports wheelchair and a year's free training in any sport they chose. She welcomed the support and continued with both sports, playing internationally for the Dutch wheelchair basketball team that won the 1997 European Championship. Tennis became a full-time preoccupation a year later. It was a decision that changed the face of the sport.

It was perhaps the upper-body strength gained as a basketball player that provided her with instant, almost scary success, as she became world number one in the sport within a year, but it may also be down to a unique advantage of her disability. Vergeer still has feeling in her left leg and transmits this extra strength diagonally to her right hand when serving, thus turning what is generally thought of as a defence in the sport into attack. There is, moreover, her ruthless sporting mentality. Like any leading athlete Vergeer knows how to exploit an opponent's weaknesses while never allowing a deficiency of her own to deter her. She has even won tournaments playing in a friend's wheelchair, which, because of being set up for someone else's height and weight, she described as like 'playing in high heels'. It didn't stop her.

After almost a year as world number one, she did not lose a single set on the way to her first gold medal, beating fellow compatriot Sharon Walraven in the Sydney 2000 Paralympic final. With Singles bronze medallist Maaike Smit she clinched the Doubles gold undefeated too. Her supremacy in the game has hardly been challenged since.

Vergeer achieved numerous Grand Slam successes before the Athens 2004 Games, where she again won gold without conceding a set. The Doubles gold was also retained with partner Smit. It was not until the Beijing 2008 Singles final, and a heated bout with fellow Dutch competitor Korie Homan, that Vergeer finally lost an Olympic set. After an even battle in the first two sets, the young pretender took a 3–1 lead in the third, but Vergeer ended her countrywoman's run and stormed to victory, winning her 349th consecutive match.

Although Vergeer is in her thirties, age is less of a barrier in Wheelchair Tennis, with athletes known to compete into their forties. That does not bode well for Vergeer's opponents, as her authority looks set to continue, especially since she conducts her domestic life in the manner of a true sporting icon. Few competitors in any field take their discipline as seriously as Vergeer does. For her, the sport is an elite one and she treats it and herself accordingly, saying she would rather train than be out partying.

Statistics
Born: 18 July 1981, Woerden, Netherlands

Paralympic Games Medals
Sydney 2000
Women's Singles....................................Gold
Women's Doubles...............................Gold

Athens 2004
Women's Singles....................................Gold
Women's Doubles...............................Gold

Beijing 2008
Women's Singles....................................Gold
Women's Doubles.............................. Silver

Left: Seen here celebrating at the Beijing 2008 Games, Vergeer knows more about dominating tennis than Rafael Nadal, Roger Federer or the Williams sisters, combined.

Right: Vergeer showing off her strong return during the gold-medal match at the Athens 2004 Paralympic Games which she went on to win.

'If you see it as an elite sport, you have to live your life like a top athlete. I'm not saying I'm a miracle woman, but winning a gold medal is more important than a party.'

VALENTINA **VEZZALI**
FENCING

ITALY

The Olympic Games are all about pushing the boundaries of your sport and hitting new heights. As such, Valentina Vezzali is a true Olympic legend, having dominated the Women's Individual Foil Competition with a determination rarely seen even at the highest levels. Her victory in that event at Beijing 2008 made her only the fourth woman ever to have won gold medals at three consecutive Games.

As a measure of Valentina Vezzali's supremacy in the Individual Foil, one fact stands out – she has lost just one of 21 fights in the Olympic Games, with an unbeaten record standing at an incredible 12 years. The Italian has a bulging trophy cabinet, with her Olympic haul taking pride of place. Three gold medals and one silver in the individual event represents a quite astonishing tally, showing her longevity and ability to produce time and again. Yet Vezzali is very much a team player. In the Team event, she has a further two golds and one bronze medal, giving her a grand total of seven separate Olympic gongs.

But do not be fooled into thinking that she saves her best for the Olympic Games. Her

quickly than in other sports. Don't tell that to Vezzali, though, as she won her third successive individual title at the Beijing 2008 Games at the age of 34.

That success completed an Olympic journey that had started in Atlanta 12 years previously. The Italian's great skill is her ability to counterattack, with her defence so strong that she can riposte to devastating effect. This was first demonstrated when she stormed her way to the final in 1996; her semi-final destruction of French opponent Laurence Modaine-Cessac was particularly impressive. In a sport where the margins are meant to be wafer-thin, the odd point here and there, the fact that Vezzali cruised into the final with a 15–7 victory was remarkable. But

Statistics
Born: 14 February 1974, Jesi, Ancona, Italy
Height: 5ft 5in (1.65m)
Weight: 119lb (54kg)

Olympic Games Medals
Atlanta 1996
Women's Team Foil..............................Gold
Women's Individual Foil................ Silver

Sydney 2000
Women's Individual Foil...................Gold
Women's Team Foil..............................Gold

Athens 2004
Women's Individual Foil...................Gold

Beijing 2008
Women's Individual Foil...................Gold
Women's Team Foil........................ Bronze

record in the World Championships is just as impressive, with five individual and six team golds illustrating how she has dominated her sport for a generation. Fencing is meant to be a sport for younger athletes, with reactions and sleight of hand supposedly slowing even more

she was to be left disappointed: Laura Badea-Carlescu of Romania proved too strong, winning 15–10 and taking gold.

That remains the last fight Vezzali has ever lost in the Individual Foil at Olympic level. But she did not come away empty-handed and won her first

Above: Vezzali celebrates winning the Women's Individual Foil gold-medal match, defeating Nam Hyun-Hee of South Korea at the Beijing 2008 Games.

Right: Vezzali parries a thrust from Hungary's Virginie Ujlaki during the Women's Team Foil bronze-medal match at Beijing 2008.

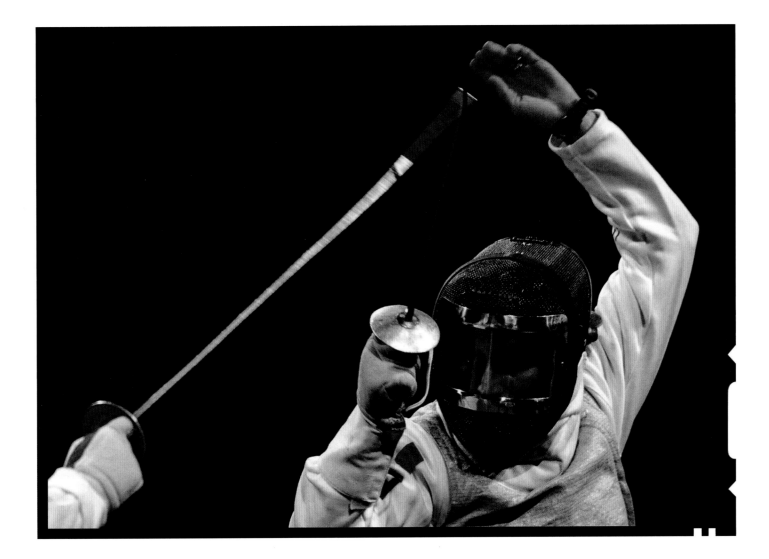

Olympic gold in Atlanta 1996 as part of the Italian team. She was to have her solo revenge four years later at the Sydney 2000 Games. There she met Badea-Carlescu in the semi-finals, and the boot was very much on the other foot as Vezzali won 15–8. Her second Olympic final was, quite simply, a breeze, as she defeated Rita Konig of Germany 15–5. And the perfect Olympic Games was complete when the Italian team retained their title, defeating Poland. As a mark of her skill, Vezzali won every one of her fights in that final.

In Athens 2004, the story was all too familiar for her opponents. A confident run to the final saw her face fellow Italian, and her great personal rival, Giovanna Trillini. Again it was to be Vezzali who walked away with the gold, winning the match 15–11. And as she headed to Beijing four years later, she knew that she was on the verge of making history by winning a third consecutive Olympic gold medal. She was made to work hard for it, though, coming up against a tough opponent in the final in the shape of South

Korean Nam Hyun-Hee. With time running out in a low-scoring fight, Vezzali was 5–4 down with just 41 seconds to go. But her experience and class carried her through, the Italian landing the winning hit with just four seconds to go. She also picked up another medal in the Team event, this time bronze, in what is likely to be the final curtain call for her Olympic career. If that is the last time we see Vezzali in action at the highest level, she will nevertheless retire as a true legend who gave everything to her sport.

'I always gave my life and soul to this sport.'

LASSE **VIRÉN**
ATHLETICS

FINLAND

Another famous 'Flying Finn', Lasse Virén is a legendary figure in long-distance running, winning the 10,000m and 5,000m 'double' at successive Olympic Games, in Munich 1972 and Montreal 1976. He famously fell during the 10,000m in Munich 1972, but remarkably got back on his feet to win gold.

Lasse Virén's achievements are all the more remarkable considering he did not make his international debut until he was 22, by which time he had already signed up as a police officer in Finland. But his rise to fame was quick. Within months he had set a new Finnish record over 5,000m and, having been taken to Kenya for a brutal training regime under coach Rolf Haikkola, set a new world record over two miles. He arrived at the Munich 1972 Games as a dark horse for a medal finish.

During his career he became legendary for timing his training regime perfectly to peak at the Olympic Games – his record shows no other major victories. And he did exactly that in 1972, winning the 10,000m with an outstanding performance. He beat Ron Clarke's seven-year-old world record, despite falling on the 12th lap following a tangle with Emiel Puttemans. The way he jumped back to his feet so quickly to rejoin the pack within 150 metres instantly marked him out as an Olympic legend, especially as he kicked for home with 600 metres to go, winning in 27:38.35. As if that wasn't enough, he then triumphed in the 5,000m, becoming only the fourth athlete ever to complete a long-distance 'double', joining Hannes Kolehmainen, Emil Zátopek and Vladimir Kuts in the record books. He won the 5,000m in 13:26.42, one second ahead of second-placed Tunisian Mohammed Gammoudi.

Four years later, in Montreal 1976, he did it again to complete a 'double double'. His victory in the 10,000m looked simple, keeping up with pacemaker Carlos Lopes of Portugal before passing him to win by 4.79 seconds. Then, in the 5,000m final, he held off the likes of Dick Quax, Rod Dixon and Brendan Foster with a devastating burst from the front over the final laps. In fact, his final 1,500 metres was so fast that his time would have placed him eighth in the 1,500m final the same year. In a thrilling finish four runners sprinted for the tape, Virén winning by less than a second.

Remarkably, he had almost missed the final altogether after controversially taking off his shoes and holding them in the air after the 10,000m final. He was accused of deliberately showing the sponsor's name to the crowd to gain publicity and banned from competing in the 5,000m. But thankfully the decision was overturned on appeal.

The Finn's powers of recovery became legendary after that, not least because he also took part in the Marathon on the day after the 5,000m final, and he finished a more than respectable fifth in 2:13:11. There was one more Olympic Games left in his legs, but his farewell in Moscow 1980 did not produce the medals he was dreaming of. He came fifth in the 10,000m, only grabbing an automatic place in the final when Ireland's John Treacy collapsed with heatstroke in the heats. And he failed to finish in the Marathon, opting to retire from international athletics shortly after the Games were completed.

It was the end of a remarkable career, which made him a national icon in Finland. After retiring, he turned to politics, holding a seat in the Finnish Parliament from 1999 until 2007.

Statistics

Born: 22 July 1949, Mryskyla, Finland
Height: 5ft 11in (1.8m)
Weight: 130lb (59kg)

Olympic Games Medals

Munich 1972

Men's 10,000m..Gold

Men's 5,000m ....Gold

Montreal 1976

Men's 10,000m..Gold

Men's 5,000m ....Gold

Below: The Finn attributed the super powers that helped him to a remarkable Olympic 'double double' to a diet of reindeer milk during training.

Right: Virén wins the 5,000m final at the Munich 1972 Games, with silver-medallist Mohammed Gammoudi (904) and bronze-medallist Ian Stewart (309) close behind.

'*Dream barriers look very high until someone climbs them.*
Then they are not barriers any more.'

WANG NAN
TABLE TENNIS

CHINA

China has dominated the world of women's Table Tennis in recent years, largely due to the stunning achievements of Wang Nan. A four-time Olympic gold medallist, Wang has only won the Singles title once, but her selfless performances in both the Doubles and Team events have made her a true legend of her sport.

Wang Nan's nickname is 'The Smiling Assassin', but you don't become a four-time Olympic champion without being teak-tough. A child prodigy after taking up the sport at the age of seven, within eight years Wang was in China's national team – and, as testament to her longevity and immense talent, she was still winning gold medals 15 years later.

Known and well liked for her happy demeanour both on and off court, she became the leader of the Chinese national team after the retirement of Deng Yaping in 1997, which marked the start of a decade of Olympic glory. A three-time World Champion before the Sydney 2000 Games, Wang was a strong favourite for Olympic gold – and the left-hander did not disappoint. She breezed into the semi-finals against Seoul 1988 Singles champion Chen Jing, and served notice of her intent with a 3–1 victory. That set up a final showdown with Wang's Doubles partner, Li Ju. The final was closer than the semi-final had been, but Wang came through in the decider to win 3–2.

That was Wang's second gold of Sydney 2000, after she and Li had stormed to victory in the Doubles two days before they faced each other in the final of the Singles. A sign of China's dominance in Table Tennis, it was their first- and second-choice teams who met in the gold-medal match – and it was Wang and Li who triumphed over Sun Jin and Yang Ying, claiming a 3–2 victory and the gold medal.

Wang won the next two World Championships, but her campaign in the Singles at the Athens 2004 Olympic Games was a disappointing affair by her high standards. A shock quarter-final defeat to Li Jia Wei of Singapore ended her hopes of a second successive gold in the event. Yet to her immense credit Wang recovered from the blow to produce a superb performance in the Doubles final, which was the following day. Partnered by Zhang Yining, who had succeeded Wang as world number one and had won gold in the Singles event, the pair stormed to the final thanks to victories over Italy, Hong Kong and China's second-choice side. Standing in their way were the South Korean duo of Lee Eun-Sil

Statistics
Born: 23 October 1978, Fushun, China
Height: 5ft 5in (1.65m)
Weight: 132lb (60kg)

Olympic Games Medals

Sydney 2000
Women's Singles ....Gold
Women's Doubles ....Gold

Athens 2004
Women's Doubles ....Gold

Beijing 2008
Women's Team ....Gold
Women's Singles .... Silver

Below: Wang was still delighted to win a silver medal for China in Beijing 2008 as she lost to fellow countrywoman Zhang Yining in the final of the Women's Singles.

Right: Wang in action against Singapore's Feng Tianwei during the Team competition gold-medal match at the Beijing 2008 Olympic Games.

and Seong Eun-Mi, but they were to prove no match for their illustrious opponents. A 4–1 victory was secured with some ease, and with it came Wang's third Olympic gold.

Despite her record Wang came under intense pressure going into the 2008 Olympic Games in her home country, but she raised her game in front of the Beijing crowd. Again she was both helped and hindered by Zhang, who denied her gold in the Singles but played a crucial role as the Chinese team won the Team event – Wang's fourth gold medal. Wang had looked back to her best in the Singles, but found Zhang to be in inspired form in the final and she lost 4–1, although the silver medal no doubt acted as some consolation.

In a quite stunning Olympic Games for the Chinese – their men took a clean sweep of medals in the Singles and Team Table Tennis events – Wang and Zhang were joined by bronze medallist Guo Yue for the Team competition. Understandably clear favourites, the trio lived up to their billing and were simply unstoppable as they hammered Singapore 3–0 in the final in another gold-medal-winning performance. Five Olympic medals, four of them gold, already make Wang a true Olympic legend.

'Table tennis is my life. I feel [it's] the end of the world if I lose a game. However, no matter how good I am, I will be surpassed sooner or later. So I just want to enjoy the game as long as I can.'

ISABELL **WERTH**
EQUESTRIAN – DRESSAGE

With eight Olympic medals, five of them gold, Isabell Werth has justifiably earned the title of 'Dressage Queen'. She is the world's most successful Dressage rider and a multiple world and European Champion. A proud German, she has competed at four Olympic Games and is a reigning champion as part of the winning German Dressage team from Beijing 2008.

Isabell Werth did not even want to be a Dressage rider. A horse fanatic, she grew up dreaming of Olympic glory in Jumping and Eventing. She certainly showed ability in those disciplines, but it was only after meeting a man known as the Doctor that she embarked in earnest on the journey that would lead her towards greatness and the donning of the tailcoat.

In 1987, at the age of 17, her neighbour Dr Schulten-Baumer invited her to ride his horses. It was the beginning of a partnership between coach and rider that would turn Werth into an outstanding competitor in Dressage. 'Apart from my parents, it was the Doctor who shaped me the most,' reflects Werth. 'For me, he will always be one of the best coaches in the world.'

On each horse given to her by Schulten-Baumer, she excelled and celebrated landmark victories, her greatest coming on a chestnut gelding called Gigolo, who became the most successful Dressage horse of all time with Werth in the saddle.

By the age of 23, the girl from the Rhineland was competing in her first Olympic Games, the Barcelona 1992 Games. She was already known as an emerging star within Dressage circles, and had a European Championship gold to her name, but few people expected such a mature performance from the young German. On Gigolo, she produced an extremely assured ride and scored 1,551 points, enough for second place in the Individual standings behind compatriot Nicole Uphoff-Becker. An all-German podium meant she picked up her first gold as part of the German team.

Four years later at the Atlanta 1996 Games she went one better and won both Dressage Team and Individual golds, registering a total of 235.09 percentage points under a newly implemented scoring system, a slim winning margin of just 2.7 over Anky van Grunsven of the Netherlands. Gigolo and Werth, still coached by the Doctor, had already cemented their place in the annals of riding history as one of the great Dressage pairings when they continued their story at the next Olympic Games, in

Sydney 2000. It was there that she claimed silver in Dressage Individual and another gold in Dressage Team, her fourth overall.

It ended a highly successful year for Werth in a number of ways, as she also qualified as a lawyer and started working for a marketing company. It was her last Games on Gigolo and heralded the end of an era in other ways as well. In 2001, she emotionally split from her mentor Dr Schulten-Baumer, the first step towards becoming a riding professional and being completely independent, eventually establishing her own training stable.

She found it difficult to replace Gigolo, though, and missed out on the Athens 2004 Games, returning at Beijing 2008 on Satchmo, on whom she had won the Dressage Individual World Championships in 2006. In Beijing, Germany resumed their domination of the Dressage Team event and took their seventh gold in succession, with Werth once again their leading rider. It brought a historic fifth gold for her, to which she added her third silver in the Dressage Individual Competition. The journey for Werth is far from over and she continues to target two more gold medals at London 2012, where, though aged 43, she will be as hungry for success as ever.

Statistics
Born: 21 July 1969, Rheinberg, Nordrhein-Westfalen, Germany
Height: 5ft 6in (1.68m)
Weight: 141lb (64kg)

Olympic Games Medals
Barcelona 1992
Dressage Team Competition.............Gold
Dressage Individual
 Competition.. Silver

Atlanta 1996
Dressage Individual
 Competition..Gold
Dressage Team Competition.............Gold

Sydney 2000
Dressage Team Competition.............Gold
Dressage Individual Competition..Silver

Beijing 2008
Dressage Team Competition.............Gold
Dressage Individual Competition..Silver

Above: Werth proudly displays her most recent silver and gold medal triumphs from the Beijing 2008 Olympic Games, won in the Dressage Team and Individual Competitions.

Right: Riding Satchmo, Werth shows the way to another gold medal in the Dressage Team Competition event at the Beijing 2008 Games.

'To me he was a friend, a teacher and a sport partner. Once in a while he might have thought of all the victories we had celebrated. Beyond the sport Gigolo had shaped my life and I remember our years with gratefulness.'

Isabell Werth on the death of her favourite horse, Gigolo

HANS GUNTER
WINKLER
EQUESTRIAN – JUMPING

GERMANY

Hans Günter Winkler won seven Olympic Games medals, including five golds, during an illustrious career that spanned six Games. He has the greatest Olympic record of any show jumper, with his most famous achievements coming on Halla, the only horse ever ridden to three Olympic gold medals.

Born to a riding instructor and brought up surrounded by horses, Hans Günter Winkler always seemed destined to become a champion in the saddle. Nobody, however, could have predicted an international career that started in 1952 and ended in 1986 after 108 showings for Germany. He remains the only jumper to win five Olympic gold medals and the only equestrian athlete in any discipline to compete and win medals at six different Olympiads.

Despite being put on horses at a young age by his father, there were no guarantees that Winkler would have the ability and commitment to establish and sustain his position at the highest level of Jumping. On the Olympic stage, with the ultimate prize at stake, he competed and won medals over a period of 20 years. He is one of just four competitors to have won medals at six different Olympics.

Winkler was one of the most popular athletes in Germany in the 1950s and 1960s, coming to the fore when he won his first German Championship in 1952. He went to the Melbourne 1956 Olympic Games as a favourite in the Equestrian events, which took place in Stockholm due to quarantine restrictions.

On Halla, his favourite mare, Winkler triumphed in both the Individual and Team Jumping events. His road to success, however, was far from smooth. The competition seemed all but over for Winkler when he pulled a groin muscle in the first round, but – with the aid of painkillers – he continued to ride, knowing the German team would be eliminated without him. Suffering dizziness and double vision, Winkler could only steer Halla around the course, but the horse was still able to produce a supreme performance and they won Individual gold. It ended an almost perfect three years of pre-eminence, following Individual Jumping World Championship victories in 1954 and 1955.

Four years later, at the Rome 1960 Games, and still on Halla, Winkler won a third Olympic gold, again as part of the German Jumping team. It was a feat he repeated, for the fourth Olympic gold of his career, at Tokyo 1964, by which time Halla had retired. He won bronze in the Team event Mexico City 1968, and the Team then achieved gold on home soil at the Munich 1972 Games four years later, where Winkler did not take part in the Individual competition.

Although individual titles eluded him after Melbourne 1956, he was ranked fifth in Rome 1960 and Mexico City 1968, while he came 16th in the field in Tokyo 1964 and 10th at Montreal 1976. The Montreal 1976 Games were his last, during which he celebrated his 50th birthday, and he collected his seventh and final medal, a silver in Team Jumping. He remains one of the most successful German Olympic athletes, second only to the great Reiner Klimke in terms of gold medals in German Equestrian competition, and he was twice named German athlete of the year, in 1955 and 1956.

Winkler finally retired in 1986, drawing to a close a wonderful career in Jumping – the most successful in Olympic history. He continues to be involved in the sport, owning a stable of horses at his German home, while running a sports marketing firm and writing books on equestrianism.

Statistics
Born: 24 July 1926, Wuppertal, Nordrhein-Westfalen, Germany
Height: 5ft 9in (1.75m)
Weight: 159lb (72kg)

Olympic Games Medals
Stockholm 1956
Individual Jumping ....Gold
Team Jumping ....Gold

Rome 1960
Team Jumping ....Gold

Tokyo 1964
Team Jumping ....Gold

Mexico City 1968
Team Jumping .... Bronze

Munich 1972
Team Jumping ....Gold

Montreal 1976
Team Jumping .... Silver

Left: Winkler wins the Team Jumping Competition in Rome 1960, his third gold medal in two Olympic Games. Fritz Thiedemann and Alwin Schockemohle were his teammates.

Right: Winkler is presented with a gold medal by IOC President Avery Brundage at the Stockholm 1956 Games. Winkler was still winning medals 20 years later.

'The decisive minutes of my entire riding career were before that final run. Victory and defeat were so close together and there was no turning back. Thank God for my mare Halla, for without this wonderful horse it would all have ended in a fiasco.'

Hans Günter Winkler on his two gold medals in Stockholm 1956

EMIL **ZATOPEK**
ATHLETICS

Many would argue that Emil Zátopek is the greatest Olympian ever. He claimed five Olympic medals overall, and his performance at the Helsinki 1952 Olympic Games has gone down in folklore. He won the 5,000m, 10,000m and the Marathon in the space of eight days. Astonishingly, Zátopek had never run a marathon before.

Emil Zátopek, who was later justifiably dubbed 'The Locomotive', dominated long-distance running from 1948 to 1954, winning 38 consecutive 10,000m races, including 11 in 1949. He set 18 world records over various distances, as well as gaining five Olympic medals and leaving the legacy of those incredible Games in Helsinki 1952.

The sixth child of a modest Czechoslovakian family, Zátopek was working at a shoe factory at the age of 16 when the compnay who employed him, Bata, sponsored a 1,500m race. Reluctantly, he entered the competition and was surprised to finish second. From there, his love affair with long-distance running thrived.

But his success in the Olympic Games came at a price. Zátopek conducted brutal training regimes that would have finished off lesser athletes, but set the standard for many who run professionally today. He would regularly run 50 sets of 400m in the morning and the afternoon, displaying a tenacity and dedication to training rarely seen in Olympic hopefuls. Zátopek's fierce system paid off as he burst on to the world scene at the London 1948 Games, setting an Olympic record on his way to winning the 10,000m. He also finished second in the 5,000m as his lung-busting sprints towards the finish line captured the imagination of the spectators, while reducing his competitors to mere also-rans.

His training in the lead-up to the Helsinki 1952 Games was extreme, with Zátopek running sets of 20 x 200m, 40 x 400m and then another 20 x 200m as part of his schedule. His rest between sets? Just a 200m jog. It seemed beyond human capability to contemplate achieving such a feat, let alone completing the training, but it all paid off in quite exceptional circumstances in Helsinki.

The first step on his ascent to greatness was the 10,000m and Zátopek easily won, beating silver medallist and arch-rival Alain Mimoun by 15 seconds to claim an Olympic record of

29:17.0. One down, two to go. The next day, Zátopek performed well in the preliminary rounds for the 5,000m and clinched a place in the final, although he was not the favourite: the West German athlete Herbert Schade had set an Olympic record in qualifying, while Belgian Gaston Reiff was the defending champion. Tactically timing his run to perfection, Zátopek reserved enough energy to make a late dash for the line. He beat Mimoun into second place again, while Schade finished third. It was another Olympic record for the fearless 'Locomotive'. On the same day as his 5,000m victory, Zátopek's wife, Dana, won the Women's Javelin Throw – success obviously ran in the family.

It was the Marathon that would confirm Zátopek as an Olympic legend. Doctors advised him not to race in the event, which was scheduled just three days after the 5,000m final, but Zátopek ignored the warnings and raced in what was his first ever attempt at that distance. Before embarking on his marathon adventure he muttered the immortal words,

Statistics
Born: 19 September 1922, Koprivnice, Czech Republic
Died: 21 November 2000
Height: 6ft (1.83m)
Weight: 159lb (72kg)

Olympic Games Medals
London 1948
Men's 10,000m...Gold
Men's 5,000m.. Silver

Helsinki 1952
Men's 10,000m...Gold
Men's 5,000m...Gold
Men's Marathon......................................Gold

Below: With the hand of a rival on his shoulder, Zátopek reflects on his triple gold success at the Helsinki 1952 Olympic Games.

Right: The Czech shows the strain as he battles to his second gold medal in the 10,000m event at the Helsinki 1952 Games.

'Men – today we die a little', but Zátopek was very much alive as he won his third gold of the Games, setting a third Olympic record after running the gruelling 26 miles in under two and a half hours.

His sensational Olympic Games treble at Helsinki 1952, and the way in which it was achieved, sets Zátopek apart from other athletes. He competed again in the Melbourne 1956 Games but couldn't claim another medal – although

his place in the pantheon of Olympic greats was already assured. As he walked away with a third gold around his neck after that Marathon victory in 1952, it was clear he was in fact a breed apart. An incredible athlete, a remarkable Olympian.

'If you want to win something, run the 100m. If you want to experience something, run a marathon.'

JAN **ZELEZNY**
ATHLETICS

CZECH REPUBLIC

Possibly the most famous javelin thrower of all time and certainly the most successful, Czech star Jan Železný is the only man to have won three Javelin Throw gold medals in Olympic history, triumphing in Barcelona 1992, Atlanta 1996 and Sydney 2000 in a career that spanned a remarkable 20 years at the very top. His intense but friendly rivalry with Britain's Steve Backley was a feature of the sport for many years.

It's a measure of Jan Železný's quality that, four years after retiring from the sport, he still holds the top five longest javelin throws of all time – and seven of the top 10. All were recorded during a golden four-year period between 1993 and 1997, including a world-record 98.48m in Jena in May 1996.

Železný first shot to fame at the age of just 22 at the Seoul 1988 Games, where he was favourite to win gold after taking the sport by storm. By that stage he was already the world-record holder, but things did not quite go to plan. Finland's Tapio Korjus beat him by 16cm to finish in first place, clinching a shock victory with the very last throw of the competition. Železný, who became famous for his competitive spirit, took that lesson to heart. Having begun his Olympic career with a silver medal, it was gold, gold, gold from then on.

Four years later at Barcelona 1992, it was his turn to taste victory with his final throw, breaking his own Olympic record by a massive 3.76m with a throw of 89.66m right at the death. At the Atlanta 1996 Games, in an intense battle with Britain's Steve Backley, he came from behind to win with a throw of 88.16 to take gold again. No javelin thrower had ever managed three Olympic golds in a row but at Sydney 2000 Železný – famous in particular for the dramatic speed of his run-up – made history. Having recovered from a serious shoulder injury two years earlier, he set a new Olympic record of 90.17m, beating Backley to emerge victorious again.

With statistics like that it's no surprise to find that athletics was very much in Železný's genes. His first coach was his father, Jaroslav, who taught him the all-important basic techniques, while his mother, Jana, was also a javelin thrower. Železný was so dominant in his chosen discipline that in the decade between 1991 and 2001 he won 106 out of the 135 competitions in which he took part, produced 34 throws over 90m, was named IAAF Athlete of the Year in 2000 and was elected a member of the IOC in 1999.

His profile reached legendary status in his home country, but in truth the whole world was fascinated by the quiet and modest athlete's intensely competitive battles with major rivals, such as Backley, Sergey Makarov, Boris Henry, Seppo Raty, Raymond Hecht and Aki Parviainen. And although the javelin specifications changed twice during his career, he can claim six world records with the various spears, proving his technique was almost perfect.

As well as Olympic Games success he was three times World Champion, but strangely never won a European Championships gold, recording only third-place finishes in 1994 and 2006 – the latter at the age of 40, after which he finally announced his retirement. He continues to be involved in the sport through his work at the IOC, and as a renowned coach.

Statistics
Born: 16 June 1966, Mlada Boleslav, Czech Republic
Height: 6ft 1in (1.85m)
Weight: 194lb (88kg)

Olympic Games Medals
Seoul 1988
Men's Javelin Throw...........................Silver

Barcelona 1992
Men's Javelin Throw..............................Gold

Atlanta 1996
Men's Javelin Throw..............................Gold

Sydney 2000
Men's Javelin Throw..............................Gold

Below: He had a friendly smile, but Železný was a fierce competitor in a career that spanned three decades and five Olympiads.

Right: Železný won his third Olympic gold medal in Sydney 2000, to go with his three World Championships titles and many world-record throws during his career.

'I don't like being a big hero. It is very difficult for Steve [Backley] never to win the Olympic Games. He is a very good friend. I say sorry to him afterwards, but we have the same dream.'

Železný shows his sporting side after pipping rival Steve Backley to gold again at the Sydney 2000 Games

TRISCHA **ZORN**
PARALYMPIC SWIMMING

Her astonishing 46 medals make Trischa Zorn the most decorated athlete in the history of the Paralympic Games. Despite her blindness, the American swimmer won 32 gold, nine silver and five bronze medals over seven Games between Arnhem 1980 and Athens 2004. She broke multiple world records and is a four-time all-American champion.

Trischa Zorn now works as a special needs teacher, helping third- and fourth-grade students to succeed despite their disabilities. If her students need inspiration, then Zorn has only to tell them her story. It is one that spans seven Paralympic Games and has seen a paradigm shift in the nature of the competition, from a marginalised sideshow to a mainstream event held in world-class stadiums in front of enthusiastic crowds. That is because the public witness real people, with real challenges and an absolute commitment to overcome the obstacles before them.

Nothing captures the Olympian spirit better than the Paralympic Games; no athletes in the world demand respect more than those who, like Zorn, have to battle against the odds. Zorn's status as an icon for her peers was highlighted when she was chosen to take the Paralympic Oath for athletes at the Atlanta 1996 Games. By then, at the age of 32, she was already established as an all-time Paralympic great.

Despite being what is classified as 'legally blind' and able to see only silhouettes, Zorn started swimming from a young age. She swam in her first disabled event in 1979 and found success well before athletes with a disability were accepted into mainstream competition. Her first Paralympic Games came in Arnhem 1980 when she was just 16 – it was the start of the most successful career of any Paralympian.

She competed in the B, B2, B1-2, B1-3, B2-3 S12, SB12 and SM12 disability categories during her 24 years of Paralympic competition, usually returning home with a considerable gold-medal haul. Zorn left Arnhem 1980 with five golds, two from Medley events and three from 100m single-stroke disciplines – in the Backstroke, Butterfly and Freestyle – and all were won in world-record times. As her profile, as well as that of disabled sport grew, after Seoul 1988, she was nominated as a candidate for *Sports Illustrated*'s Sportswoman of the Year in 1988.

Zorn set an incredible seven world records at the Barcelona 1992 Paralympic Games as she

Statistics
Born: 1 June 1964, Orange, California, USA

Paralympic Games Medals
Arnhem 1980
Women's 100m Backstroke B ....Gold
Women's 100m Butterfly B ....Gold
Women's 100m Freestyle B ....Gold
Women's 4 x 50m Individual
    Medley Relay B...Gold
Women's 4 x 100m Individual
    Medley Relay B..Gold

New York 1984
Women's 100m Backstroke B2...........Gold
Women's 100m Butterfly B2 ....Gold
Women's 100m Freestyle B2 ....Gold
Women's 200m Individual
    Medley B2...Gold
Women's 400m Individual
    Medley B2...Gold

Seoul 1988
Women's 50m Breaststroke B2 ....Gold
Women's 50m Freestyle B2 ....Gold
Women's 100m Backstroke B2...........Gold
Women's 100m Breaststroke B2........Gold
Women's 100m Butterfly B2 ....Gold
Women's 100m Freestyle B2 ....Gold
Women's 200m Breaststroke B2........Gold
Women's 200m Individual
    Medley B2...Gold
Women's 400m Freestyle B2...............Gold
Women's 400m Individual
    Medley B2...Gold

Left: 'It is my passion to affect people's lives in a positive way, to show them that anything is possible,' said the winning American swimmer.

Right: Zorn cuts powerfully through the water, making her the most decorated ever Paralympic Games athlete.

won 10 gold medals and two silvers, making her comfortably the top medallist at the Games. She again topped the medals table at the Atlanta 1996 Games four years later, where she won two gold, three silver and three bronze medals in her homeland. Zorn won four silvers and a bronze at the Sydney 2000 Games and trained as hard as ever before returning for a final Games in Athens 2004, now aged 40, where she won her last Paralympic medal, a bronze in the 100m Backstroke S12.

An iconic champion in the pool and an inspirational person away from competition, in January 2005 Zorn was one of eight athletes honoured during the New Year celebrations in Times Square, New York. It marked the end of a long and triumphant career that coincided with a new era in Paralympic sport. Zorn is the swimming queen: she overcame the odds, refused to give up on her dream and became the most successful Paralympian of all time. Her stunning record will continue to inspire athletes with a disability who themselves dream of becoming champions in the future.

Barcelona 1992

Women's 50m Freestyle B2 .... Gold
Women's 100m Backstroke B2 .... Gold
Women's 100m Breaststroke B1-2 ..... Gold
Women's 100m Freestyle B2 .... Gold
Women's 200m Backstroke B1-2 .... Gold
Women's 200m Breaststroke B1-3 .... Gold
Women's 200m Medley B2 .... Gold
Women's 400m Medley B1-3 .... Gold
Women's 4 x 100m Freestyle
   Relay B1-3 .... Gold
Women's 4 x 100m Medley
   Relay B1-3 .... Gold
Women's 100m Butterfly B2-3 .... Silver
Women's 400m Freestyle B2-3 .... Silver

Atlanta 1996

Women's 100m Backstroke B2 .... Gold
Women's 200m Individual
   Medley B2 .... Gold
Women's 50m Freestyle B2 .... Silver
Women's 400m Freestyle B2 .... Silver
Women's 4 x 100m Medley
   Relay B1-3 .... Silver
Women's 100m Breaststroke B2 .... Bronze
Women's 100m Freestyle B2 .... Bronze
Women's 4 x 100m Freestyle
   Relay B1-3 .... Bronze

Sydney 2000

Women's 100m Backstroke S12 .... Silver
Women's 100m Breaststroke SB12 .... Silver
Women's 100m Butterfly S12 .... Silver
Women's 200m Individual
   Medley SM12 .... Silver
Women's 50m Freestyle S12 .... Bronze

Athens 2004

Women's 100m Backstroke S12 ..... Bronze

OLYMPIC AND PARALYMPIC GAMES RECORDS

The scale of the Olympic and Paralympic Games means that thousands of athletes have taken part since the inception of the modern Summer Games in 1896 – Beijing 2008 alone hosted more than 15,000 athletes. But Olympic and Paralympic glory is not just about medals tables, it is as much as about endeavour and passion as racking up wins. And, of course, the differing nature of each sport means that some events yield higher medal counts than others. Nevertheless, on the following pages you will find the cream of the gold-medal winners, those who have won a hat-trick of golds or more, along with all the silver, bronze and total medals won.

HOST CITIES

Olympic Games

Athens	1896
Paris	1900
St. Louis	1904
London	1908
Stockholm	1912
Antwerp	1920
Paris	1924
Amsterdam	1928
Los Angeles	1932
Berlin	1936
London	1948
Helsinki	1952
Melbourne	1956
Rome	1960
Tokyo	1964
Mexico City	1968
Munich	1972
Montreal	1976
Moscow	1980
Los Angeles	1984
Seoul	1988
Barcelona	1992
Atlanta	1996
Sydney	2000
Athens	2004
Beijing	2008

Paralympic Games

Rome	1960
Tokyo	1964
Tel Aviv	1968
Heidelberg	1972
Toronto	1976
Arnhem	1980
Stoke Mandeville and New York	1984
Seoul	1988
Barcelona	1992
Atlanta	1996
Sydney	2000
Athens	2004
Beijing	2008

Right: The Women's field tackles the daunting water jump during the 3,000m Steeplechase at the Beijing 2008 Olympic Games.

This table lists the most successful Summer Olympic and Paralympic athletes, with three golds or more. Their rank (R) is determined by the most number of gold (G) medals won. Silver (S), bronze (B) and total (TOT) medals are also given, along with competition dates.

OLYMPIC MEN

R	ATHLETE	SPORT(S)	G	S	B	TOT	DATES
1	Phelps, Michael (USA)	Swimming	14	0	2	16	2004–08
2	Nurmi, Paavo (FIN)	Athletics	9	3	0	12	1920–28
3	Spitz, Mark (USA)	Swimming	9	1	1	11	1968–72
4	Lewis, Carl (USA)	Athletics	9	1	0	10	1984–96
5	Kato, Sawao (JPN)	Gymnastics	8	3	1	12	1968–76
6	Biondi, Matt (USA)	Swimming	8	2	1	11	1984–92
7	Ewry, Ray (USA)	Athletics	8	0	0	8	1900–08
8	Andrianov, Nikolay (USSR)	Gymnastics	7	5	3	15	1972–80
9	Shakhlin, Boris (USSR)	Gymnastics	7	4	2	13	1956–64
10	Chukarin, Viktor (USSR)	Gymnastics	7	3	1	11	1952–56
11	Gerevich, Aladár (HUN)	Fencing	7	1	2	10	1932–60
13	Mangiarotti, Edoardo (ITA)	Fencing	6	5	2	13	1936–60
14	Van Innis, Hubert (BEL)	Archery	6	3	0	9	1900–20
15	Nakayama, Akinori (JPN)	Gymnastics	6	2	2	10	1968–72
16	Fredriksson, Gert (SWE)	Canoeing	6	1	1	8	1948–60
17	Shcherbo, Vitaly (BEL)	Gymnastics	6	0	4	10	1992–96
18	Klimke, Reiner (GER)	Equestrian	6	0	2	8	1964–88
19	Kovács, Pál (HUN)	Fencing	6	0	1	7	1936–60
20	Kárpáti, Rudolf (HUN)	Fencing	6	0	0	6	1948–60
	Nadi, Nedo (ITA)	Fencing	6	0	0	6	1912–20
22	Ono, Takashi (JPN)	Gymnastics	5	4	4	13	1952–64
23	Osburn, Carl (USA)	Shooting	5	4	2	11	1912–24
24	Hall, Jr., Gary (USA)	Swimming	5	3	2	10	1996–2004
25	Thorpe, Ian (AUS)	Swimming	5	3	1	9	2000–04
26	Ritola, Ville (FIN)	Athletics	5	3	0	8	1924–28
27	Endo, Yukio (JPN)	Gymnastics	5	2	0	7	1960–68
	Peirsol, Aaron (USA)	Swimming	5	2	0	7	2000–08
29	Tsukahara, Mitsuo (JPN)	Gymnastics	5	1	3	9	1968–76
30	Jager, Tom (USA)	Swimming	5	1	1	7	1984–92
	Lee, Willis (USA)	Shooting	5	1	1	7	1920
	Winkler, Hans Günter (GER)	Equestrian	5	1	1	7	1956–76
33	Heida, Anton (USA)	Gymnastics	5	1	0	6	1904
	Lilloe-Olsen, Ole (NOR)	Shooting	5	1	0	6	1920–24
	Schollander, Don (USA)	Swimming	5	1	0	6	1964–68
36	Lane, Al (USA)	Shooting	5	0	1	6	1912–20
	Redgrave, Steve (GBR)	Rowing	5	0	1	6	1984–2000
	Weissmuller, Johnny (USA)	Swimming, Water Polo	5	0	1	6	1924–28
39	Fisher, Morris (USA)	Shooting	5	0	0	5	1920–24
40	Popov, Aleksandr (RUS)	Swimming	4	5	0	9	1992–2000
41	Carlberg, G. Vilhelm (SWE)	Shooting	4	4	0	8	1908–24
42	Miez, Georges (SUI)	Gymnastics	4	3	1	8	1924–36
	Olsen, Otto (NOR)	Shooting	4	3	1	8	1920–24
44	Patzaichin, Ivan (ROU)	Canoeing	4	3	0	7	1968–84
45	Nemov, Aleksey (RUS)	Gymnastics	4	2	6	12	1996–2000
46	Matthes, Roland (GDR)	Swimming	4	2	2	8	1968–76
47	Liberg, Einar (NOR)	Shooting	4	2	1	7	1908–24
48	Delfino, Giuseppe (ITA)	Fencing	4	2	0	6	1952–64
	Gaudin, Lucien (FRA)	Fencing	4	2	0	6	1920–28
	d'Oriola, Christian (FRA)	Fencing	4	2	0	6	1948–56
51	Daniels, Charlie (USA)	Swimming	4	1	2	7	1904–08
	Lezak, Jason (USA)	Swimming	4	1	2	7	2000–08
	Spooner, Lloyd (USA)	Shooting	4	1	2	7	1920
54	Décugis, Max (FRA)	Tennis	4	1	1	6	1900–20
	Rose, Murray (AUS)	Swimming	4	1	1	6	1956–60
	Sidyak, Viktor (USSR)	Fencing	4	1	1	6	1968–80
57	Artyomov, Vladimir (USSR)	Gymnastics	4	1	0	5	1988
	Ferguson, Ian (NZL)	Canoeing	4	1	0	5	1984–88
	Fonst, Ramón (CUB)	Fencing	4	1	0	5	1900–04
	Hoy, Chris (GBR)	Cycling	4	1	0	5	2000–08
	Kolehmainen, Hannes (FIN)	Athletics	4	1	0	5	1912–20
	Louganis, Greg (USA)	Diving	4	1	0	5	1976–88
	Muratov, Valentin (USSR)	Gymnastics	4	1	0	5	1952–56
	Naber, John (USA)	Swimming	4	1	0	5	1976
	Puliti, Oreste (ITA)	Fencing	4	1	0	5	1920–28
	Pahud de Mortanges, Charles (NED)	Equestrian	4	1	0	5	1924–32
	Sheppard, Mel (USA)	Athletics	4	1	0	5	1908–12
	Zátopek, Emil (CZE)	Athletics	4	1	0	5	1948–52
69	Kitajima, Kosuke (JPN)	Swimming	4	0	2	6	2004–08
	Kulcsár, Győző (HUN)	Fencing	4	0	2	6	1964–76
71	Hurley, Marcus (USA)	Cycling	4	0	1	5	1904
	Li, Xiaopeng (CHN)	Gymnastics	4	0	1	5	2000–08
	Olsen, Jon (USA)	Swimming	4	0	1	5	1992–96
	Pozdnyakov, Stanislav (RUS)	Fencing	4	0	1	5	1992–2004
	Zampori, Giorgio (ITA)	Gymnastics	4	0	1	5	1912–22
	Beerbaum, Ludger (GER)	Equestrian	4	0	0	4	1988–2004
77	Darnyi, Tamás (HUN)	Swimming	4	0	0	4	1988–92
	Dillard, Harrison (USA)	Athletics	4	0	0	4	1948–52
	Elvstrøm, Paul (DEN)	Sailing	4	0	0	4	1948–60
	Fuchs, Jenő (HUN)	Fencing	4	0	0	4	1908–12
	Johnson, Michael (USA)	Athletics	4	0	0	4	1992–2000
	Korzeniowski, Robert (POL)	Athletics	4	0	0	4	1996–2004
	Kraenzlein, Al (USA)	Athletics	4	0	0	4	1900
	Krayzelburg, Lenny (USA)	Swimming	4	0	0	4	2000–04
	Krovopuskov, Viktor (USSR)	Fencing	4	0	0	4	1976–80
	Oerter, Al (USA)	Athletics	4	0	0	4	1956–68
	Owens, Jesse (USA)	Athletics	4	0	0	4	1936
	Pavesi, Carlo (ITA)	Fencing	4	0	0	4	1952–60
	Pinsent, Matthew (GBR)	Rowing	4	0	0	4	1992–2004
	Radmilovic, Paul (GBR)	Swimming, Water Polo	4	0	0	4	1908–20
	Saint Cyr, Henri (SWE)	Equestrian	4	0	0	4	1952–56
	Salnikov, Vladimir (USSR)	Swimming	4	0	0	4	1980–88
	Schuhmann, Carl (GER)	Gymnastics, Wrestling	4	0	0	4	1896
	Virén, Lasse (FIN)	Athletics	4	0	0	4	1972–76
95	Dityatin, Aleksandr (USSR)	Gymnastics	3	6	1	10	1976–80
96	Gaudini, Giulio (ITA)	Fencing	3	4	2	9	1928–36
97	Cattiau, Philippe (FRA)	Fencing	3	4	1	8	1920–36
	Ducret, Roger (FRA)	Fencing	3	4	1	8	1920–28
99	Kenmotsu, Eizo (JPN)	Gymnastics	3	3	3	9	1968–76
	Swahn, Alfred (SWE)	Shooting	3	3	3	9	1908–24
101	Hackett, Grant (AUS)	Swimming	3	3	1	7	2000–08
102	Van Den Hoogenband, Pieter (NED)	Swimming	3	2	2	7	2000–04
103	Eyser, George (USA)	Gymnastics	3	2	1	6	1904
	Gross, Michael (FRG)	Swimming	3	2	1	6	1984–88
	Holmann, Knut (NOR)	Canoeing	3	2	1	6	1992–2000
	Li, Ning (CHN)	Gymnastics	3	2	1	6	1984
	Natvig, Harald (NOR)	Shooting	3	2	1	6	1920–24
	Nazlymov, Vladimir (USSR)	Fencing	3	2	1	6	1968–80
	Rose, Ralph (USA)	Athletics	3	2	1	6	1904–12
	Weingärtner, Hermann (GER)	Gymnastics	3	2	1	6	1896
111	Balczó, András (HUN)	Modern Pentathlon	3	2	0	5	1960–72
	Beresford, Jr, Jack (GBR)	Rowing	3	2	0	5	1920–36
	Davis, Josh (USA)	Swimming	3	2	0	5	1996–2000
	Dibiasi, Klaus (ITA)	Diving	3	2	0	5	1964–76
	Kahanamoku, Duke (USA)	Swimming	3	2	0	5	1912–24
	Morales, Pablo (USA)	Swimming	3	2	0	5	1984–92
	Schumann, Ralf (GER)	Shooting	3	2	0	5	1988–2008
	Yang, Wei (CHN)	Gymnastics	3	2	0	5	2000–08
119	Frey, Konrad (GER)	Gymnastics	3	1	2	6	1936
	Lochte, Ryan (USA)	Swimming	3	1	2	6	2004–08
	Schwarzmann, Alfred (GER)	Gymnastics	3	1	2	6	1936–52
	Stukelj, Leon (YUG)	Gymnastics	3	1	2	6	1924–36
	Swahn, Oscar (SWE)	Shooting	3	1	2	6	1908–20
	Wiggins, Bradley (GBR)	Cycling	3	1	2	6	2000–08
125	Bluhm, Kay (GER)	Canoeing	3	1	1	5	1988–96
	Cornaggia-Medici, Giancarlo (ITA)	Fencing	3	1	1	5	1928–36
	Crocker, Ian (USA)	Swimming	3	1	1	5	2000–08
	Dittmer, Andreas (GER)	Canoeing	3	1	1	5	1996–2004
	Gyarmati, Dezső (HUN)	Water Polo	3	1	1	5	1948–64
	Hencken, John (USA)	Swimming	3	1	1	5	1972–76
	Huhtanen, Veikko (FIN)	Gymnastics	3	1	1	5	1948
	MacDonald, Paul (NZL)	Canoeing	3	1	1	5	1984–88
	Morelon, Daniel (FRA)	Cycling	3	1	1	5	1964–76
	Rossi, Antonio (ITA)	Canoeing	3	1	1	5	1992–2004
	Whitfield, Mal (USA)	Athletics	3	1	1	5	1948–52
	Xiong, Ni (CHN)	Diving	3	1	1	5	1988–2000
137	Ainslie, Ben (GBR)	Sailing	3	1	0	4	1996–2008
	Azaryan, Albert (USSR)	Gymnastics	3	1	0	4	1956–60
	Bekele, Kenenisa (ETH)	Athletics	3	1	0	4	2004–08
	Claudius, Leslie (IND)	Hockey	3	1	0	4	1948–60
	Flanagan, John (USA)	Athletics	3	1	0	4	1900–08
	Flatow, Alfred (GER)	Gymnastics	3	1	0	4	1896
	Gutsche, Torsten (GER)	Canoeing	3	1	0	4	1992–96
	Heath, Mike (USA)	Swimming	3	1	0	4	1984
	Hickcox, Charlie (USA)	Swimming	3	1	0	4	1968
	Hillman, Harry (USA)	Athletics	3	1	0	4	1904–08
	Hoy, Andrew (AUS)	Equestrian	3	1	0	4	1992–2000
	Karelin, Aleksandr (RUS)	Wrestling	3	1	0	4	1988–2000
	Lewis, Steve (USA)	Athletics	3	1	0	4	1988–92
	Lightbody, Jim (USA)	Athletics	3	1	0	4	1904–08
	Mankin, Valentin (USSR)	Sailing	3	1	0	4	1968–80

R	ATHLETE	SPORT(S)	G	S	B	TOT	DATES
	McLane, Jimmy (USA)	Swimming	3	1	0	4	1948–52
	Nadi, Aldo (ITA)	Fencing	3	1	0	4	1920
	Neri, Romeo (ITA)	Gymnastics	3	1	0	4	1928–32
	Nordvik, Hans (NOR)	Shooting	3	1	0	4	1912–24
	Prinstein, Meyer (USA)	Athletics	3	1	0	4	1900–04
	Riccardi, Franco (ITA)	Fencing	3	1	0	4	1928–36
	Rouse, Jeff (USA)	Swimming	3	1	0	4	1992–96
	Rousseau, Florian (FRA)	Cycling	3	1	0	4	1996–2000
	Saneyev, Viktor (USSR)	Athletics	3	1	0	4	1968–80
	Schümann, Jochen (GER)	Sailing	3	1	0	4	1976–2000
	Singh, Udham (IND)	Hockey	3	1	0	4	1952–64
	Wariner, Jeremy (USA)	Athletics	3	1	0	4	2004–08
	Železný, Jan (CZE)	Athletics	3	1	0	4	1988–2000
165	Helm, Rüdiger (GDR)	Canoeing	3	0	3	6	1976–80
166	Aaltonen, Paavo (FIN)	Gymnastics	3	0	2	5	1948–52
	Berczelly, Tibor (HUN)	Fencing	3	0	2	5	1936–52
	Fenton, Dennis (USA)	Shooting	3	0	2	5	1920–24
	Fiedler, Jens (GER)	Cycling	3	0	2	5	1992–2004
	Taylor, Henry (GBR)	Swimming	3	0	2	5	1908–20
171	Bilozerchev, Dmitry (USSR)	Gymnastics	3	0	1	4	1988
	Dimas, Pyrros (GRE)	Weightlifting	3	0	1	4	1992–2004
	Doherty, Reggie (GBR)	Tennis	3	0	1	4	1900–08
	Ebbesen, Eskild (DEN)	Rowing	3	0	1	4	1996–2008
	Frigerio, Ugo (ITA)	Athletics	3	0	1	4	1920–32
	Kabos, Endre (HUN)	Fencing	3	0	1	4	1932–36
	Kárpáti, György (HUN)	Water Polo	3	0	1	4	1952–64
	Lavrov, Andrey (RUS)	Handball	3	0	1	4	1988–2004
	Montgomery, Jim (USA)	Swimming	3	0	1	4	1976
	Sheridan, Martin (USA)	Athletics	3	0	1	4	1904–08
	Stäheli, Konrad (SUI)	Shooting	3	0	1	4	1900
	Tomkins, James (AUS)	Rowing	3	0	1	4	1992–2004
183	Abbagnale, Agostino (ITA)	Rowing	3	0	0	3	1988–2000
	Benedek, Tibor (HUN)	Water Polo	3	0	0	3	2000–08
	Biros, Péter (HUN)	Water Polo	3	0	0	3	2000–08
	Bolt, Usain (JAM)	Athletics	3	0	0	3	2008
	Braglia, Alberto (ITA)	Gymnastics	3	0	0	3	1908–12
	Brietzke, Siegfried (GDR)	Rowing	3	0	0	3	1972–80
	Buhan, Jéhan (FRA)	Fencing	3	0	0	3	1948–52
	Burton, Michael (USA)	Swimming	3	0	0	3	1968–72
	Carey, Rick (USA)	Swimming	3	0	0	3	1984
	Chand, Dhyan (IND)	Hockey	3	0	0	3	1928–36
	Charpentier, Robert (FRA)	Cycling	3	0	0	3	1936
	Chukhray, Sergey (USSR)	Canoeing	3	0	0	3	1976–80
	Clark, Steven Edward (USA)	Swimming	3	0	0	3	1960–64
	Cloetens, Edmond (BEL)	Archery	3	0	0	3	1920
	Costello, Paul (USA)	Rowing	3	0	0	3	1920–28
	Davis, Glenn (USA)	Athletics	3	0	0	3	1956–60
	Fenyvesi, Csaba (HUN)	Fencing	3	0	0	3	1968–72
	Francis, Ranganandhan (IND)	Hockey	3	0	0	3	1948–56
	Frederick, Karl (USA)	Shooting	3	0	0	3	1920
	Gaines, Rowdy (USA)	Swimming	3	0	0	3	1984
	Ginn, Drew (AUS)	Rowing	3	0	0	3	1996–2008
	Hahn, Archie (USA)	Athletics	3	0	0	3	1904
	Houser, Bud (USA)	Athletics	3	0	0	3	1924–28
	Ivanov, Vyacheslav (USSR)	Rowing	3	0	0	3	1956–64
	Jackson, Joe (USA)	Shooting	3	0	0	3	1920
	Johansson, Ivar (SWE)	Wrestling	3	0	0	3	1932–36
	Hochschorner, Pavol (SVK)	Canoeing	3	0	0	3	2000–08
	Hochschorner, Peter (SVK)	Canoeing	3	0	0	3	2000–08
	Kakiasvili, Akakios (EUN)	Weightlifting	3	0	0	3	1992–2000
	Kammerer, Zoltán (HUN)	Canoeing	3	0	0	3	2000–04
	Karppinen, Pertti (FIN)	Rowing	3	0	0	3	1976–84
	Kásás, Tamás (HUN)	Water Polo	3	0	0	3	2000–08
	Kelly, Sr, Jack (USA)	Rowing	3	0	0	3	1920–24
	Kharkov, Sergey (RUS)	Gymnastics	3	0	0	3	1988–96
	Kiraly, Karch (USA)	Beach Volleyball, Volleyball	3	0	0	3	1984–96
	Kiss, Gergő (HUN)	Water Polo	3	0	0	3	2000–08
	Lemming, Eric (SWE)	Athletics, Tug-Of-War	3	0	0	3	1900–12
	Ma, Lin (CHN)	Table Tennis	3	0	0	3	2004–08
	Masson, Paul (FRA)	Cycling	3	0	0	3	1896
	Meade, Richard (GBR)	Equestrian	3	0	0	3	1968–72
	Medved, Aleksandr (USSR)	Wrestling	3	0	0	3	1964–72
	Molnár, Tamás (HUN)	Water Polo	3	0	0	3	2000–08
	Morozov, Vladimir (USSR)	Canoeing	3	0	0	3	1964–72
	Morrow, Bobby Joe (USA)	Athletics	3	0	0	3	1956
	Mutlu, Halil (TUR)	Weightlifting	3	0	0	3	1996–2004
	Nomura, Tadahiro (JPN)	Judo	3	0	0	3	1996–2004
	Norling, Daniel (SWE)	Equestrianism, Gymnastics	3	0	0	3	1908–20
	Papp, László (HUN)	Boxing	3	0	0	3	1948–56

R	ATHLETE	SPORT(S)	G	S	B	TOT	DATES
	Parfyonovich, Vladimir (USSR)	Canoeing	3	0	0	3	1980
	Rajcsányi, László (HUN)	Fencing	3	0	0	3	1936–52
	Ross, Norman (USA)	Swimming	3	0	0	3	1920
	Ryan, Matt (AUS)	Equestrian	3	0	0	3	1992–2000
	Sadovy, Yevgeny (EUN)	Swimming	3	0	0	3	1992
	Savón, Félix (CUB)	Boxing	3	0	0	3	1992–2000
	Saytiyev, Buvaisa (RUS)	Wrestling	3	0	0	3	1996–2008
	Schriver, Ollie (USA)	Shooting	3	0	0	3	1920
	Singh Gentle, Randhir (IND)	Hockey	3	0	0	3	1948–56
	Singh, Sr, Balbir (IND)	Hockey	3	0	0	3	1948–56
	Smith, Charles (GBR)	Water Polo	3	0	0	3	1908–20
	Snell, Peter (NZL)	Athletics	3	0	0	3	1960–64
	Stevenson, Teófilo (CUB)	Boxing	3	0	0	3	1972–80
	Storcz, Botond (HUN)	Canoeing	3	0	0	3	2000–04
	Süleymanoğlu, Naim (TUR)	Weightlifting	3	0	0	3	1988–96
	Szécsi, Zoltán (HUN)	Water Polo	3	0	0	3	2000–08
	Taylor, Angelo (USA)	Athletics	3	0	0	3	2000–08
	Van Moer, Edmond (BEL)	Archery	3	0	0	3	1920
	Van Der Voort Van Zijp, Adolf (NED)	Equestrian	3	0	0	3	1924–28
	Westergren, Carl (SWE)	Wrestling	3	0	0	3	1920–32
	Wilkinson, George (GBR)	Water Polo	3	0	0	3	1900–12
	Wykoff, Frank (USA)	Athletics	3	0	0	3	1928–36
	Zhdanovich, Viktor (USSR)	Fencing	3	0	0	3	1960–64
	Zou, Kai (CHN)	Gymnastics	3	0	0	3	2008

OLYMPIC WOMEN

R	ATHLETE	SPORT(S)	G	S	B	TOT	DATES
1	Latynina, Larissa (USSR)	Gymnastics	9	5	4	18	1956–64
2	Fischer-Schmidt, Birgit (GER)	Canoeing	8	4	0	12	1980–2004
3	Thompson, Jenny (USA)	Swimming	8	3	1	12	1992–2004
4	Čáslavská, Věra (CZE)	Gymnastics	7	4	0	11	1960–68
5	Otto, Kristin (GDR)	Swimming	6	0	0	6	1988
	Van Dyken, Amy (USA)	Swimming	6	0	0	6	1996–2000
7	Keleti, Ágnes (HUN)	Gymnastics	5	3	2	10	1952–56
8	Comăneci, Nadia (ROU)	Gymnastics	5	3	1	9	1976–80
9	Werth, Isabell (GER)	Equestrian	5	3	0	8	1992–2008
10	Astakhova, Polina (USSR)	Gymnastics	5	2	3	10	1956–64
11	Elisabeta Oleniuc-Lipă (ROU)	Rowing	5	2	1	8	1984–2004
12	Egerszegi, Krisztina (HUN)	Swimming	5	1	1	7	1988–96
	Vezzali, Valentina (ITA)	Fencing	5	1	1	7	1996–2008
14	Nelli Kim (USSR)	Gymnastics	5	1	0	6	1976–80
	Georgeta Damian-Andrunache (ROU)	Rowing	5	0	1	6	2000–08
16	Torres, Dara (USA)	Swimming	4	4	4	12	1984–2008
17	Ender, Kornelia (GDR)	Swimming	4	4	0	8	1972–76
	Fraser, Dawn (AUS)	Swimming	4	4	0	8	1956–64
19	Turishcheva, Lyudmila (USSR)	Gymnastics	4	3	2	9	1968–76
20	de Bruijn, Inge (NED)	Swimming	4	2	2	8	2000–04
21	Guo, Jingjing (CHN)	Diving	4	2	0	6	2000–08
	Korbut, Olga (USSR)	Gymnastics	4	2	0	6	1972–76
23	Trillini, Giovanna (ITA)	Fencing	4	1	3	8	1992–2008
24	Kim, Soo-Nyung (KOR)	Archery	4	1	1	6	1988–2000
	Ignat, Doina (ROU)	Rowing	4	1	1	6	1992–2008
	Novikova-Belova, Yelena (USSR)	Fencing	4	1	1	6	1968–80
	Zijlaard-Van Moorsel, Leontien (NED)	Cycling	4	1	1	6	2000–04
28	Ashford, Evelyn (USA)	Athletics	4	1	0	5	1984–92
	Evans, Janet (USA)	Swimming	4	1	0	5	1988–92
	Fu, Mingxia (CHN)	Diving	4	1	0	5	1992–2000
	Klochkova, Yana (UKR)	Swimming	4	1	0	5	2000–04
	Szabo, Ecaterina (ROU)	Gymnastics	4	1	0	5	1984
	Wang, Nan (CHN)	Table Tennis	4	1	0	5	2000–08
34	Boron, Kathrin (GER)	Rowing	4	0	1	5	1992–2008
	Edwards, Teresa (USA)	Basketball	4	0	1	5	1984–2000
	Susanu, Viorica (ROU)	Rowing	4	0	1	5	2000–08
	Wagner-Augustin, Katrin (GER)	Canoeing	4	0	1	5	2000–08
38	Blankers-Koen, Fanny (NED)	Athletics	4	0	0	4	1948
	Cuthbert, Betty (AUS)	Athletics	4	0	0	4	1956–64
	Davydova, Anastasiya (RUS)	Synchronised Swimming	4	0	0	4	2004–08
	Deng, Yaping (CHN)	Table Tennis	4	0	0	4	1992–96
	Eckert-Wöckel, Bärbel (GDR)	Athletics	4	0	0	4	1976–80
	Leslie, Lisa (USA)	Basketball	4	0	0	4	1996–2008
	McCormick, Pat (USA)	Diving	4	0	0	4	1952–56
	Uphoff-Becker, Nicole (GER)	Equestrian	4	0	0	4	1988–92
	Yermakova, Anastasiya (RUS)	Synchronised Swimming	4	0	0	4	2004–08

R	ATHLETE	SPORT(S)	G	S	B	TOT	DATES
	Zhang, Yining(CHN)	Table Tennis	4	0	0	4	2004–08
48	Van Grunsven, Theodora (NED)	Equestrian	3	5	0	8	1992–2008
49	Coughlin, Natalie (USA)	Swimming	3	4	4	11	2004–08
50	Jones, Leisel (AUS)	Swimming	3	4	1	8	2000–08
	Thomas, Petria (AUS)	Swimming	3	4	1	8	1996–2004
52	Pollack, Andrea (GDR)	Swimming	3	3	0	6	1976–80
53	Andersson, Agneta (SWE)	Canoeing	3	2	2	7	1984–96
	Szewińska-Kirszenstein, Irena (POL)	Athletics	3	2	2	7	1964–76
55	Silivaş, Daniela (ROU)	Gymnastics	3	2	1	6	1988
	Stecher, Renate (GDR)	Athletics	3	2	1	6	1972–76
57	Griffith Joyner, Florence (USA)	Athletics	3	2	0	5	1984–88
	Portwich, Ramona (GER)	Canoeing	3	2	0	5	1988–96
59	Amǎnar, Simona (ROU)	Gymnastics	3	1	3	7	1996–2000
	Strickland de la Hunty, Shirley (AUS)	Athletics	3	1	3	7	1948–56
61	Joyner-Kersee, Jackie (USA)	Athletics	3	1	2	6	1984–96
	Lenton-Trickett, Libby (AUS)	Swimming	3	1	2	6	2004–08
63	Boginskaya, Svetlana (EUN)	Gymnastics	3	1	1	5	1988–92
	Campbell-Brown, Veronica (JAM)	Athletics	3	1	1	5	2000–08
	Georgescu, Elena (ROU)	Rowing	3	1	1	5	1992–2008
	Gorokhova, Galina (USSR)	Fencing	3	1	1	5	1960–72
	Gould, Shane (AUS)	Swimming	3	1	1	5	1972
	Meagher, Mary T. (USA)	Swimming	3	1	1	5	1984–88
	Pipotǎ-Burcicǎ, Constanţa (ROU)	Rowing	3	1	1	5	1992–2008
	Torrence, Gwen (USA)	Athletics	3	1	1	5	1992–96
71	Berg, Laura (USA)	Softball	3	1	0	4	1996–2008
	Brisco-Hooks, Valerie (USA)	Athletics	3	1	0	4	1984–88
	Bryzgina, Olga (EUN)	Athletics	3	1	0	4	1988–92
	Gulbin-Engel-Krämer, Ingrid (GDR)	Diving	3	1	0	4	1960–64
	Hogshead, Nancy (USA)	Swimming	3	1	0	4	1984
	Janics, Natasa (HUN)	Canoeing	3	1	0	4	2004–08
	Mastenbroek, Rie (NED)	Swimming	3	1	0	4	1936
	Metschuck, Caren (GDR)	Swimming	3	1	0	4	1980
	Nothnagel-Von Seck, Anke (GER)	Canoeing	3	1	0	4	1988–92
	Park, Seong-Hyeon (KOR)	Archery	3	1	0	4	2004–08
	Petrenko-Samusenko, Tatyana (USSR)	Fencing	3	1	0	4	1960–72
	Press, Tamara (USSR)	Athletics	3	1	0	4	1960–64
	Von Saltza, Chris (USA)	Swimming	3	1	0	4	1960
	Stouder, Sharon (USA)	Swimming	3	1	0	4	1964
	Tyus, Wyomia (USA)	Athletics	3	1	0	4	1964–68
86	Martino, Angel (USA)	Swimming	3	0	3	6	1992–96
87	Fernandez, Ana Ibis (CUB)	Volleyball	3	0	1	4	1992–2004
	Heddle, Kathleen (CAN)	Rowing	3	0	1	4	1992–96
	Khvedosyuk-Pinayeva, Lyudmila (USSR)	Canoeing	3	0	1	4	1964–72
	McBean, Marnie (CAN)	Rowing	3	0	1	4	1992–96
	Rudolph, Wilma (USA)	Athletics	3	0	1	4	1956–60
	Smith, Michelle (IRL)	Swimming	3	0	1	4	1996
93	Ballanger, Félicia (FRA)	Cycling	3	0	0	3	1996–2000
	Bell, Regla (CUB)	Volleyball	3	0	0	3	1992–2000
	Belote, Melissa (USA)	Swimming	3	0	0	3	1972
	Bennett, Brooke (USA)	Swimming	3	0	0	3	1996–2000
	Bleibtrey, Ethelda (USA)	Swimming	3	0	0	3	1920
	Brusnikina, Olga (RUS)	Synchronised Swimming	3	0	0	3	2000–04
	Caulkins, Tracy (USA)	Swimming	3	0	0	3	1984
	Costa, Marlenis (CUB)	Volleyball	3	0	0	3	1992–2000
	Devers, Gail (USA)	Athletics	3	0	0	3	1992–96
	Fernandez, Lisa (USA)	Softball	3	0	0	3	1996–2004
	Gafencu, Liliana (ROU)	Rowing	3	0	0	3	1996–2004
	Gato, Idalmis (CUB)	Volleyball	3	0	0	3	1992–2000
	Haislett, Nicole (USA)	Swimming	3	0	0	3	1992
	Harrigan, Lori (USA)	Softball	3	0	0	3	1996–2004
	Hawkes, Rechelle (AUS)	Hockey	3	0	0	3	1988–2000
	Henry, Jodie (AUS)	Swimming	3	0	0	3	2004
	Howell, Matilda Scott (USA)	Archery	3	0	0	3	1904
	Izquierdo, Lilia (CUB)	Volleyball	3	0	0	3	1992–2000
	Kazankina, Tatyana (USSR)	Athletics	3	0	0	3	1976–80
	Kiselyova, Mariya (RUS)	Synchronised Swimming	3	0	0	3	2000–04
	Krause, Barbara (GDR)	Swimming	3	0	0	3	1980
	Luis, Mireya (CUB)	Volleyball	3	0	0	3	1992–2000
	Madison, Helene (USA)	Swimming	3	0	0	3	1932
	Meyer, Debbie (USA)	Swimming	3	0	0	3	1968
	Neilson, Sandy (USA)	Swimming	3	0	0	3	1972
	Norelius, Martha (USA)	Swimming	3	0	0	3	1924–28
	O'Brien-Amico, Leah (USA)	Softball	3	0	0	3	1996–2004
	Pérec, Marie-José (FRA)	Athletics	3	0	0	3	1992–96
	Ponor, Cǎtǎlina (ROU)	Gymnastics	3	0	0	3	2004
	Reinisch, Rica (GDR)	Swimming	3	0	0	3	1980

R	ATHLETE	SPORT(S)	G	S	B	TOT	DATES
	Rice, Steph (AUS)	Swimming	3	0	0	3	2008
	Richter, Ulrike (GDR)	Swimming	3	0	0	3	1976
	Smith, Katie (USA)	Basketball	3	0	0	3	2000–08
	Staley, Dawn (USA)	Basketball	3	0	0	3	1996–2004
	Steinseifer, Carrie (USA)	Swimming	3	0	0	3	1984
	Swoopes, Sheryl (USA)	Basketball	3	0	0	3	1996–2004
	Tappin, Ashley (USA)	Swimming	3	0	0	3	1992–2000
	Theodorescu, Monica (GER)	Equestrian	3	0	0	3	1988–96
	Torres, Regla (CUB)	Volleyball	3	0	0	3	1992–2000
	Williams, Venus (USA)	Tennis	3	0	0	3	2000–08
	Yun, Mi-Jin (KOR)	Archery	3	0	0	3	2000–04
	Zabelina, Aleksandra (USSR)	Fencing	3	0	0	3	1960–72

PARALYMPIC MEN

R	ATHLETE	SPORT(S)	G	S	B	TOT	DATES
1	Marson, Roberto (ITA)	Wheelchair Fencing, Athletics, Swimming	16	7	3	26	1964–76
2	Jacobsson, Jonas (SWE)	Shooting	16	1	8	25	1980–2008
3	Kenny, Mike (GBR)	Swimming	16	0	0	16	1976–88
4	Nietlispach, Franz (SUI)	Athletics, Cycling	14	6	2	22	1976–2008
5	Edgson, Michael (CAN)	Swimming	14	2	0	16	1984–92
6	Frei, Heinz (SUI)	Athletics, Cycling	13	6	5	22	1984–2008
7	Trondsen, Erling (NOR)	Swimming	13	6	1	20	1976–92
8	Dodson, Bart (USA)	Athletics	13	3	4	20	1984–2000
9	Morgan, John (USA)	Swimming	13	2	0	15	1984–92
10	Henker, Siegmar (GER)	Archery, Athletics, Shooting, Swimming	12	9	2	23	1976–96
11	McIsaac, Timothy (CAN)	Swimming	11	6	4	21	1976–88
12	Roberts, David (GBR)	Swimming	11	4	1	16	2000–08
13	Bergman, Uri (ISR)	Swimming	11	0	1	12	1976–88
14	Pawlowski, Arkadiusz (POL)	Swimming	10	3	5	18	1980–2000
15	Sullivan, Timothy (AUS)	Athletics	10	0	0	10	2000–08
16	Pedersen, Noel (NOR)	Swimming	9	9	3	21	1988–2000
17	Holmes, Christopher (GBR)	Swimming	9	5	1	15	1988–2000
18	Lachaud, Christian (FRA)	Wheelchair Fencing	9	2	2	13	1976–2000
	Owen, Ed (USA)	Athletics, Swimming, Wheelchair Basketball	9	2	2	13	1964–88
20	Hennaert, Andre (FRA)	Wheelchair Fencing, Table Tennis	9	1	6	16	1976–92
21	Pearson, Lee (GBR)	Equestrian	9	0	0	9	2000–08
	Stein, R. (USA)	Athletics	9	0	0	9	1960–64
23	Emmel, Manfred (GER)	Athletics, Swimming, Table Tennis	8	7	0	15	1968–2008
24	Pancalli, Luca (ITA)	Swimming	8	6	1	15	1984–96
25	Oribe, Ricardo (ESP)	Swimming	8	5	1	14	1992–2008
26	Lindmann, Eric (FRA)	Swimming	8	4	6	18	1992–2004
27	Huot, Benoit (CAN)	Swimming	8	4	4	16	2000–08
28	Cowdrey, Matthew (AUS)	Swimming	8	4	2	14	2004–08
	Wu, Walter (CAN)	Swimming	8	4	2	14	1996–2004
30	Matthews, Robert (GBR)	Athletics	8	4	1	13	1984–2004
31	Bellance, Arthur (FRA)	Wheelchair Fencing	8	2	2	12	1980–96
	Rodriguez, Sebastian (ESP)	Swimming	8	2	2	12	2000–08
33	Hildebrandt, Frits (NED)	Swimming	8	2	0	10	1976–84
34	Weber, Edund (GER)	Athletics, Table Tennis	8	2	1	11	1972–88
35	Thompson, James (USA)	Swimming	8	1	2	11	1988–2000
36	Schroeder, Karl (GER)	Athletics, Swimming	8	0	0	8	1980–84
	Surgeoner, Robin (GBR)	Swimming	8	0	0	8	1984–92
38	Pinard, Pascal (FRA)	Swimming	7	5	6	18	1992–2004
39	Dabrowski, Jerzy (POL)	Athletics, Volleyball (Standing)	7	4	2	13	1980–2008
	Issorat, Claude (FRA)	Athletics	7	4	2	13	1992–2004
41	Van Winkel, Paul (BEL)	Athletics	7	4	1	12	1980–92
42	Olsson, Anders (SWE)	Swimming	7	3	4	14	1980–2008
43	Foppolo, David (FRA)	Swimming	7	3	2	12	1980–96
44	Pacault, Yvon (FRA)	Wheelchair Fencing	7	3	0	10	1988–2000
45	Gerein, Clayton (CAN)	Athletics, Swimming	7	2	5	14	1984–2008
	Koeberle, Heinrich (GER)	Athletics	7	2	5	14	1984–2000
47	de Vidi, Alvise (ITA)	Athletics, Swimming	7	2	4	12	1988–2004
48	Jerome, John (USA)	Athletics	7	2	2	11	1976–88
49	Houtsma, Alwin (NED)	Swimming	7	2	1	10	1996–2000
	Valdez, Eusebio (MEX)	Athletics	7	2	1	10	1976–1984
51	Conde, Javier (ESP)	Athletics	7	2	0	9	1992–2004
52	Robeson, Scott (USA)	Swimming	7	1	3	11	1976–80
53	Boldt, Arnold (CAN)	Athletics	7	1	0	8	1976–92
54	Taylor, T. (GBR)	Lawn Bowls, Table Tennis, Snooker	7	0	4	11	1964–84
55	Kolly, Urs (SUI)	Athletics	7	0	1	8	1992–2008
	Perry, B. (FRA)	Athletics, Swimming	7	0	1	8	1976–80

R	ATHLETE	SPORT(S)	G	S	B	TOT	DATES
57	Owczarek, Miroslaw (POL)	Swimming	6	9	1	16	1976–92
58	Sleczka, Krzysztof (POL)	Swimming	6	8	4	18	1984–2000
59	Anderson, James (GBR)	Swimming	6	7	0	13	1992–2004
60	Fuller, Neil (AUS)	Athletics	6	6	3	15	1992–2004
61	de Groot, Alwin (NED)	Swimming	6	5	2	13	1992–96
	Silva, Clodoaldo (BRA)	Swimming	6	5	2	13	2000–08
63	Francis, Heath (AUS)	Athletics	6	4	3	13	2000–08
	de Vos, Marc (BEL)	Archery, Athletics	6	4	2	12	1960–88
65	Szlezak, Jerzy (POL)	Athletics	6	4	0	10	1984–92
	Woelk, Holger (GER)	Swimming	6	4	0	10	1984–92
67	Thompson, Dick (GBR)	Athletics, Table Tennis, Wheelchair Fencing	6	3	5	14	1960–72
68	Rossi, Franco (ITA)	Swimming, Table Tennis, Wheelchair Fencing	6	3	4	13	1960–72
	Spiess, Guenter West (GER)	Athletics, Wheelchair Fencing	6	3	4	13	1976–96
	Wanger, Joseph (ISR)	Swimming	6	3	4	13	1972–88
71	He, Junquan (CHN)	Swimming	6	3	2	11	2000–08
72	Machowczyk, Ryszard (POL)	Swimming	6	3	1	10	1972–80
73	Rosenast, Hans (SUI)	Athletics, Table Tennis	6	3	0	9	1972–92
	Wojciechowski, Andrzej (POL)	Swimming	6	3	0	9	1984–88
75	Petersson, John (DEN)	Swimming	6	2	7	15	1984–2000
76	Durand, Pascal (FRA)	Wheelchair Fencing	6	2	4	12	1988–2004
77	Kindred, Sascha (GBR)	Swimming	6	2	3	11	1996–2008
	Short, Russell (AUS)	Athletics	6	2	3	11	1988–2008
	So, Wa Wai (HKG)	Athletics	6	2	3	11	1996–2008
80	Jauhiainen, Harri (FIN)	Athletics	6	2	2	10	1980–88
	Scott, Christopher (AUS)	Cycling	6	2	2	10	1996–2008
82	Kenny, Darren (GBR)	Cycling	6	2	0	8	2004–08
	Kers, M. (NED)	Swimming	6	2	0	8	1976–80
84	Monsalvo, Eduardo (MEX)	Athletics, Swimming	6	1	3	10	1976–96
85	Lee, Hae Gon (KOR)	Table Tennis	6	1	2	9	1988–2004
86	Badid, Mustapha (FRA)	Athletics	6	1	1	8	1984–96
	Clark, Raymond (SWE)	Athletics	6	1	1	8	1980–84
	Hermans, Alex (BEL)	Athletics	6	1	1	8	1980–2000
	Sun, Hai Tao (CHN)	Athletics	6	1	1	8	1996–2004
	Szpojnarowicz, Marek (POL)	Swimming	6	1	1	8	1984–92
91	Bouallegue, Maher (TUN)	Athletics	6	1	0	7	2000–04
92	Thrupp, Darren (AUS)	Athletics	6	0	3	9	1988–2008
93	Larson, David (USA)	Athletics	6	0	2	8	1988–2000
94	Hagai, Baruch (ISR)	Swimming, Table Tennis	6	0	1	7	1964–88
	Kreidel, Thomas (GER)	Table Tennis	6	0	1	7	1984–96
96	Guo, Wei (CHN)	Athletics	6	0	0	6	2000–08
	Laveborn, Mats (SWE)	Athletics	6	0	0	6	1984–88
	Pedersen, Cato Zahl (NOR)	Athletics	6	0	0	6	1980–84
	Worthington, Jeff (USA)	Athletics	6	0	0	6	1988
100	Kawai, Junichi (JPN)	Swimming	5	9	7	21	1992–2008
101	Bugarin, Kingsley (AUS)	Swimming	5	8	6	19	1984–2000
102	Pinto, Shlomo (ISR)	Swimming	5	8	1	14	1976–1992
103	Kelly, Daniel (USA)	Swimming	5	7	5	17	1992–2000
104	Erasmus, Daniel (RSA)	Athletics, Lawn Bowls	5	6	1	12	1964–72
105	Muirhead, James (GBR)	Swimming	5	5	3	13	1976–84
106	Cairns, Kenneth (GBR)	Swimming	5	5	2	12	1984–2004
	Golombek, Gregor (GDR)	Athletics	5	5	2	12	1980–88
	Makarau, Raman (BLR)	Swimming	5	5	2	12	2000–08
109	Schuhbauer, Johann (GER)	Athletics	5	4	6	15	1968–88
110	Torres, Javier (ESP)	Swimming	5	4	5	14	1992–2008
111	Lofstrom, Lars (SWE)	Athletics, Wheelchair Basketball	5	4	2	11	1972–96
112	Duval, Julius (USA)	Athletics	5	4	1	10	1972–80
	Reimer, Eugene (CAN)	Athletics	5	4	1	10	1968–80
114	Renalson, V. (AUS)	Weightlifting	5	3	2	10	1964–76
115	Gudgeon, Gary (AUS)	Swimming	5	3	1	9	1980–84
	Jezek, Jiri (CZE)	Cycling	5	3	1	9	2000–08
	Reelie, Richard (CAN)	Athletics	5	3	1	9	1988–2004
	Stokkel, Johannes (NED)	Swimming	5	3	1	9	1988–92
119	Christen, Lukas (SUI)	Athletics	5	3	0	8	1992–2000
	Pereira, Luis Claudio (BRA)	Athletics	5	3	0	8	1984–88
121	Biela, Grzegorz (POL)	Swimming	5	2	3	10	1976–84
122	Pych, Miroslaw (POL)	Athletics	5	2	2	9	1992–2008
123	Prieto, Juan Antonio (ESP)	Athletics	5	2	1	8	1992–2000
	Rosier, Jean (FRA)	Wheelchair Fencing	5	2	1	8	1992–2000
125	Beez, Alois (GER)	Athletics	5	2	0	7	1976–84
	Ellis, D. (GBR)	Swimming	5	2	0	7	1964–76
	Lombaard, Fanie (RSA)	Athletics	5	2	0	7	2000–04
128	Figl, Robert (GER)	Athletics	5	1	6	12	1988–2004
129	Ozaki, Mineho (JPN)	Athletics	5	1	5	11	1984–2008
130	Smyrnov, Viktor (UKR)	Swimming	5	1	4	10	2004–08
131	Kujala, Pekka (FIN)	Athletics	5	1	2	8	1976–92
	Levy, Moshe (ISR)	Swimming	5	1	2	8	1968–92
	Prossl, W. (GER)	Athletics	5	1	2	8	1960–72
	Requena, Julio (ESP)	Athletics	5	1	2	8	1992–2000
135	Fung, Ying Ki (HKG)	Wheelchair Fencing	5	1	1	7	2000–04
	Li, Qiang (CHN)	Athletics, Table Tennis	5	1	1	7	2000–08
	More, Cyril(FRA)	Wheelchair Fencing	5	1	1	7	1996–2008
138	Braet, Achiel (BEL)	Athletics	5	1	0	6	1976–80
	Easton, Robert (CAN)	Athletics	5	1	0	6	1984–88
	Einarsson, Mats (SWE)	Swimming	5	1	0	6	1988
	Fidalgo, Alfonso (ESP)	Athletics	5	1	0	6	1992–2000
	Johansson, Thomas (SWE)	Shooting	5	1	0	6	1996–2004
	Keay, Colin (GBR)	Athletics	5	1	0	6	1984–88
	Meredith, Shawn (USA)	Athletics	5	1	0	6	1992–96
145	Christensen, Anders (DEN)	Swimming	5	0	5	10	1984–92
146	Chepel, Oleg (BLR)	Athletics	5	0	3	8	1988–2000
	Nugent, Rodney (AUS)	Athletics	5	0	3	8	1988–92
	Strokin, Andrey (RUS)	Swimming	5	0	3	8	2000–08
149	Mosterd, Johan (NED)	Swimming	5	0	2	7	1984–88
	Rogo, Renzo (ITA)	Swimming, Wheelchair Fencing	5	0	2	7	1960–64
151	Allek, Mohamed Algeria	Athletics	5	0	1	6	1996–2008
	Betega, G. (FRA)	Swimming	5	0	1	6	1980–84
	Jokinen, Kimmo (FIN)	Table Tennis	5	0	1	6	1984–2000
	Marklein, Errol (GER)	Athletics	5	0	1	6	1980–92
	Modabber Raz, Ghader (IRI)	Athletics	5	0	1	6	1996–2000
156	Wening, Jason (USA)	Swimming	5	0	1	6	1992–2000
157	Lecours, Stephane (CAN)	Swimming	5	0	0	5	1988
	Magner, Jorgen (SWE)	Swimming	5	0	0	5	1988
	Surala, Andrzej (POL)	Swimming	5	0	0	5	1980
	Walker, Michael (GBR)	Athletics	5	0	0	5	1988–92
161	Kueschall, Rainer (SUI)	Athletics, Table Tennis	4	10	6	20	1968–1992
162	Noble, Paul (GBR)	Swimming	4	8	1	13	1984–2000
163	Simon, Heinz (GER)	Archery, Athletics, Swimming, Table Tennis	4	7	1	12	1964–88
164	Kimmig, Holger (GER)	Swimming	4	6	5	15	1992–2000
165	Van Buiten, Andre (NED)	Swimming	4	6	0	10	1980–92
166	Rodriguez, Jose Manuel (ESP)	Athletics, Boccia	4	5	2	11	1984–2008
167	Hainey, Tomas (CAN)	Swimming	4	5	0	9	1984–92
168	Ferraris, Giovanni (ITA)	Snooker, Table Tennis, Wheelchair Fencing	4	4	5	13	1960–76
169	Woods, Marc (GBR)	Swimming	4	4	2	10	1988–2004
170	Dias, Daniel (BRA)	Swimming	4	4	1	9	2008
	Taiganidis, Charalampos (GRE)	Swimming	4	4	1	9	2004–08
172	Oehler, Dennis (USA)	Athletics	4	3	3	10	1988–96
173	Jorgensen, Henrik (DEN)	Athletics, Boccia	4	3	2	9	1984–2004
	Leicht, Dieter (GER)	Wheelchair Fencing	4	3	2	9	1972–92
	Manson-Bishop, Leslie (RHO)	Athletics, Swimming	4	3	2	9	1964–72
	Thatcher, Noel (GBR)	Athletics	4	3	2	9	1984–2004
	Wallrodt, Bruce (AUS)	Athletics	4	3	2	9	1988–2004
178	Hui, Charn Hung (HKG)	Wheelchair Fencing	4	3	1	8	2000–08
	Koysub, Supachai (THA)	Athletics	4	3	1	8	2000–08
	Pauwels, Hans (BEL)	Swimming	4	3	1	8	1984–88
181	Tisserant, Guy (FRA)	Athletics, Table Tennis	4	3	0	7	1984–96
182	Jeannin, Daniel (FRA)	Athletics, Swimming, Table Tennis	4	2	5	11	1968–88
	Williams, Paul (GBR)	Athletics	4	2	5	11	1984–2004
184	Citerne, Robert (FRA)	Wheelchair Fencing	4	2	3	9	1988–2008
	Petersen, Wolfgang (GER)	Athletics	4	2	3	9	1988–96
	Wollmert, Jochen (GER)	Table Tennis	4	2	3	9	1992–2008
187	Nortmann, Hermann (GER)	Archery, Athletics	4	2	2	8	1984–2004
188	de Almeida Coelho, Paulo (POR)	Athletics	4	2	1	7	1992–2004
	Berg, Matthias (GER)	Athletics	4	2	1	7	1980–88
	Nourafshan, Mokhtar (IRI)	Athletics	4	2	1	7	1988–2004
	Sanchez, Jose Antonio (ESP)	Athletics	4	2	1	7	1992–2000
	Tomaszewski, Ryszard (POL)	Athletics, Powerlifting, Weightlifting	4	2	1	7	1980–96
	Tynan, Ronan (IRL)	Athletics	4	2	1	7	1984–88
194	Bjoernstad, Helge (NOR)	Swimming	4	2	0	6	1992–96
	Hammond, Gregory (AUS)	Swimming	4	2	0	6	1984–88
	Osborn, David (USA)	Athletics	4	2	0	6	1988
	Thomsen, Henrik (DEN)	Athletics	4	2	0	6	1980–84
198	Dunne, Gerard (IRL)	Swimming	4	1	4	9	1984–2000
	Ghysel, Eric (FRA)	Swimming	4	1	4	9	1984–88
200	Kim, Kyung Mook (KOR)	Table Tennis	4	1	5	10	1992–2008

R	ATHLETE	SPORT(S)	G	S	B	TOT	DATES
201	Kozon, Bogdan (POL)	Swimming	4	1	3	8	1984–88
202	Aleksyeyev, Dmytro (UKR)	Swimming	4	1	2	7	2004–08
	Clark, Ray (USA)	Athletics	4	1	2	7	1972–76, 1996
	Govaerts, Benny (BEL)	Athletics	4	1	2	7	1988–2004
	Jung, Keum Jong (KOR)	Powerlifting, Weightlifting	4	1	2	7	1984–2008
	Mangano, Santo (ITA)	Shooting	4	1	2	7	1984–96
	Martin, Peter (NZL)	Athletics	4	1	2	7	1996–2004
	Musil, Roman (CZE)	Athletics, Cycling	4	1	2	7	2000–08
	Russell, Eric (AUS)	Athletics	4	1	2	7	1976–80, 1992
210	Becke, Tom (USA)	Athletics, Powerlifting, Swimming	4	1	1	6	1980–84
	Du, Jianping (CHN)	Swimming	4	1	1	6	2008
	Josefiak, Hans (GER)	Athletics	4	1	1	6	1976–84
	Kale, Duane (NZL)	Swimming	4	1	1	6	1996
	Kim, Du Chun (KOR)	Athletics	4	1	1	6	1988–2000
	Li, Duan (CHN)	Athletics	4	1	1	6	2000–04
	Mashchenko, Oleksandr (UKR)	Swimming	4	1	1	6	2000–08
	Nielsen, Jorn (DEN)	Athletics	4	1	1	6	1976–80
	Shelton, Michael (GBR)	Lawn Bowls, Snooker	4	1	1	6	1960–76
	Son, Hoon (KOR)	Athletics	4	1	1	6	1988–92
220	Ajibola, Adeoye	Athletics	4	1	0	5	1992–96
	Bellot, Pierre (FRA)	Swimming	4	1	0	5	1992–96
	Brasil, Andre (BRA)	Swimming	4	1	0	5	2008
	Dahl, Stephan (DEN)	Swimming	4	1	0	5	1984
	Gunnerup, Harald (NOR)	Swimming	4	1	0	5	1960–76
	Khadr, Metwali Ahmed (EGY)	Athletics	4	1	0	5	1976–84
	Lindberg, Bengt (SWE)	Powerlifting, Weightlifting	4	1	0	5	1972–96
	Patchett, W. (AUS)	Athletics	4	1	0	5	1976–80
	Sjogren, Hans (SWE)	Swimming	4	1	0	5	1984
	Strauch, Abraham (ISR)	Weightlifting	4	1	0	5	1976–92
	Tangen, Bjorn (NOR)	Athletics	4	1	0	5	1980–84
	Volpentest, Tony (USA)	Athletics	4	1	0	5	1992–2000
232	Modra, Kieran (AUS)	Cycling, Swimming	4	0	4	8	1988–2008
233	Bradshaw, S. (GBR)	Archery, Table Tennis	4	0	3	7	1968–80
	Lebedinsky, Andrey (RUS)	Shooting	4	0	3	7	1996–2008
	Yin, Jianhua (CHN)	Swimming	4	0	3	7	2000–04
236	An, Tae Sung (KOR)	Archery	4	0	2	6	1998–2008
237	Alsup, Ronnie (USA)	Athletics	4	0	1	5	1984–92
	Kovar, Martin (CZE)	Swimming	4	0	1	5	1996–2004
	Miller, D. (NZL)	Athletics	4	0	1	5	1972–84
	Pawlik, Andrzej (POL)	Athletics	4	0	1	5	1976–80
	Pistorius, Oscar (RSA)	Athletics	4	0	1	5	2004–08
	Veraksa, Maksym (UKR)	Swimming	4	0	1	5	2008
243	Andrews, Danny (USA)	Athletics	4	0	0	4	2004–08
	Chapuis, J. M. (FRA)	Archery	4	0	0	4	1976–1984
	Cheung, Wai Leung (HKG)	Wheelchair Fencing	4	0	0	4	1996
	Czyz, Wojtek (GER)	Athletics	4	0	0	4	2004–08
	Enhamed, Enhamed (ESP)	Swimming	4	0	0	4	2008
	Fornalczyk, Ryszard (POL)	Weightlifting	4	0	0	4	1984–2004
	Jeszenszky, Attila (HUN)	Swimming	4	0	0	4	1984
	Kalmykov, Vadim (USSR)	Athletics	4	0	0	4	1988
	Kohl, Manfred (GER)	Volleyball (Standing)	4	0	0	4	1988–2000
	Lee, Hak Young (KOR)	Archery	4	0	0	4	1984–2004
	Magnet, Wolfgang (AUT)	Swimming	4	0	0	4	1976–80
	Matsson, J. (SWE)	Athletics	4	0	0	4	1984
	Nitz, Paul (USA)	Athletics	4	0	0	4	1992–2004
	Ramsey, Phil (USA)	Swimming	4	0	0	4	1964
	Slaugh, D. (USA)	Archery	4	0	0	4	1964
	Smyth, Paul (IRL)	Lawn Bowls	4	0	0	4	1980–84
	Walden, Robert (AUS)	Swimming	4	0	0	4	1984–88
	Whitman, Jack (USA)	Archery	4	0	0	4	1960–64
	Zhang, Lixin (CHN)	Athletics	4	0	0	4	2008
262	Heir, Douglas (USA)	Athletics	3	7	2	12	1984–2000
263	Bolotin, Ron (ISR)	Swimming	3	5	3	11	1980–2000
	Crisp, James (GBR)	Swimming	3	5	3	11	2000–04
265	Punko, Sergei (BLR)	Swimming	3	5	2	10	2000–08
	Ockvirk, Robert (USA)	Athletics, Swimming	3	5	2	10	1972–80
267	Fearnley, Kurt (AUS)	Athletics	3	5	1	9	2000–08
268	Haber, Peter (GER)	Athletics	3	5	0	8	1992–2000
	Wolf, Nachman (ISR)	Athletics	3	5	0	8	1984–2000
270	Adams, Jeffrey (CAN)	Athletics	3	4	6	13	1988–2004
271	Levis, Reno (USA)	Archery, Athletics	3	4	3	10	1968–80
	Loi, Vittorio (ITA)	Wheelchair Fencing	3	4	3	10	1968–80
	Planchon, C. (FRA)	Wheelchair Fencing	3	4	3	10	1964–80
274	Dempsey, Michael (USA)	Table Tennis	3	4	2	9	1972–2000
	McGregor, Kerrod (AUS)	Athletics	3	4	2	9	1984–96
	Kerr, Gary (USA)	Athletics, Table Tennis	3	4	2	9	1972–80
	Noorduin, Willem (NED)	Athletics	3	4	2	9	1988–2008
	Williamson, David (USA)	Athletics	3	4	2	9	1968–76
279	Gomez, Said (PAN)	Athletics	3	4	1	8	1992–2008
	Leek, Peter (AUS)	Swimming	3	4	1	8	2008
	Loeffler, Stefan (GER)	Swimming	3	4	1	8	1992–96
	Rubin, Arieh (ISR)	Swimming, Table Tennis	3	4	1	8	1968–76
283	Coultas, Nigel (GBR)	Athletics	3	4	0	7	1988–92
	Leonard, Dan (CAN)	Athletics	3	4	0	7	1980–84
285	Bergeron, Dean (CAN)	Athletics	3	3	5	11	1996–2008
286	Thomas, Cyril (GBR)	Wheelchair Fencing	3	3	4	10	1964–88
	Viger, Andre (CAN)	Athletics	3	3	4	10	1980–96
288	de la Bourdonnaye, Gilles (FRA)	Table Tennis	3	3	3	9	1992–2008
	Johann, Jurgen (GER)	Athletics	3	3	3	9	1976–88
	Lindsay, John (AUS)	Athletics	3	3	3	9	1998–2004
	Van Ophem, Remi (BEL)	Athletics	3	3	3	9	1972–88
292	Fitzgerald, M. (CAN)	Athletics	3	3	2	8	1980–84
	Chan, Kam Loi (HKG)	Wheelchair Fencing	3	3	2	8	1992–2004
	Prestat (FRA)	Wheelchair Fencing	3	3	2	8	1968–76
	Smith, Greg (AUS)	Athletics, Wheelchair Rugby	3	3	2	8	1992–2008
	Vidal, Daniel (ESP)	Swimming	3	3	2	8	2000–08
297	Andersson, Per (SWE)	Swimming	3	3	1	7	1984–88
	Fuertes, Juan (ESP)	Swimming	3	3	1	7	1992–96
	Kikolski, Waldemar (POL)	Athletics	3	3	1	7	1992–2000
	Krauz, Jan (POL)	Athletics	3	3	1	7	1976–84
	Nederman, Lars-Ove (SWE)	Swimming	3	3	1	7	1984–88
	Poulisse, Marcel (NED)	Swimming	3	3	1	7	1984–88
	Pringle, Malcolm (RSA)	Athletics	3	3	1	7	1996–2004
	Wahoram, Prawat (THA)	Athletics	3	3	1	7	2000–08
305	Amarouche, Farid (FRA)	Athletics	3	3	0	6	1988–1992
	Du, Jian Ping (CHN)	Swimming	3	3	0	6	2004
	Fraczyk, Stanislaw (AUT)	Table Tennis	3	3	0	6	1996–2008
	Lund, Peter (DEN)	Swimming	3	3	0	6	1992
	Mulder, Jan (NED)	Cycling	3	3	0	6	1992–2004
310	Manganaro, Aldo (ITA)	Athletics	3	2	4	9	1988–2004
	Payton, Stephen (GBR)	Athletics	3	2	4	9	1996–2008
312	Mastro, James (USA)	Athletics, Judo, Wrestling	3	2	3	8	1980–84, 1992–2000
	Tammel, Eef (NED)	Shooting	3	2	3	8	1984–92
314	Bohm, Hans-Joachim (GER)	Wheelchair Fencing	3	2	2	7	1972–84
	Frasure, Brian (USA)	Athletics	3	2	2	7	2000–08
	Haslam, P. (GBR)	Shooting, Snooker	3	2	2	7	1972–84
	Kwong, Wai Ip (HKG)	Wheelchair Fencing	3	2	2	7	1992–2004
	Lapalme, Denis (CAN)	Athletics, Swimming	3	2	2	7	1976–80, 1988–92
	Long, Giles (GBR)	Swimming	3	2	2	7	1996–2004
	Nilsson, Tore (SWE)	Swimming	3	2	2	7	1976–80
	Takada, Toshihiro (JPN)	Athletics	3	2	2	7	2004–08
322	Bec, Serge (FRA)	Wheelchair Fencing	3	2	1	6	1964–68
	Cid, Antonio (ESP)	Boccia	3	2	1	6	1992–2004
	Cohen, Izhar (ISR)	Swimming	3	2	1	6	1998–2008
	Hansen, R. (CAN)	Athletics	3	2	1	6	1980–84
	Izlakar, Franjo Slovenia	Athletics	3	2	1	6	1980–2000
	Martinson, Jim (USA)	Athletics	3	2	1	6	1980–84
	Xiong, Xiao Ming (CHN)	Swimming	3	2	1	6	2000–04
329	Arnold, Daniel (GER)	Table Tennis	3	2	0	5	2000–08
	Barnbeck, Heinz (GER)	Swimming	3	2	0	5	1984–88
	Boerstler, B. (GER)	Table Tennis	3	2	0	5	1972–80
	Bundgaard, Christian (DEN)	Swimming	3	2	0	5	1992–2008
	Fedyna, Oleksii (UKR)	Swimming	3	2	0	5	2008
	Grun, Guy (BEL)	Archery	3	2	0	5	1968–88
	Hernandez, Salvador (MEX)	Athletics	3	2	0	5	1996–2008
	Roselle, Ronald (NED)	Swimming	3	2	0	5	1984
	Steiner (GER)	Archery, Athletics, Table Tennis	3	2	0	5	1972–76
	Verner, S. (SWE)	Swimming	3	2	0	5	1976
	Winger, Dean (USA)	Swimming	3	2	0	5	1980
340	Hong, Suk Man (KOR)	Athletics	3	1	3	7	2004–08
341	Chida, Farhat (TUN)	Athletics	3	1	2	6	2004–08
	Hahnengress, Jochen (GER)	Swimming	3	1	2	6	1988–92
	Haynes, Winford (USA)	Athletics	3	1	2	6	1976–96
	Kurfess, Thomas (GER)	Table Tennis	3	1	2	6	1988–2000
	Register, Freeman (USA)	Athletics	3	1	2	6	1992–2000
346	Bridgeman, Ken (GBR)	Lawn Bowls	3	1	1	5	1980–88
	Brinkman, C. (USA)	Athletics	3	1	1	5	1976–80
	Hess, Wolfgang (GER)	Shooting	3	1	1	5	1988
	de Hoop, Gerrie (NED)	Swimming	3	1	1	5	1980–84

R	ATHLETE	SPORT(S)	G	S	B	TOT	DATES
	Marin, Angel (ESP)	Athletics	3	1	1	5	1988–92
	Miller, Stephen (GBR)	Athletics	3	1	1	5	1996–2008
	Osland, Stig (NOR)	Swimming	3	1	1	5	1980–84
	Othmar, Carsten (GER)	Swimming	3	1	1	5	1984
	Reyes, Juan Ignacio (MEX)	Swimming	3	1	1	5	2000–04
	Roth, Harald (AUT)	Athletics	3	1	1	5	1984–92
	Sakelarov, Gueorgui (BUL)	Athletics	3	1	1	5	1988–2000
	Schmidberger, R. (GER)	Archery	3	1	1	5	1972–80
	Schmidt, Detlef (GER)	Swimming	3	1	1	5	1992–2000
	Sulisalo, Timo (FIN)	Athletics	3	1	1	5	1976–88
	Ten, Ricardo (ESP)	Swimming	3	1	1	5	1996–2008
	Wrobel, Andrzej (POL)	Athletics	3	1	1	5	1992–2000
362	Ahmed, Gomma G. (EGY)	Powerlifting	3	1	0	4	1988–2004
	Arefyev, Artem (RUS)	Athletics	3	1	0	4	2004–08
	Flamengo, Jean-Louis (FRA)	Swimming	3	1	0	4	1992–96
	Fujimoto, Satoshi (JPN)	Judo	3	1	0	4	1996–2008
	Gagnon, Philippe (CAN)	Swimming	3	1	0	4	2000
	Golkar Azghandi, Ali (IRI)	Volleyball (Sitting)	3	1	0	4	1992–2004
	Hajek, Rudolf (AUT)	Table Tennis	3	1	0	4	1988–2004
	Kim, Byoung Young (KOR)	Table Tennis	3	1	0	4	2000–08
	Kleynhans, Ebert (RSA)	Swimming	3	1	0	4	1996–2004
	Kokarev, Dmitry (RUS)	Swimming	3	1	0	4	2008
	Langenhoven, Hilton (RSA)	Athletics	3	1	0	4	2004–08
	Li, Huzhao (CHN)	Athletics	3	1	0	4	2008
	Neppl, James (USA)	Athletics, Goalball	3	1	0	3	1980–88
	Nielsen, Hans Lykkestrig (DEN)	Equestrian	3	1	0	4	1984
	Robin, Jean-Philippe (FRA)	Table Tennis	3	1	0	4	2000, 2008
	Skaret, Frank (SWE)	Swimming	3	1	0	4	1976–80
	Smith, H. (USA)	Athletics	3	1	0	4	1964–68
	Teuber, Michael (GER)	Cycling	3	1	0	4	2000–08
	Wang, Xiao Fu (CHN)	Swimming	3	1	0	4	2004
	Zanarotto, Germano (ITA)	Wheelchair Fencing	3	1	0	4	1968–72
382	Eiriksson, Olafur (ISL)	Swimming	3	0	6	9	1988–96
383	Minor, R. (CAN)	Athletics	3	0	4	7	1976–84
384	Collado, Jesus (ESP)	Swimming	3	0	3	6	2000–08
	Dukai, Geza (HUN)	Swimming	3	0	3	6	1984–88
	Peeters, Michel (FRA)	Table Tennis	3	0	3	6	1980–2000
	Szekeres, Pal (HUN)	Wheelchair Fencing	3	0	3	6	1992–2008
388	Cho, Hyun Kwan (KOR)	Archery	3	0	2	5	1988–2008
	Churchill, Kenneth (GBR)	Athletics	3	0	2	5	1992–2004
	Cibone, Thierry (FRA)	Athletics	3	0	2	5	2000–08
	Cundy, Jody (GBR)	Swimming	3	0	2	5	1996–2008
	Lee, Hong Gu (KOR)	Archery	3	0	2	5	2000–08
	Matthews, Tim (AUS)	Athletics	3	0	2	5	1996–2004
	Pedrajas, Jose (ESP)	Swimming	3	0	2	5	1988–96
	Vereczkei, Zsolt (HUN)	Swimming	3	0	2	5	1992–2008
396	Ball, Greg (AUS)	Cycling	3	0	1	4	2000–08
	Bone, Jamie (CAN)	Athletics	3	0	1	4	1988
	Butler, Daniel (USA)	Swimming	3	0	1	4	1992–2000
	Ge, Yang (CHN)	Table Tennis	3	0	1	4	2004–08
	Hardy, Jeffrey (AUS)	Swimming	3	0	1	4	1996–2000
	Jackson, Simon (GBR)	Judo	3	0	1	4	1988–2004
	Kang, Seong Hoon (KOR)	Table Tennis	3	0	1	4	1992–2004
	Paz, Marcelino (BRA)(ESP)	Athletics	3	0	1	4	1988–92
	Rosenbaum, R. (USA)	Swimming	3	0	1	4	1964–72
	Sanchez-Guijo, Enrique (ESP)	Athletics	3	0	1	4	1996–2000
	Shaw, James (CAN)	Athletics	3	0	1	4	1996–2004
	Wanyoike, Henry (KEN)	Athletics	3	0	1	4	2000–08
	Xu, Qing (CHN)	Swimming	3	0	1	4	2004–08
409	Adesoji, Adekundo A. (NIG)	Athletics	3	0	0	3	2004
	Axelsson, Thomas (SWE)	Table Tennis	3	0	0	3	1984–96
	Bruno, Frank (CAN)	Athletics	3	0	0	3	1992–96
	Cai, Zusheng (CHN)	Swimming	3	0	0	3	1988–92
	Casinos, David (ESP)	Athletics	3	0	0	3	2000–08
	Cougouille, Didier (FRA)	Swimming	3	0	0	3	1984
	Danilik, Aliaksandr (BLR)	Cycling	3	0	0	3	2000–04
	Dengerink, Carlo (NED)	Football 7-a-side	3	0	0	3	1988–92
	Eriksson, Hikan (SWE)	Athletics	3	0	0	3	1984
	Finder, Piotr (POL)	Swimming	3	0	0	3	1988
	Fink, Walter (AUT)	Athletics	3	0	0	3	1976–80
	Firouzi, Parviz (IRI)	Volleyball (Sitting)	3	0	0	3	1992–2000
	Fowler, V. (AUS)	Swimming	3	0	0	3	1964
	Frey, Martin (SUI)	Athletics	3	0	0	3	1984
	Van Geel, Joris (NED)	Swimming	3	0	0	3	1988
	Giebel, Josef (GER)	Volleyball (Standing)	3	0	0	3	1988–92
	Grgic, Pavo (GER)	Volleyball (Standing)	3	0	0	3	1992–2000
	Guntlisbergen, Peter (NED)	Football 7-a-side	3	0	0	3	1988–92
	Heersink, Paul (NED)	Football 7-a-side	3	0	0	3	1988–96
	Heinrich, Bernd (GER)	Volleyball (Standing)	3	0	0	3	1988–2000
	Hou, Bin (CHN)	Athletics	3	0	0	3	1996–2004
	Hull, Peter (GBR)	Swimming	3	0	0	3	1988–92
	de Jong, Arno (NED)	Football 7-a-side	3	0	0	3	1988–2000
	Karlsson, Arne (SWE)	Powerlifting, Weightlifting	3	0	0	3	1980–92
	Kashfia, Ali (IRI)	Volleyball (Sitting)	3	0	0	3	1988–96
	Kiley, David (USA)	Athletics	3	0	0	3	1976
	Kirwa, Henry Kiprono (KEN)	Athletics	3	0	0	3	2008
	Kone, Oumar Basakoulba (CIV)	Athletics	3	0	0	3	1996–2008
	Louwrens, Michael (RSA)	Athletics	3	0	0	3	1996–2008
	Macedo, Jose (POR)	Boccia	3	0	0	3	1996–2004
	Magennis, E. (AUS)	Lawn Bowls	3	0	0	3	1972–76, 1984
	Mannila, Tauno (FIN)	Athletics	3	0	0	3	1976
	Mitchell, Royal (USA)	Athletics	3	0	0	3	2000–08
	Mueller, Oliver (GER)	Volleyball (Standing)	3	0	0	3	1992–2000
	Noe, Michael (USA)	Athletics	3	0	0	3	1992
	O'Hanlon, Evan (AUS)	Athletics	3	0	0	3	2008
	Pendleton, Rick (AUS)	Swimming	3	0	0	3	2004–08
	Prado, Lucas (BRA)	Athletics	3	0	0	3	2008
	Raymond, Serge (CAN)	Athletics	3	0	0	3	1998–2002
	Van Rensburg (RSA)	Athletics	3	0	0	3	1972
	Rubner, Bernd (GER)	Swimming	3	0	0	3	1984
	Ruiz, Mariano (ESP)	Athletics	3	0	0	3	1988–2000
	Salavatian, Aliakbar (IRI)	Volleyball (Sitting)	3	0	0	3	1992–2000
	Sayovo, Jose Armando (ANG)	Athletics	3	0	0	3	2004
	Schmidl, Bernard (GER)	Volleyball (Standing)	3	0	0	3	1992–2000
	Shivani Mahjori, Ahmad (IRI)	Volleyball (Sitting)	3	0	0	3	1988–96
	Smyk, Zbigniew (POL)	Swimming	3	0	0	3	1980
	Soleimanikhoramdasht, Majid (IRI)	Volleyball (Sitting)	3	0	0	3	1992–2000
	Sommer, Elmar (GER)	Volleyball (Standing)	3	0	0	3	1992–96
	Vogel, Bernd (GER)	Powerlifting	3	0	0	3	1992–2004
	de Vries, Jaap (NED)	Football 7-a-side	3	0	0	3	1988–2000
	Weissenfels, Josef (GER)	Volleyball (Standing)	3	0	0	3	1988–96
	Zhang, Hai Dong (CHN)	Powerlifting	3	0	0	3	1996–2004

PARALYMPIC WOMEN

R	ATHLETE	SPORT(S)	G	S	B	TOT	DATES
1	Zorn, Trischa (USA)	Swimming	32	9	5	46	1980–2004
2	Hess, Beatrice (FRA)	Swimming	15	4	0	19	1996–2004
3	Narita, Mayumi (JPN)	Swimming	15	3	2	20	1996–2008
4	Petitclerc, Chantal (CAN)	Athletics	14	5	2	21	1992–2008
5	Popovich, Erin (USA)	Swimming	14	5	0	19	2000–08
6	Hengst, Claudia (GER)	Swimming	13	4	8	25	1988–2004
7	Batalova, Rima (RUS)	Athletics	13	2	2	17	1988–2008
8	Rubin-Rosenbaum, Zipora (ISR)	Athletics, Swimming, Table Tennis	11	4	6	21	1964–80, 1988
9	Grey-Thompson, Tanni (GBR)	Athletics	11	4	1	16	1988–2004
	Santamarta, Purificacion (ESP)	Athletics	11	4	1	16	1980–2004
11	Harriman, Maragaret (RSA)	Archery, Dartchery, Lawn Bowls, Swimming	11	2	4	17	1960–76, 1996
12	Scutti, Maria (ITA)	Athletics, Swimming, Table Tennis, Wheelchair Fencing	10	3	2	15	1960
13	Tjernberg, Magdalena (SWE)	Swimming	10	3	0	13	1984–88
14	Scott, Elizabeth (USA)	Swimming	10	2	5	17	1992–2000
15	Du Toit, Natalie (RSA)	Swimming	10	1	0	11	2004–2008
16	Ruiter, Marijke (NED)	Swimming, Wheelchair Basketball	10	0	1	11	1972–76, 1988
17	Hansen, Connie (DEN)	Athletics	9	4	1	14	1984–92
18	Sauvage, Louise (AUS)	Athletics	9	4	0	13	1992–2004
19	Cooper, Priya (AUS)	Swimming	9	3	4	16	1992–2000
20	Bryant, Carol (GBR)	Athletics, Swimming, Table Tennis, Wheelchair Fencing	9	2	5	16	1964–76

R	ATHLETE	SPORT(S)	G	S	B	TOT	DATES
21	Quell, Margit (GER)	Athletics, Swimming	9	2	2	13	1972–88
22	Buggenhagen, Marianne (GER)	Athletics	9	1	2	12	1992–2008
23	Ahrenstrand, Annelie (SWE)	Swimming	9	1	0	10	1980–84
	Vaughan, M. (GBR)	Swimming	9	1	0	10	1976–80
	Zhu, Hong Yan (CHN)	Swimming	9	1	0	10	2000–04
26	Toso, Anna Maria (ITA)	Athletics, Swimming, Table Tennis, Wheelchair Fencing	8	10	2	20	1960–64
27	Lauridsen, Ingrid (DEN)	Athletics	8	5	4	17	1980–92
28	Cornejo, Josefina (MEX)	Athletics, Swimming, Table Tennis	8	5	1	14	1976–80
	Rimmer, Eve M. (NZL)	Archery, Athletics, Swimming	8	5	1	14	1968–80
30	Hixson, Rosalie (USA)	Athletics, Lawn Bowls, Swimming, Table Tennis	8	4	6	18	1964–76
31	Siegers, Britta (GER)	Swimming	8	4	1	13	1984–92, 2004
32	Soto, Juana (MEX)	Athletics	8	3	3	14	1980–92, 2000
33	Kosmala, Elizabeth (AUS)	Shooting	8	3	0	11	1980–2004
34	Cable, Candace (USA)	Athletics	8	2	2	12	1980, 1988–96
35	Kuhnel, R. (AUT)	Swimming, Table Tennis	8	1	3	12	1960–68
36	Bouw, Joanne (CAN)	Athletics	8	0	2	10	1984–96
37	Dixon, Stephanie (CAN)	Swimming	7	10	2	19	2000–08
38	Cote, Kirby (CAN)	Swimming	7	6	0	13	2000–08
39	Newstead, Jennifer (NZL)	Swimming	7	2	1	10	1992–96
40	Michel, Yvette (CAN)	Swimming	7	2	0	9	1980–84
41	Long, Jessica (USA)	Swimming	7	1	1	9	2004–08
42	Zhang, Xiaoling (CHN)	Table Tennis	7	0	2	9	1988, 1996–2008
43	Lake, Josee (CAN)	Swimming	7	0	0	7	1980–84
44	Sandoval, Martha (MEX)	Athletics, Swimming, Table Tennis	6	6	0	12	1976–80
45	Forder, V. (GBR)	Archery, Athletics, Swimming, Wheelchair Fencing	6	4	1	11	1964–68
46	Freeman, T. (AUS)	Athletics	6	4	0	10	1972–76
47	Hopf, Yvonne (GER)	Swimming	6	3	2	11	1992–96
48	Schweizer, Rosa (AUT)(SUI)	Archery, Athletics, Table Tennis	6	3	0	9	1972–84
49	Hakonardottir, Kristin (ISL)	Swimming	6	2	4	12	1988–2004
50	Brandewie, Debra (USA)	Swimming	6	2	1	9	1988
51	El Hannouni, Assia (FRA)	Athletics	6	2	0	8	2004–08
	Hageraats, Ineke (NED)	Swimming	6	2	0	8	1980–84
	Mucz, Joanne (CAN)	Swimming	6	2	0	8	1984–92
54	Carracelas, Sara (ESP)	Swimming	6	1	3	10	1996–2008
55	Barr, Isabel (GBR)	Swimming	6	1	2	9	1980–88
56	Balta, Stephania (CAN)	Athletics	6	1	0	7	1980–84
	Bisquolm, Elisabeth (SUI)	Athletics, Table Tennis	6	1	0	7	1976–80
	Franks, Lisa (CAN)	Athletics, Wheelchair Basketball	6	1	0	7	2000–08
	Gustafson, M. (CAN)	Athletics, Swimming	6	1	0	7	1984
	Her Beek, L. (NED)	Swimming	6	1	0	7	1976
61	Farrell, Anne (CAN)	Athletics	6	0	2	8	1980–84
	Peiro, Ana (ESP)	Swimming	6	0	2	8	1984–88
	Zander (GER)	Athletics, Swimming	6	0	2	8	1960
64	Rowley, Janet (USA)	Athletics	6	0	1	7	1980–88
65	Bevard, M. (USA)	Swimming	6	0	0	6	1984
	Buddelmeyer, Petra (GER)	Athletics	6	0	0	6	1984–88
	Gonzalez, Arancha (Aranzazu) (ESP)	Swimming	6	0	0	6	1992–96
	Paton, Siobhan (AUS)	Swimming	6	0	0	6	2000
	Saker, M. (SWE)	Athletics	6	0	0	6	1984
	Sloan, Jessica (CAN)	Swimming	6	0	0	6	2000
71	Burton, Janice (GBR)	Swimming	5	10	5	20	1984–96
72	Bailey, Sarah (GBR)	Swimming	5	8	3	16	1992–2004
73	Carlton, Kathryne Lynne (USA)	Athletics	5	8	2	15	1980–2000
74	Stidever, Jane (GBR)	Equestrian, Swimming	5	5	6	16	1984–2004
75	Blackburn, Jane (GBR)	Archery, Athletics, Lawn Bowls, Table Tennis	5	4	2	11	1972–92
76	Al-Romi, Adelah (KUW)	Athletics	5	4	1	10	1980–92
77	Perales, Maria Teresa (ESP)	Swimming	5	3	8	16	2000–08
78	Cochetti, S. (ARG)	Athletics, Swimming	5	3	4	12	1964–68
	Driscoll, Jean (USA)	Athletics	5	3	4	12	1988–2000
80	Gonzalez, Doramitzi (MEX)	Swimming	5	3	3	11	2000–08
81	Mielech, Zofia (POL)	Athletics	5	3	2	10	1980–88, 1996
82	Kim, Im Yeon (KOR)	Shooting	5	3	1	9	1992–2008
83	Bourgain, Josette (FRA)	Wheelchair Fencing	5	3	0	8	1980, 1992–96
	Gilchrist, Lynnette (RHO)	Athletics, Swimming	5	3	0	8	1964
85	Adamik, Malgorzata (POL)	Swimming	5	2	5	12	1980–92
87	Owczarczyk, Krystyna (POL)	Athletics	5	2	5	12	1972–84
87	Prieur, Martine (FRA)	Athletics	5	2	4	11	1984–88
88	Buck, Gwen (GBR)	Lawn Bowls, Swimming, Table Tennis	5	2	3	10	1964–76
89	Goodrich, Judy (CAN)	Athletics, Swimming, Wheelchair Basketball	5	2	1	8	1984–92
	Pohl, Daniela (GER)	Swimming	5	2	1	8	1992–2000
91	Anderson (GBR)	Archery, Lawn Bowls, Swimming, Table Tennis	5	2	0	7	1960, 1972
	Duine, L. L. (NED)	Swimming	5	2	0	7	1976
93	Donaldson, Karen (USA)	Athletics, Swimming	5	1	3	9	1972–80
94	Berger-Waldenegg (AUT)	Athletics, Swimming, Table Tennis	5	1	2	8	1960
	Fantato, Paola (ITA)	Archery	5	1	2	8	1988–2004
96	Caspers, Barbara (AUS)	Shooting	5	1	1	7	1980–88
	McIntosh, Lisa (AUS)	Athletics	5	1	1	7	2000–08
98	Van Der Benden (NED)	Swimming	5	1	0	6	1968–72
	Beraudias, Agnes (FRA)	Swimming	5	1	0	6	1984–92
	Chan, Yui Chong (HKG)	Wheelchair Fencing	5	1	0	6	2004–08
	Edmondson, Elizabeth (AUS)	Swimming	5	1	0	6	1964–68
	Martin, P. (USA)	Athletics, Swimming	5	1	0	6	1976–80
	Pierre, Beatrice (FRA)	Swimming	5	1	0	6	1984–88
	Runyan, Marla (USA)	Athletics	5	1	0	6	1992
	Vergeer, Esther (NED)	Wheelchair Tennis	5	1	0	6	2000–08
	Yu, Chui Yee (HKG)	Wheelchair Fencing	5	1	0	6	2004–08
107	Winters, Amy (AUS)	Athletics	5	0	2	7	1996–2004
108	Evertsen, J. (NED)	Swimming	5	0	0	5	1976
	Foulds, P. (GBR)	Swimming	5	0	0	5	1960–64
	Ignaczuk, G. (POL)	Swimming	5	0	0	5	1980
	Ogorzelska, Agnieszka (POL)	Swimming	5	0	0	5	1980
	Romero, Jolanda (NED)	Swimming	5	0	0	5	1984
	Simpson, Tham (USA)	Athletics	5	0	0	5	1984–88
	Swanepoel, C. (GER)	Swimming	5	0	0	5	1980
115	Tjernberg, Gabriella (SWE)	Swimming	4	12	1	17	1984–92
116	Santos, Adria (BRA)	Athletics	4	8	1	13	1988–2008
117	Gallagher, Rosaleen (IRL)	Archery, Athletics, Swimming, Table Tennis	4	6	11	21	1968–88
118	Schwanger, Laura (USA)	Athletics, Rowing	4	6	2	12	1988–96, 2008
119	Goldstein, Ora (ISR)	Athletics, Swimming	4	5	3	12	1968–76
120	Cross, Tracey (AUS)	Swimming	4	5	1	10	1992–2000
121	Myers, Sharon (USA)	Athletics, Swimming	4	4	7	15	1972–80
122	Torres, Leticia (MEX)	Athletics	4	3	6	13	1988–2004
123	Lundborg, Monika (SWE)	Swimming	4	3	2	9	1980–84
124	Dashwood, Gemma (AUS)	Swimming	4	3	1	8	1996–2000
	Sivakova, Tamara (BLR)	Athletics	4	3	1	8	1992–2008
126	Luncher, Joyce (USA)	Swimming	4	3	0	7	1996
	Nesheim, Eva (NOR)	Swimming	4	3	0	7	1992–96
	Rahn, Sharon (USA)	Athletics, Swimming	4	3	0	7	1976–80
129	Picot, Patricia (FRA)	Wheelchair Fencing	4	2	4	10	1992–2008
130	Olarte, S. (ARG)	Athletics	4	2	2	8	1964–68
131	Leybovitch, Keren Or (ISR)	Swimming	4	2	1	7	2000–04
132	Joscelyne, Barbara (GBR)	Athletics	4	2	0	6	1980–84
	Scharf, Ilse (AUT)	Swimming, Table Tennis	4	2	0	6	1960, 1968–76
134	Valle, Patricia (MEX)	Swimming	4	1	3	8	1996–2008
135	Price, M. (GBR)	Athletics, Swimming	4	1	2	7	1980
	Schad, Petra (GER)	Athletics, Swimming	4	1	2	7	1980–92
137	Bedla, Barbara (POL)	Athletics	4	1	1	6	1976–80
	Dunham, Anne (GBR)	Equestrian	4	1	1	6	1996–2008
	Llorens, Lisa (AUS)	Athletics	4	1	1	6	1996–2000
140	Bouwmeester, Ans (NED)	Athletics	4	1	0	5	1984–88
	Van Duyn, Annemiek (NED)	Swimming	4	1	0	5	1984
	Fauche, J. (CAN)	Swimming	4	1	0	5	1984
	Howie, B. (GBR)	Athletics	4	1	0	5	1972–80
	Innes, Caroline (GBR)	Athletics	4	1	0	5	1992–2000
	Liebrecht (GER)	Archery, Athletics, Swimming	4	1	0	5	1972–76
	Pettersen, H. (NOR)	Swimming	4	1	0	5	1984
	Raes, Liesbeth (NED)	Swimming	4	1	0	5	1984
	Wang, Fang (CHN)	Athletics	4	1	0	5	2004–08
149	Wyrzykowska, Marta (POL)	Wheelchair Fencing	4	0	2	6	2000–04

R	ATHLETE	SPORT(S)	G	S	B	TOT	DATES
150	Van Buren-Schmidt, I. (NED)	Table Tennis	4	0	1	5	1972–80
	Hagel, Susan (USA)	Archery, Dartchery, Wheelchair Basketball	4	0	1	5	1976–96
152	Choptain, D. (CAN)	Swimming	4	0	0	4	1976
	Delorme, P. (FRA)	Swimming	4	0	0	4	1984
	Dosimont, D. (FRA)	Athletics	4	0	0	4	1980
	Edwards, Susan (USA)	Athletics	4	0	0	4	1988–92
	Eiler, Barbara (USA)	Swimming	4	0	0	4	1984
	Gettinger, Cynthia (USA)	Swimming	4	0	0	4	1988
	Hilberink, H. (NED)	Swimming	4	0	0	4	1972–76 1976–80
	Krajewska, Lucyna (POL)	Swimming	4	0	0	4	1980, 1988
	Patton, C. (USA)	Athletics, Swimming	4	0	0	4	1980
161	Loiseau, Ludivine (FRA)	Swimming	3	7	2	12	1996–2004
162	Espenhayn, Kay (GER)	Swimming	3	7	1	11	1996–2000
163	Rosenbaum, Ruth (USA)	Athletics, Table Tennis	3	6	1	10	1976–96
164	McEleny, Margaret (GBR)	Swimming	3	5	7	15	1992–2004
165	Mishani (ISR)	Athletics, Swimming, Table Tennis	3	5	3	11	1964–68
166	Bertini, Mariella (ITA)	Wheelchair Fencing	3	5	0	8	1984–2000
167	Ceeney, Daphne (AUS)	Archery, Athletics, Swimming, Table Tennis, Wheelchair Fencing	3	4	4	11	1960–64
168	Gull, Beverley (GBR)	Swimming	3	4	1	8	1988–92
	Zhao, Jihong (CHN)	Athletics	3	4	1	8	1984–92
170	Lamsbach, Ruth (GER)	Athletics, Swimming, Table Tennis, Wheelchair Basketball	3	3	5	11	1968–92
171	Pairoux, Genevieve (FRA)	Swimming	3	3	3	9	1988–92, 2008
172	Hattingh (RSA)	Athletics, Lawn Bowls, Table Tennis	3	3	1	7	1968–72
	Norris, Karen (USA)	Swimming	3	3	1	7	1992–2000
	Webb, Katrina (AUS)	Athletics	3	3	1	7	1996–2004
175	Coates, Deanna (GBR)	Shooting	3	3	2	8	1984–2008
176	Kortekaas, M. (NED)	Athletics, Swimming	3	3	0	6	1976–80
	Xu, Hong Yan (CHN)	Athletics	3	3	0	6	1996–2004
178	Gotell, Chelsey (CAN)	Swimming	3	2	7	12	2000–08
179	Borre, Ingrid (BEL)	Table Tennis	3	2	2	7	1984–96
	Campo, Danielle (CAN)	Swimming	3	2	2	7	2000–04
	Voboril, Ingrid (AUT)	Athletics, Table Tennis	3	2	2	7	1968–76
	Whitsell, Karissa (USA)	Cycling	3	2	2	7	2000–08
183	Beyer, G. (GER)	Athletics	3	2	1	6	1984
	Grand Maison, Valerie (CAN)	Swimming	3	2	1	6	2008
	Pape, Christiane (GER)	Table Tennis	3	2	1	6	1988, 1996–2004
	Weninger, Christiane (GER)	Table Tennis	3	2	1	6	1984–92
	Williams, Leone (JAM)	Athletics, Swimming	3	2	1	6	1972, 1980
188	Eriksson, Kerstin (SWE)	Swimming	3	2	0	5	1980–84
	Ieretti, A. (CAN)	Athletics	3	2	0	5	1984
	Nobumoto, Hiromi (JPN)	Athletics	3	2	0	5	1980
	Proust, Stephanie (FRA)	Swimming	3	2	0	5	1984
	Scherney, Andrea (AUT)	Athletics	3	2	0	5	1996–2008
	Van Den Bosch, Monique (NED)	Wheelchair Tennis	3	2	0	5	1988–92
194	Monaco, Irene (ITA)	Archery, Athletics, Swimming, Table Tennis, Wheelchair Fencing	3	1	6	10	1964–68, 1980–84
195	Quinlan, Darleen (USA)	Athletics	3	1	5	9	1972–80
196	Van de Cappelle, Murielle (FRA)	Wheelchair Fencing	3	1	2	6	1996–2000
	Jaenicke, Britta (GER)	Athletics	3	1	2	6	1988–2000
	Kopp, Heidi (GER)	Swimming	3	1	2	6	1988–92
	Malchan, Ayala (ISR)	Wheelchair Fencing	3	1	2	6	1968–80
	Walker, Elisabeth (CAN)	Swimming	3	1	2	6	1992–2004
201	Anderson, Nancy (USA)	Athletics, Boccia, Swimming	3	1	1	5	1984–92
	Bey, Elena-Marie (USA)	Swimming	3	1	1	5	1976
	Brunner, Helena (AUS)	Swimming	3	1	1	5	1984
	Cloonan, Morna (IRL)	Athletics, Swimming, Table Tennis	3	1	1	5	1984
	Dodd, Lorraine (AUS)	Athletics, Swimming	3	1	1	5	1968
	Hagen, Vibeke (NOR)	Swimming	3	1	1	5	1980–84
	Hlavackova, Bela (CZE)	Swimming	3	1	1	5	2004–08
	Nannenberg, Jacqueline (NED)	Swimming	3	1	1	5	1988–96
	Polasik, Jadwiga (POL)	Wheelchair Fencing	3	1	1	5	1996–2004
	Quinn, Alison (AUS)	Athletics	3	1	1	5	1992–2000
	Vandierendonck, Chantal (NED)	Wheelchair Tennis	3	1	1	5	1988–96
	Zajac, Brenda (USA)	Athletics	3	1	1	5	1988
213	Chen, Wei Hong (CHN)	Table Tennis	3	1	0	4	2000–04
	Fiadotava, Iryna (BLR)	Cycling	3	1	0	4	2000–08
	Floer, Marga (GER)	Athletics, Swimming	3	1	0	4	1968–72
	Hunter, Ellen (GBR)	Cycling	3	1	0	4	2004–08
	Jouravliova, Raissa (USSR)	Athletics	3	1	0	4	1988
	Karlsson, Cecilia (SWE)	Swimming	3	1	0	4	1988
	Lafaye Marziou, Isabelle (FRA)	Table Tennis	3	1	0	4	2000–04
	Lei, Lina (CHN)	Table Tennis	3	1	0	4	2004–08
	Liu, Mei Li (CHN)	Table Tennis	3	1	0	4	2000–04
	McGlynn, Aileen (GBR)	Cycling	3	1	0	4	2004–08
	Moeller, Reinhild (GER)	Athletics	3	1	0	4	1984–88
	Mora, J. (USA)	Athletics	3	1	0	4	1984
	Pacquette, J. (CAN)	Athletics	3	1	0	4	1976
	Pascoe, Sophie (NZL)	Swimming	3	1	0	4	2008
	Ren, Gui Xiang (CHN)	Table Tennis	3	1	0	4	2000–04
	Roberts, Ann Marie (USA)	Athletics	3	1	0	4	1980–84
	Rutherford, Mikhaila (USA)	Swimming	3	1	0	4	2004
	Shannon, Leann (USA)	Athletics	3	1	0	4	1996
231	Barr, Dianne (GBR)	Swimming	3	0	3	6	1988–92
	Bulleri, Sabrina (ITA)	Athletics	3	0	3	6	1984–88
	Smit, Maaike (NED)	Wheelchair Basketball, Wheelchair Tennis	3	0	3	6	1988–2004
	Tustain, Nicola (GBR)	Equestrian	3	0	3	6	2000–04
235	Currie, Anne (AUS)	Swimming	3	0	2	5	1984, 1992
	Luo, Fuqun (CHN)	Table Tennis	3	0	2	5	1996–2000
	Van Rijswijk, Joke (NED)	Athletics	3	0	2	5	1980–88
238	Abbott, Marni (CAN)	Wheelchair Basketball	3	0	1	4	1992–2004
	Andrey, Zita (SUI)	Athletics	3	0	1	4	1984–88
	Benoit, Chantal (CAN)	Wheelchair Basketball	3	0	1	4	1992–2008
	Dong, Qiming (CHN)	Swimming	3	0	1	4	1996–2004
	Ferguson, Tracey (CAN)	Wheelchair Basketball	3	0	1	4	1992–2008
	Garcia, Anais (ESP)	Swimming	3	0	1	4	1996–2004
	Krempien, Jennifer (CAN)	Wheelchair Basketball	3	0	1	4	1992–2008
	Kutrowski, Linda (CAN)	Wheelchair Basketball	3	0	1	4	1988–2004
	Misciagna, Laura (ITA)	Athletics	3	0	1	4	1984–88
	Ohama, Kendra (CAN)	Wheelchair Basketball	3	0	1	4	1992–2008
	Woodcock, Brenda (GBR)	Athletics, Swimming	3	0	1	4	1984
249	Arriens-Kappens (NED)	Swimming	3	0	0	3	1960
	Benhama, Sanaa (MAR)	Athletics	3	0	0	3	2008
	Cohen, Ariela (ISR)	Swimming	3	0	0	3	1976
	Cole, G. (CAN)	Athletics	3	0	0	3	1980
	Criddle, Deborah (GBR)	Equestrian	3	0	0	3	2000–08
	Desmarets, Murielle (FRA)	Wheelchair Fencing	3	0	0	3	1984–88
	Fu, Taoying (CHN)	Powerlifting	3	0	0	3	2000–08
	Goddard, M. (GBR)	Athletics	3	0	0	3	1980
	Harper, Aileen (GBR)	Athletics	3	0	0	3	1984
	Huang, Lisha (CHN)	Athletics	3	0	0	3	2008
	Jaaroa, Merja (SWE)	Athletics	3	0	0	3	1984
	Jansen, Janet (NED)	Athletics	3	0	0	3	1988
	Kristiansen, C. (CAN)	Swimming	3	0	0	3	1980
	Mayer (GER)	Swimming	3	0	0	3	1972
	Omar, Fatma (EGY)	Powerlifting	3	0	0	3	2000–08
	Onfroy (FRA)	Athletics	3	0	0	3	1980
	Pankova, Tamara (EUN)	Athletics	3	0	0	3	1988–92
	Savchenko, Oxana (RUS)	Swimming	3	0	0	3	2008
	Schyff (RSA)	Swimming	3	0	0	3	1972
	Schafhausen, I. (GER)	Athletics	3	0	0	3	1980
	Semenova, Olga (RUS)	Athletics	3	0	0	3	2000–08
	Stilwell, Michelle (CAN)	Athletics, Wheelchair Basketball	3	0	0	3	2000, 2008
	Swann, Anne (GBR)	Athletics	3	0	0	3	1984
	White, Kim (GBR)	Athletics	3	0	0	3	1984

INDEX

1km Time Trial
Chris Hoy................................76-7

1km Time Trial Bicycle CP Div 3/4 (men's)
Darren Kenny........................ 90-1

1km Time Trial CP3 (men's)
Darren Kenny........................ 90-1

1km Time Trial LC2 (mixed)
Jiří Ježek 78-9

3m Springboard (men's)
Greg Louganis......................106-7

3 x 25m Individual Medley 1B (women's)
Isabel Newstead 116-17

4 x 50m Freestyle B (women's)
Trisha Zorn............................208-9

4 x 50m Freestyle Relay 20 Points (men's)
David Roberts.........................148-9

4 x 50m Individual Medley Relay B (women's)
Trisha Zorn 208-9

4 x 100m Freestyle Relay (men's)
Ian Thorpe 182-3
Mark Spitz 162-3
Matt Biondi 24-5
Michael Phelps 136-7

4 x 100m Freestyle Relay (women's)
Dara Torres 188-9
Jenny Thompson 180-1

4 x 100m Freestyle Relay 34 Points (men's)
David Roberts.........................148-9
Sarah Storey..........................166-7

4 x 100m Freestyle Relay B1-3 (women's)
Trisha Zorn............................208-9

4 x 100m Freestyle Relay S7-10 (women's)
Sarah Storey..........................166-7

4 x 100m Individual Medley Relay B (women's)
Trisha Zorn 208-9

4 x 100m Medley Relay (men's)
Ian Thorpe 182-3
Mark Spitz 162-3
Matt Biondi 24-5
Michael Phelps 136-7

4 x 100m Medley Relay (women's)
Dara Torres 188-9
Jenny Thompson 180-1

4 x 100m Medley Relay 34 Points (men's)
David Roberts.........................148-9

4 x 100m Medley Relay B1-3 (women's)
Trisha Zorn............................208-9

4 x 100m Medley Relay S7-10 (women's)
Sarah Storey..........................166-7

4 x 100m Relay (men's)
Carl Lewis...............................102-3
Jesse Owens 128-9
Usain Bolt...............................30-1
Valery Borzov.......................... 32-3

4 x 100m Relay (women's)
Betty Cuthbert 44-5
Evelyn Ashford.........................18-19
Fanny Blankers-Koen 26-7
Gwen Torrance.........................186-7
Irena Szewińska........................ 174-5
Merlene Ottey..........................126-7
Shirley Strickland 168-9
Wilma Rudolph 150-1

4 x 100m Relay TW3-4 (women's)
Tanni Grey-Thompson 70-1

4 x 200m Freestyle Relay (men's)
Ian Thorpe 182-3
Mark Spitz 162-3
Matt Biondi 24-5
Michael Phelps 136-7

4 x 200m Freestyle Relay (women's)
Jenny Thompson 180-1

4 x 400m Relay (men's)
Michael Johnson 80-1

4 x 400m Relay (women's)
Gwen Torrance.........................186-7
Valerie Brisco-Hooks......................34-5

10m Platform (men's)
Greg Louganis........................106-7

25m Backstroke 1B (women's)
Isabel Newstead 116-17

25m Backstroke 1C (women's)
Isabel Newstead 116-17

25m Breaststroke 1B (women's)
Isabel Newstead 116-17

25m Breaststroke 1C (women's)
Isabel Newstead 116-17

25m Butterfly 1B (women's)
Isabel Newstead 116-17

25m Freestyle 1B (women's)
Isabel Newstead 116-17

25m Freestyle 1C (women's)
Isabel Newstead 116-17

50m Breaststroke B2 (women's)
Trisha Zorn............................208-9

50m Freestyle (men's)
Matt Biondi 24-5

50m Freestyle (women's)
Dara Torres 188-9

50m Freestyle B2 (women's)
Trisha Zorn............................208-9

50m Freestyle S7 (men's)
David Roberts.........................148-9

50m Freestyle S9 (women's)
Natalie Du Toit 48-9

50m Freestyle S12 (women's)
Trisha Zorn............................208-9

60m (men's)
Alvin Kraenzlein...........................98-9

80m Hurdles (women's)
Fanny Blankers-Koen 26-7
Shirley Strickland 168-9

100m (men's)
Carl Lewis...............................102-3
Jesse Owens 128-9
Usain Bolt...............................30-1
Valery Borzov.......................... 32-3

100m (women's)
Betty Cuthbert 44-5
Evelyn Ashford.........................18-19
Fanny Blankers-Koen 26-7
Gwen Torrance.........................186-7
Irena Szewińska........................ 174-5
Merlene Ottey..........................126-7
Shirley Strickland 168-9
Wilma Rudolph 150-1

100m Backstroke B (women's)
Trisha Zorn............................208-9

100m Backstroke B2 (women's)
Trisha Zorn............................208-9

100m Backstroke S7 (men's)
David Roberts.........................148-9

100m Backstroke S12 (women's)
Trisha Zorn............................208-9

100m Backstroke S9 (women's)
Natalie Du Toit 48-9

100m Backstroke S10 (women's)
Sarah Storey..........................166-7

100m Backstroke S12 (women's)
Trisha Zorn............................208-9

100m Breaststroke B1-2 (women's)
Trisha Zorn............................208-9

100m Breaststroke B2 (women's)
Trisha Zorn............................208-9

100m Breaststroke SB9 (women's)
Sarah Storey..........................166-7

100m Breaststroke SB10 (women's)
Sarah Storey..........................166-7

100m Breaststroke SB12 (women's)
Trisha Zorn............................208-9

100m Butterfly (men's)
Mark Spitz 162-3
Matt Biondi 24-5
Michael Phelps 136-7

100m Butterfly (women's)
Dara Torres 188-9

100m Butterfly B (women's)
Trisha Zorn............................208-9

100m Butterfly B2 (women's)
Trisha Zorn............................208-9

100m Butterfly B2-3 (women's)
Trisha Zorn............................208-9

100m Butterfly S9 (women's)
Natalie Du Toit 48-9

100m Butterfly S12 (women's)
Trisha Zorn............................208-9

100m Freestyle (men's)
Ian Thorpe 182-3
Mark Spitz 162-3
Matt Biondi 24-5

100m Freestyle (women's)
Dara Torres 188-9
Jenny Thompson 180-1

100m Freestyle 1B (women's)
Isabel Newstead 116-17

100m Freestyle B (women's)
Trisha Zorn............................208-9

100m Freestyle B2 (women's)
Trisha Zorn............................208-9

100m Freestyle S7 (men's)
David Roberts.........................148-9

100m Freestyle S9 (women's)
Natalie Du Toit 48-9

100m Freestyle S10 (women's)
Sarah Storey..........................166-7

100m T44 (men's)
Oscar Pistorius 140-1

100m T52 (women's)
Tanni Grey-Thompson 70-1

100m T53 (women's)
Chantal Petitclerc........................ 134-5
Tanni Grey-Thompson 70-1

100m T54 (women's)
Chantal Petitclerc........................ 134-5

100m TW3 (women's)
Tanni Grey-Thompson 70-1

100 TW4 (women's)
Louise Sauvage 154-5

110m Hurdles (men's)
Alvin Kraenzlein...........................98-9

200m (men's)
Carl Lewis...............................102-3
Jesse Owens 128-9
Michael Johnson........................ 80-1
Usain Bolt...............................30-1
Valery Borzov.......................... 32-3

200m (women's)
Betty Cuthbert 44-5
Fanny Blankers-Koen 26-7
Gwen Torrance.........................186-7
Irena Szewińska........................ 174-5
Marie-José Pérec......................... 132-3
Merlene Ottey..........................126-7
Valerie Brisco-Hooks....................34-5
Wilma Rudolph 150-1

200m Backstroke B1-2 (women's)
Trisha Zorn............................208-9

200m Breaststroke B1-3 (women's)
Trisha Zorn 208-9

200m Breaststroke B2 (women's)
Trisha Zorn............................208-9

200m Butterfly (men's)
Mark Spitz 162-3
Michael Phelps 136-7

200m Freestyle (men's)
Ian Thorpe 182-3
Mark Spitz 162-3
Matt Biondi 24-5
Michael Phelps 136-7

200m Hurdles (men's)
Alvin Kraenzlein...........................98-9
Harry Hillman..........................72-3

200m Individual Medley (men's)
Michael Phelps 136-7

200m Individual Medley B2 (women's)
Trisha Zorn............................208-9

200m Individual Medley SM7 (men's)
David Roberts.........................148-9

200m Individual Medley SM9 (women's)
Natalie Du Toit 48-9

200m Individual Medley SM10 (women's)
Sarah Storey..........................166-7

200m Individual Medley SM12 (women's)
Trisha Zorn............................208-9

200m T44 (men's)
Oscar Pistorius 140-1

200m T52 (women's)
Tanni Grey-Thompson 70-1

200m T53 (women's)
Chantal Petitclerc........................ 134-5
Tanni Grey-Thompson 70-1

200m T54 (women's)
Chantal Petitclerc........................ 134-5

200m TW3 (women's)
Tanni Grey-Thompson 70-1

200m TW4 (women's)
Chantal Petitclerc........................ 134-5
Louise Sauvage 154-5

400m (men's)
Harry Hillman..........................72-3
Michael Johnson 80-1

400m (women's)
Betty Cuthbert 44-5
Irena Szewińska 174-5
Marie-José Pérec 132-3
Valerie Brisco-Hooks....................34-5

400m 3 (women's)
Tanni Grey-Thompson 70-1

400m Freestyle (men's)
Ian Thorpe 182-3

400m Freestyle (women's)
Rebecca Adlington...................... 10-11

400m Freestyle B2 (women's)
Trisha Zorn............................208-9

400, Freestyle B2-3 (women's)
Trisha Zorn............................208-9

400m Freestyle S7 (men's)
David Roberts.........................148-9

400m Freestyle S9 (women's)
Natalie Du Toit 48-9

400m Freestyle S10 (women's)
Sarah Storey..........................166-7

400m Hurdles (men's)
Edwin Moses 112-13
Harry Hillman..........................72-3

400m Individual Medley (men's)
Michael Phelps 136-7

400, Individual Medley B1-3 (women's)
Trisha Zorn............................208-9

400m Individual Medley B2 (women's)
Trisha Zorn............................208-9

400m T44 (men's)
Oscar Pistorius 140-1

400m T52 (women's)
  Tanni Grey-Thompson 70-1
400m T53 (women's)
  Chantal Petitclerc......................134-5
  Louise Sauvage 154-5
  Tanni Grey-Thompson 70-1
400m T54 (women's)
  Chantal Petitclerc......................134-5
  Louise Sauvage 154-5
400m TW3 (women's)
  Tanni Grey-Thompson 70-1
400m TW4 (women's)
  Louise Sauvage 154-5
800m (men's)
  Peter Snell.............................160-1
  Sebastian Coe 38-9
800m (women's)
  Kelly Holmes.............................74-5
800m Freestyle (women's)
  Rebecca Adlington......................10-11
800m T52 (women's)
  Tanni Grey-Thompson 70-1
800m T53 (women's)
  Chantal Petitclerc......................134-5
  Louise Sauvage 154-5
  Tanni Grey-Thompson 70-1
800m T54 (women's)
  Chantal Petitclerc......................134-5
  Louise Sauvage 154-5
800m TW3 (women's)
  Tanni Grey-Thompson 70-1
800m TW4 (women's)
  Chantal Petitclerc......................134-5
  Louise Sauvage 154-5
1,500m (men's)
  Hicham El-Guerrouj.......................52-3
  Kipchoge Keino...........................88-9
  Paavo Nurmi.............................120-1
  Peter Snell.............................160-1
  Sebastian Coe 38-9
1,500m (women's)
  Kelly Holmes.............................74-5
1,500m T52-53 (women's)
  Chantal Petitclerc......................134-5
  Louise Sauvage 154-5
1,500m T54 (women's)
  Chantal Petitclerc......................134-5
  Louise Sauvage 154-5
3,000m Steeplechase (men's)
  Kipchoge Keino...........................88-9
  Paavo Nurmi.............................120-1
  Ville Ritola.............................146-7
3000m Team (men's)
  Paavo Nurmi.............................120-1
  Ville Ritola.............................146-7
5,000 m (men's)
  Alain Mimoun..........................110-11
  Emil Zátopek 204-5
  Hicham El-Guerrouj.......................52-3
  Kipchoge Keino...........................88-9
  Lasse Viren.............................196-7
  Paavo Nurmi.............................120-1
  Ville Ritola.............................146-7
5,000m T52-53 (women's)
  Louise Sauvage 154-5
5,000m T54 (women's)
  Louise Sauvage 154-5
10,000m (men's)
  Alain Mimoun..........................110-11
  Emil Zátopek 204-5
  Haile Gebrselassie......................66-7
  Lasse Viren.............................196-7
  Paavo Nurmi.............................120-1
  Ville Ritola.............................146-7

Adlington, Rebecca 10-11
Ainslie, Ben 12-13
Air Pistol 1A-1C (women's)
  Isabel Newstead 116-17
Air Pistol 2-6 (women's)
  Isabel Newstead 116-17
Air Pistol SH1 (women's)
  Isabel Newstead 116-17
Alekseyev, Vasily 14-15
Ali, Muhammad 36-7
Amsterdam Olympic Games 1928
  Paavo Nurmi 120-1
  Ville Ritola 146-7
Andrianov, Nikola 16-17, 87
Antwerp Olympic Games 1920
  Hubert Van Innis 190-1
  Paavo Nurmi 120-1
Archery (men's)
  Hubert Van Innis 190-1
Archery (women's)
  Kim Soo-Nyung 92-3
Arnhem Paralympic Games 1980
  Arnold Boldt 28-9
  Isabel Newstead 116-17
  Philip Craven 42-3
  Trisha Zorn.............................208-9
Ashford, Evelyn 18-19
Athens Olympic Games 1896
  Robert Garrett 64-5
Athens Olympic Games 2004
  Ben Ainslie 12-13
  Birgit Fischer...........................56-7
  Carolina Kluft 94-5
  Chris Hoy...............................76-7
  Elisabeta Oleniuc-Lipă 124-5
  Hicham El-Guerrouj.......................52-3
  Ian Thorpe 182-3
  Jenny Thompson 180-1
  Kelly Holmes.............................74-5
  Matthew Pinsent.........................138-9
  Michael Phelps.........................136-7
  Wang Nan 198-9
  Ricardo Santos 152-3
  Ryoko Tani 176-7
  Stanislav Pozdniakov....................142-3
  Tadahiro Nomura 118-19
  Torben Grael 68-9
  Valentina Vezzali 194-5
Athens Paralympic Games 2004
  Darren Kenny 90-1
  David Roberts...........................148-9
  Esther Vergeer 192-3
  Isabel Newstead 116-17
  Jiří Ježek 78-9
  Lee Pearson 130-1
  Louise Sauvage 154-5
  Natalie Du Toit.........................48-9
  Oscar Pistorius 140-1
  Sarah Storey...........................166-7
  Tanni Grey-Thompson 70-1
  Trisha Zorn.............................208-9
Athletics (men's)
  Abebe Bikila 22-3
  Al Oerter 122-3
  Alain Mimoun 110-11
  Alvin Kraenzlein 98-9
  Arnold Boldt 28-9
  Daley Thompson.........................178-9
  Dick Fosbury 58-9
  Edwin Moses 112-13
  Emil Zátopek 204-5
  Haile Gebrselassie......................66-7
  Harry Hillman 72-3
  Hicham El-Guerrouj.......................52-3

Jan Železný 206-7
Jesse Owens 128-9
Jim Thorpe 184-5
Kipchoge Keino..........................88-9
Lasse Viren.............................196-7
Michael Johnson 80-1
Oscar Pistorius 140-1
Paavo Nurmi 120-1
Peter Snell 160-1
Robert Garrett 64-5
Sebastian Coe 38-9
Usain Bolt.............................30-1
Valery Borzov 32-3
Ville Ritola 146-7
Athletics (women's)
  Betty Cuthbert 44-5
  Carolina Kluft 94-5
  Chantal Petitclerc......................134-5
  Evelyn Ashford 18-19
  Gwen Torrance 186-7
  Irena Szewińska 174-5
  Isabel Newstead 116-17
  Jackie Joyner-Kersee.................... 82-3
  Kelly Holmes.............................74-5
  Louise Sauvage 154-5
  Marie-José Pérec 132-3
  Merlene Ottey...........................126-7
  Shirley Strickland 168-9
  Tanni Grey-Thompson 70-1
  Valerie Brisco-Hooks.................... 34-5
  Wilma Rudolph 150-1
Atlanta Olympic Games 1996
  Aleksandr Karelin 84-5
  Alexei Nemov...........................114-15
  Ben Ainslie 12-13
  Birgit Fischer...........................56-7
  Carl Lewis 102-3
  David Douillet 46-7
  Elisabeta Oleniuc-Lipă 124-5
  Gwen Torrance 186-7
  Haile Gebrselassie......................66-7
  Isabell Werth 200-1
  Jackie Joyner-Kersee.................... 82-3
  Jan Železný 206-7
  Jeannie Longo 104-5
  Jenny Thompson 180-1
  Marie-José Pérec 132-3
  Matthew Pinsent.........................138-9
  Merlene Ottey...........................126-7
  Michael Johnson 80-1
  Fu Mingxia 62-3
  Naim Süleymanoğlu 170-1
  Ryoko Tani 176-7
  Stanislav Pozdniakov....................142-3
  Steve Redgrave 144-5
  Susi Susanti 172-3
  Tadahiro Nomura 118-19
  Teresa Edwards..........................50-1
  Torben Grael 68-9
  Valentina Vezzali 194-5
Atlanta Paralympic Games 1996
  Chantal Petitclerc......................134-5
  Louise Sauvage 154-5
  Sarah Storey...........................166-7
  Tanni Grey-Thompson 70-1
  Trisha Zorn.............................208-9
Au Chapelet (men's)
  Hubert Van Innis 190-1
Au Cordon Doré (men's)
  Hubert Van Innis 190-1
Badminton (women's)
  Susi Susanti 172-3
Balance Beam Competition (women's)
  Larissa Latynina........................100-1

Nadia Comaneci 40-1
Olga Korbut 96-7
Barcelona Olympic Games 1992
  Aleksandr Karelin 84-5
  Birgit Fischer...........................56-7
  Carl Lewis 102-3
  Dara Torres 188-9
  David Douillet 46-7
  Elisabeta Oleniuc-Lipă 124-5
  Evelyn Ashford 18-19
  Gwen Torrance 186-7
  Isabell Werth 200-1
  Jackie Joyner-Kersee.................... 82-3
  Jan Železný 206-7
  Jeannie Longo 104-5
  Jenny Thompson 180-1
  Marie-José Pérec 132-3
  Matt Biondi 24-5
  Matthew Pinsent.........................138-9
  Merlene Ottey...........................126-7
  Michael Johnson 80-1
  Fu Mingxia 62-3
  Naim Süleymanoğlu 170-1
  Ryoko Tani 176-7
  Kim Soo-Nyung 92-3
  Stanislav Pozdniakov....................142-3
  Steve Redgrave 144-5
  Susi Susanti 172-3
  Teresa Edwards..........................50-1
Barcelona Paralympic Games 1992
  Arnold Boldt 28-9
  Chantal Petitclerc......................134-5
  Louise Sauvage 154-5
  Sarah Storey...........................166-7
  Tanni Grey-Thompson 70-1
  Trisha Zorn.............................208-9
Basketball
  Teresa Edwards..........................50-1
Beach Volleyball (men's)
  Ricardo Santos 152-3
Beamon, Bob.........................20-1, 58
Beijing Olympic Games 2008
  Ben Ainslie 12-13
  Chris Hoy...............................76-7
  Dara Torres 188-9
  Isabell Werth 200-1
  Michael Phelps.........................136-7
  Wang Nan 198-9
  Rebecca Adlington.......................10-11
  Ricardo Santos 152-3
  Ryoko Tani 176-7
  Usain Bolt.............................30-1
  Valentina Vezzali 194-5
Beijing Paralympic Games 2008
  David Roberts...........................148-9
  Darren Kenny 90-1
  Esther Vergeer 192-3
  Jiří Ježek 78-9
  Lee Pearson 130-1
  Natalie Du Toit.........................48-9
  Oscar Pistorius 140-1
  Sarah Storey...........................166-7
Berlin Olympic Games 1936
  Edoardo Mangiarotti 108-9
  Jesse Owens 128-9
Bikila, Abebe 22-3
Biondi, Matt..............................24-5
Blankers-Koen, Fanny 26-7
Boldt, Arnold 28-9
Bolt, Usain.............................30-1
Borzov, Valery 32-3
Boston, Ralph 20
Boxing
  Cassius Clay 36-7

Teofilo Stevenson 164-5
Brisco-Hooks, Valerie 34-5
Canoe sprint (men's)
    Gert Fredrickson 60-1
Canoe sprint (women's)
    Birgit Fischer.............................. 56-7
Clay, Cassius................................. 36-7
Coe, Sebastian............................... 38-9
Comaneci, Nadia 40-1, 96
Craven, Philip 42-3
Cuthbert, Betty 44-5
Cycling (Road)
    Darren Kenny 90-1
    Jeannie Longo.............................104-5
    Jiří Ježek 78-9
Cycling (Track)
    Chris Hoy..................................76-7
    Darren Kenny 90-1
    Jiří Ježek 78-9
    Sarah Storey...............................166-7
Decathlon (men's)
    Daley Thompson.......................178-9
    Jim Thorpe................................184-5
Discus Throw (men's)
    Al Oerter..................................122-3
    Robert Garrett 64-5
Discus Throw 1B (women's)
    Isabel Newstead 116-17
Diving (men's)
    Greg Louganis..........................106-7
Diving (women's)
    Fu Mingxia 62-3
Double Sculls (2x)
    (women's)
    Elisabeta Oleniuc-Lipă.............. 124-5
Douillet, David.............................. 46-7
Dressage
    Isabell Werth 200-1
    Lee Pearson.............................. 130-1
Du Toit, Natalie 48-9
Edwards, Teresa...........................50-1
Eights (8+) (women's)
    Elisabeta Oleniuc-Lipă 124-5
El-Guerrouj, Hicham.........................52-3
Equestrian
    Hans Günter Winkler.................. 202-3
    Isabell Werth 200-1
    Lee Pearson.............................. 130-1
Ewry, Ray....................................54-5
Fencing (men's)
    Edoardo Mangiarotti.................. 108-9
    Stanislav Pozdniakov.................142-3
Fencing (women's)
    Valentina Vezzali 194-5
Finn
    Ben Ainslie 12-13
Fischer, Birgit...............................56-7
Floor Competition (men's)
    Alexei Nemov..............................114-15
    Nikolai Andrianov 16-17
    Sawao Kato 86-7
Floor Competition (women's)
    Larissa Latynina..........................100-1
    Nadia Comaneci 40-1
    Olga Korbut 96-7
Fosbury, Dick 58-9
Fours (4+/4-) (men's)
    Matthew Pinsent.......................138-9
    Steve Redgrave...........................144-5
Fredrickson, Gert 60-1
Fu Mingxia 62-3
Garrett, Robert 64-5
Gebrselassie, Haile 66-7
Grael, Torben 68-9

Greco-Roman Wrestling
    Aleksandr Karelin 84-5
Grey-Thompson, Tanni 70-1
Gymnastics (men's)
    Alexei Nemov..............................114-15
    Boris Shakhlin 156-7
    Nikolai Andrianov 16-17
    Sawao Kato 86-7
Gymnastics (women's)
    Larissa Latynina..........................100-1
    Nadia Comaneci 40-1
    Olga Korbut 96-7
Heidelberg Paralympic Games 1972
    Philip Craven 42-3
Helsinki Olympic Games 1952
    Alain Mimoun 110-11
    Edoardo Mangiarotti 108-9
    Emil Zátopek 204-5
    Gert Fredrickson 60-1
    Shirley Strickland 168-9
    Udham Singh...............................158-9
Heptathlon (women's)
    Carolina Kluft 94-5
    Jackie Joyner-Kersee...................... 82-3
High Jump (men's)
    Dick Fosbury 58-9
    Ray Ewry..................................54-5
    Robert Garrett 64-5
High Jump A1 (men's)
    Arnold Boldt 28-9
High Jump A2 (men's)
    Arnold Boldt 28-9
High Jump A2A9 (men's)
    Arnold Boldt 28-9
High Jump D (men's)
    Arnold Boldt 28-9
Hockey (men's)
    Udham Singh...............................158-9
Holmes, Kelly................................74-5
Horizontal Bars Competition (men's)
    Alexei Nemov..............................114-15
    Boris Shakhlin 156-7
    Nikolai Andrianov 16-17
    Sawao Kato 86-7
Horse Vault Competition (women's)
    Larissa Latynina..........................100-1
Hoy, Chris....................................76-7
Individual All-Around Competition (men's)
    Alexei Nemov..............................114-15
    Boris Shakhlin 156-7
    Nikolai Andrianov 16-17
    Sawao Kato 86-7
Individual All-Around Competition (women's)
    Larissa Latynina..........................100-1
    Nadia Comaneci..........................40-1
Individual Archery (men's)
    Hubert Van Innis 190-1
Individual Cross-Country (men's)
    Paavo Nurmi 120-1
    Ville Ritola................................146-7
Individual Epée (men's)
    Edoardo Mangiarotti 108-9
Individual Foil (men's)
    Edoardo Mangiarotti 108-9
Individual Foil (women's)
    Valentina Vezzali 194-5
Individual Jumping Competition (men's)
    Hans Günter Winkler.................. 202-3
Individual Pursuit Bicycle CP Div 3 (men's)
    Darren Kenny 90-1
Individual Pursuit CP3 (men's)
    Darren Kenny 90-1
Individual Pursuit LC1-2/CP4 (women's)
    Sarah Storey...............................166-7

Individual Pursuit LC2 (men's)
    Jiří Ježek 78-9
Individual Pursuit LC2 (mixed)
    Jiří Ježek 78-9
Individual Road Race (women's)
    Jeannie Longo.............................104-5
Individual Road Race LC3-4/CP3 (men's)
    Darren Kenny 90-1
Individual Sabre (men's)
    Stanislav Pozdniakov...................142-3
Individual Time Trial (women's)
    Jeannie Longo.............................104-5
Individual Time Trial CP3 (men's)
    Darren Kenny 90-1
Individual Time Trial LC1-2/CP4
    (women's)
    Sarah Storey...............................166-7
Individual Time Trial LC2 (men's)
    Jiří Ježek 78-9
Javelin Throw (men's)
    Jan Železný 206-7
Javelin Throw 1B (women's)
    Isabel Newstead..........................116-17
Johnson, Michael........................34, 80-1
Joyner-Kersee, Jackie........................ 82-3
Judo (men's)
    David Douillet 46-7
    Tadahiro Nomura 118-19
Judo (women's)
    Ryoko Tani 176-7
Karelin, Aleksandr.......................... 84-5
Kato, Sawao..........................16, 86-7
Keino, Kipchoge..............................88-9
Keirin
    Chris Hoy..................................76-7
Kim Soo-Nyung 92-3
Kluft, Carolina...................82-3, 94-5
Korbut, Olga 96-7
Kraenzlein, Alvin 98-9
Laser
    Ben Ainslie 12-13
Latynina, Larissa 56, 100-1
Lewis, Carl 26, 102-3
London Olympic Games 1908
    Harry Hillman...........................72-3
    Ray Ewry..................................54-5
London Olympic Games 1948
    Alain Mimoun 110-11
    Edoardo Mangiarotti 108-9
    Emil Zátopek 204-5
    Fanny Blankers-Koen 26-7
    Gert Fredrickson 60-1
    Shirley Strickland 168-9
Long Jump (men's)
    Alvin Kraenzlein 98-9
    Bob Beamon................................20-1
    Carl Lewis 102-3
    Jesse Owens 128-9
    Ray Ewry..................................54-5
    Robert Garrett 64-5
Long Jump (women's)
    Irena Szewińska 174-5
    Jackie Joyner-Kersee...................... 82-3
Long Jump A2A9 (men's)
    Arnold Boldt 28-9
Long Jump D (men's)
    Arnold Boldt 28-9
Longo, Jeannie.............................104-5
Los Angeles Olympic Games 1984
    Carl Lewis 102-3
    Daley Thompson.......................178-9
    Dara Torres 188-9
    Edwin Moses..............................112-13
    Elisabeta Oleniuc-Lipă 124-5

Evelyn Ashford............................18-19
Greg Louganis............................106-7
Jackie Joyner-Kersee...................... 82-3
Merlene Ottey.............................126-7
Sebastian Coe 38-9
Steve Redgrave...........................144-5
Teresa Edwards...........................50-1
Torben Grael 68-9
Valerie Brisco-Hooks.....................34-5
Louganis, Greg 63, 106-7
Mang, Rudolf 14-15
Mangiarotti, Edoardo 108-9
Marathon (men's)
    Abebe Bikila 22-3
    Alain Mimoun 110-11
    Emil Zátopek 204-5
Melbourne Olympic Games 1956
    Al Oerter..................................122-3
    Alain Mimoun 110-11
    Betty Cuthbert 44-5
    Boris Shakhlin 156-7
    Edoardo Mangiarotti 108-9
    Gert Fredrickson 60-1
    Larissa Latynina..........................100-1
    Shirley Strickland 168-9
    Udham Singh...............................158-9
    Wilma Rudolph 150-1
Men Star (Keelboat)
    Torben Grael 68-9
Mennea, Pietro 80
Mexico City Olympic Games 1968
    Al Oerter..................................122-3
    Bob Beamon.........................20-1, 58
    Dick Fosbury 58-9
    Hans Günter Winkler.................. 202-3
    Irena Szewińska 174-5
    Kipchoge Keino..............................88-9
    Mark Spitz................................162-3
    Sawao Kato 86-7
Mimoun, Alain 110-11
Montreal Olympic Games 1976
    Edwin Moses..............................112-13
    Greg Louganis............................106-7
    Hans Günter Winkler.................. 202-3
    Irena Szewińska 174-5
    Lasse Viren 196-7
    Nadia Comaneci..........................40-1
    Nikolai Andrianov 16-17
    Olga Korbut 96-7
    Sawao Kato 86-7
    Teofilo Stevenson.......................164-5
    Valery Borzov 32-3
    Vasily Alekseyev 14-15
Moscow Olympic Games 1980
    Birgit Fischer...............................56-7
    Daley Thompson.......................178-9
    Merlene Ottey.............................126-7
    Nadia Comaneci 40-1
    Nikolai Andrianov 16-17
    Sebastian Coe 38-9
    Teofilo Stevenson 164-5
Moses, Edwin 112-13
Munich Olympic Games 1972
    Hans Günter Winkler.................. 202-3
    Irena Szewińska 174-5
    Kipchoge Keino..............................88-9
    Lasse Viren 196-7
    Mark Spitz................................162-3
    Nikolai Andrianov 16-17
    Olga Korbut 96-7
    Sawao Kato 86-7
    Teofilo Stevenson 164-5
    Valery Borzov 32-3
    Vasily Alekseyev 14-15

New York/Stoke Mandeville Paralympic
  Games (1984)
    Arnold Boldt 28-9
    Isabel Newstead 116-17
    Philip Craven 42-3
    Trisha Zorn 208-9
Newstead, Isabel 116-17
Nomura, Tadahiro 118-19
Nurmi, Paavo 52, 120-1
Oerter, Al 122-3
Oleniuc-Lipă, Elisabeta 124-5
Open Sailing (Keelboat)
    Torben Grael 68-9
Open Star (Keelboat)
    Torben Grael 68-9
Ottey, Merlene 126-7
Owens, Jesse 20, 26, 98, 128-9
Pairs (2+/2-) (men's)
    Matthew Pinsent 138-9
    Steve Redgrave 144-5
Parallel Bars Competition (men's)
    Alexei Nemov 114-15
    Boris Shakhlin 156-7
    Nikolai Andrianov 16-17
    Sawao Kato 86-7
Paralympic Athletics
    Arnold Boldt 28-9
    Chantal Petitclerc 134-5
    Isabel Newstead 116-17
    Louise Sauvage 154-5
    Oscar Pistorius 140-1
    Tanni Grey-Thompson 70-1
Paralympic Cycling
    Darren Kenny 90-1
    Jiří Ježek 78-9
    Sarah Storey 166-7
Paralympic Equestrian
    Lee Pearson 130-1
Paralympic Shooting
    Isabel Newstead 116-17
Paralympic Swimming
    David Roberts 148-9
    Isabel Newstead 116-17
    Natalie Du Toit 48-9
    Sarah Storey 166-7
    Trisha Zorn 208-9
Paris Olympic Games 1900
    Alvin Kraenzlein 98-9
    Hubert Van Innis 190-1
    Ray Ewry 54-5
    Robert Garrett 64-5
Paris Olympic Games 1924
    Paavo Nurmi 120-1
    Ville Ritola 146-7
Pearson, Lee 130-1
Pentathlon (men's)
    Jim Thorpe 184-5
Pérec, Marie-José 34, 132-3
Petitclerc, Chantal 134-5
Phelps, Michael 16, 136-7
Pinsent, Matthew 138-9, 144-5
Pistorius, Oscar 140-1
Pommel Horse (men's)
    Alexei Nemov 114-15
    Boris Shakhlin 156-7
    Nikolai Andrianov 16-17
    Sawao Kato 86-7
Pozdniakov, Stanislav 142-3
Quadruple Sculls (4x) (women's)
    Elisabeta Oleniuc-Lipă 124-5
Redgrave, Steve 138, 144-5
Rings Competition (men's)
    Boris Shakhlin 156-7
    Nikolai Andrianov 16-17

Sawao Kato 86-7
Ritola, Ville 146-7
Road Race CP Div 3 (men's)
    Darren Kenny 90-1
Road Race LC2 (men's)
    Jiří Ježek 78-9
Road Race LC2 (mixed)
    Jiří Ježek 78-9
Rome Olympic Games 1960
    Abebe Bikila 22-3
    Al Oerter 122-3
    Boris Shakhlin 156-7
    Cassius Clay 36-7
    Edoardo Mangiarotti 108-9
    Gert Fredrickson 60-1
    Hans Günter Winkler 202-3
    Larissa Latynina 100-1
    Peter Snell 160-1
    Udham Singh 158-9
    Wilma Rudolph 150-1
Rowing (men's)
    Matthew Pinsent 138-9
    Steve Redgrave 144-5
Rowing (women's)
    Elisabeta Oleniuc-Lipă 124-5
Rudolph, Wilma 150-1
Sailing
    Ben Ainslie 12-13
    Torben Grael 68-9
St. Louis Olympic Games 1904
    Harry Hillman 72-3
    Ray Ewry 54-5
Santos, Ricardo 152-3
Sauvage, Louise 154-5
Seoul Olympic Games 1988
    Aleksandr Karelin 84-5
    Birgit Fischer 56-7
    Carl Lewis 102-3
    Dara Torres 188-9
    Edwin Moses 112-13
    Elisabeta Oleniuc-Lipă 124-5
    Evelyn Ashford 18-19
    Greg Louganis 106-7
    Jackie Joyner-Kersee 82-3
    Jan Železný 206-7
    Matt Biondi 24-5
    Kim Soo-Nyung 92-3
    Steve Redgrave 144-5
    Teresa Edwards 50-1
    Torben Grael 68-9
    Valerie Brisco-Hooks 34-5
Seoul Paralympic Games 1988
    Arnold Boldt 28-9
    Isabel Newstead 116-17
    Philip Craven 42-3
    Tanni Grey-Thompson 70-1
    Trisha Zorn 208-9
Shakhlin, Boris 156-7
Shooting (women's)
    Isabel Newstead 116-17
Shot Put (men's)
    Robert Garrett 64-5
Shot Put 1B (women's)
    Isabel Newstead 116-17
Singh, Udham 158-9
Snell, Peter 160-1
Sprint
    Chris Hoy 76-7
Spitz, Mark 162-3
Stevenson, Teofilo 164-5
Stockholm Olympic Games 1912
    Hans Günter Winkler 202-3
    Jim Thorpe 184-5
Storey, Sarah 166-7

Strickland, Shirley 168-9
Süleymanoğlu, Naim 170-1
Susanti, Susi 172-3
Swimming (men's)
    David Roberts 148-9
    Ian Thorpe 182-3
    Mark Spitz 162-3
    Matt Biondi 24-5
    Michael Phelps 136-7
Swimming (women's)
    Dara Torres 188-9
    Isabel Newstead 116-17
    Jenny Thompson 180-1
    Natalie Du Toit 48-9
    Rebecca Adlington 10-11
    Sarah Storey 166-7
    Trisha Zorn 208-9
Sydney Olympic Games 2000
    Aleksandr Karelin 84-5
    Alexei Nemov 114-15
    Ben Ainslie 12-13
    Birgit Fischer 56-7
    Chris Hoy 76-7
    Dara Torres 188-9
    David Douillet 46-7
    Elisabeta Oleniuc-Lipă 124-5
    Haile Gebrselassie 66-7
    Hicham El-Guerrouj 52-3
    Ian Thorpe 182-3
    Isabell Werth 200-1
    Jan Železný 206-7
    Jeannie Longo 104-5
    Jenny Thompson 180-1
    Kelly Holmes 74-5
    Matthew Pinsent 138-9
    Merlene Ottey 126-7
    Michael Johnson 80-1
    Fu Mingxia 62-3
    Wang Nan 198-9
    Ricardo Santos 152-3
    Ryoko Tani 176-7
    Kim Soo-Nyung 92-3
    Stanislav Pozdniakov 142-3
    Steve Redgrave 144-5
    Tadahiro Nomura 118-19
    Teresa Edwards 50-1
    Torben Grael 68-9
    Valentina Vezzali 194-5
Sydney Paralympic Games 2000
    Chantal Petitclerc 134-5
    David Roberts 148-9
    Esther Vergeer 192-3
    Isabel Newstead 116-17
    Jiří Ježek 78-9
    Lee Pearson 130-1
    Louise Sauvage 154-5
    Sarah Storey 166-7
    Tanni Grey-Thompson 70-1
    Trisha Zorn 208-9
Szewińska, Irena 174-5
Table Tennis (women's)
    Wang Nan 198-9
Tani, Ryoko 176-7
Team Archery (men's)
    Hubert Van Innis 190-1
Team Competition (men's)
    Alexei Nemov 114-15
    Boris Shakhlin 156-7
    Nikolai Andrianov 16-17
    Sawao Kato 86-7
Team Competition (women's)
    Larissa Latynina 100-1
    Nadia Comaneci 40-1
    Olga Korbut 96-7

Team Cross-Country (men's)
    Paavo Nurmi 120-1
    Ville Ritola 146-7
Team Epée (men's)
    Edoardo Mangiarotti 108-9
Team Foil (men's)
    Edoardo Mangiarotti 108-9
Team Foil (women's)
    Valentina Vezzali 194-5
Team Jumping Competition (men's)
    Hans Günter Winkler 202-3
Team Portable Apparatus Competition
  (women's)
    Larissa Latynina 100-1
Team Sabre (men's)
    Stanislav Pozdniakov 142-3
Team Sprint (men's)
    Chris Hoy 76-7
Team Sprint LC1-4 CP3/4 (men's)
    Darren Kenny 90-1
    Jiří Ježek 78-9
Thompson, Daley 178-9
Thompson, Jenny 180-1
Thorpe, Ian 182-3
Thorpe, Jim 184-5
Tokyo Olympic Games 1964
    Abebe Bikila 22-3
    Al Oerter 122-3
    Betty Cuthbert 44-5
    Boris Shakhlin 156-7
    Hans Günter Winkler 202-3
    Irena Szewińska 174-5
    Larissa Latynina 100-1
    Peter Snell 160-1
    Udham Singh 158-9
Toronto Paralympic Games 1976
    Arnold Boldt 28-9
    Philip Craven 42-3
Torrence, Gwen 186-7
Torres, Dara 188-9
Triple Jump (men's)
    Ray Ewry 54-5
    Robert Garrett 64-5
Uneven Bars Competition (women's)
    Larissa Latynina 100-1
    Nadia Comaneci 40-1
    Olga Korbut 96-7
Van Innis, Hubert 190-1
Vault Competition (men's)
    Alexei Nemov 114-15
    Boris Shakhlin 156-7
    Nikolai Andrianov 16-17
Vergeer, Esther 192-3
Vessali, Valentina 194-5
Viren, Lasse 196-7
Wang Nan 198-9
Weightlifting
    Naim Süleymanoğlu 170-1
    Vasily Alekseyev 14-15
Werth, Isabell 200-1
Wheelchair Basketball
    Philip Craven 42-3
Wheelchair Tennis
    Esther Vergeer 192-3
Winkler, Hans Günter 202-3
Wrestling
    Aleksandr Karelin 84-5
Zátopek, Emil 110, 204-5
Železný, Jan 206-7
Zorn, Trischa 208-9

ACKNOWLEDGEMENTS

The publishers would like to thank the following sources for their kind permission to reproduce the pictures in this book.

Action Images: /Joe Chan/Reuters: 198; /Claro Cortes/Reuters: 48; /Stuart Franklin: 139; /Tony Gentile/Reuters: 143; /Richard Heathcote: 155; /Michael Lecker/Reuters: 183; /Reuters: 47, 92, 118; /Sporting Pictures: 75, 165, 196; /Bobby Yip/Reuters: 130

Corbis: /Richard Bailey: 117; /Universal/TempSport: 14

Getty Images: 33, 39, 65, 120, 121, 123, 146; /AFP: 18, 40, 86, 96, 102, 108, 113, 151, 162, 197; /Vincent Almavy/AFP: 104; /Odd Andersen/AFP: 114; /Brian Bahr: 193; /Al Bello: 136, 182, 189; /Milos Bicanski: 131; /Hamish Blair: 154; /Shaun Botterill: 173, 181; /Frederic J. Brown/AFP: 91; /Clive Brunskill: 138; /Martin Bureau/AFP: 195; /David Cannon: 144; /Central Press: 36; /China Photos: 78, 79; /Timothy Clary/AFP: 188; /Thomas Coex/AFP: 153; /Phil Cole: 70, 71; /Corr/AFP: 111; /Chris Covatta/NBAE: 50; /Adrian Dennis/AFP: 115; /John Dominis/Time & Life Pictures: 32, 88, 89, 97, 101; /Tony Duffy: 34, 35, 82, 174; /Franck Fife/AFP: 94; /Stu Forster: 67, 74; /Romeo Gacad/AFP: 126, 127, 133; /Cate Gillon: 90; /Alexander Hassenstein/Bongarts: 56, 85, 125; /David Hecker/AFP: 200; /Patrick Hertzog/AFP: 46; /Hulton Archive: 156; /Jed Jacobsohn: 31, 51; /Liu Jin/AFP: 135, 148; /Fan Jun/Landov: 137; /Mark Kauffman/Time & Life Pictures: 205; /Keystone: 110; /Toshifumi Kitamura/AFP: 63, 119; /Patrick Kovarik/AFP: 105; /Ron Kuntz/AFP: 25, 83; /Robert Laberge: 152; /Nick Laham: 11; /Francois Xavier Marit/AFP: 30; /Maxim Marmur/AFP: 124; /Clive Mason: 69; /Aris Messinis/AFP: 209; /New York Daily News: 180; /Guang Niu: 166; /Joe Patronite: 19; /Popperfoto: 22, 23, 37, 55, 64, 99, 150, 168, 170, 202; /Mike Powell: 80, 81, 187; /Steve Powell: 179; /Adam Pretty: 8-9; /Ben Radford: 12; /Mark Ralston/AFP: 134, 140; /Co Rentmeester/Time & Life Pictures: 163; /Art Rickerby/Time & Life Pictures: 161; /Rolls Press/Popperfoto: 15, 20, 21; /Pascal Rondeau: 107; /Ezra Shaw: 194; /George Silk/Time & Life Pictures: 44, 160; /Cameron Spencer: 77; /Michael Steele: 6-7, 95, 207; /Henri Szwarc/Bongarts: 142; /Bob Thomas: 38, 100, 172, 178; /Topical Press Agency: 72, 184, 185; /Topical Press Agency/Hulton Archive: 54; /Nick Wilson: 145; /Greg Wood/AFP: 62

Hindu Images: 158, 159

Press Association Images: /ABACA: 52; /AP: 17, 26, 27, 45, 58, 59, 204; /Greg Baker/AP: 49; /David Bookstaver/AP: 29; /Kin Cheung/AP: 201; /Dave Cicero/AP: 122; /Gareth Copley: 149; /DPA: 28, 87, 98, 103, 128; /Elizabeth Dalziel/AP: 192; /David Davies: 68; /Charles Dharapak/AP: 176, 177; /Zhang Duo/Landov: 167; /Empics Sport: 129, 147; /Ng Han Guan/AP: 42; /David Jones: 13; /Katsumi Kasahara/AP: 208; /Fei Maohua/Landov: 10; /Tony Marshall: 53, 93, 132, 186, 206; /Andrew Milligan: 5, 76; /Rebecca Naden: 171; /Andrew Parsons: 116; /S&G and Barratts: 16, 24, 41, 60, 61, 106, 112, 164, 169, 175; /Neal Simpson: 84; /Chitose Suzuki/AP: 199; /Mark J. Terrill/AP: 57; /Topham Picturepoint: 73, 157, 203; /Aubrey Washington: 66; /Chen Xiaowei/Landov: 141

Private Collection: 43, 191

Topfoto.co.uk: 109

Every effort has been made to acknowledge correctly and contact the source and/or copyright holder of each picture and Carlton Books Limited apologises for any unintentional errors or omissions, which will be corrected in future editions of this book.